FILSON CLUB PUBLICATIONS
NUMBER TWENTY-NINE

The Anti-Slavery Movement In Kentucky

PRIOR TO 1850

BY

ASA EARL MARTIN

FILSON CLUB PUBLICATION—NUMBER TWENTY-NINE

The
Anti-Slavery Movement
In Kentucky

PRIOR TO 1850

BY

ASA EARL MARTIN
Assistant Professor of American History,
The Pennsylvania State College

NEGRO UNIVERSITIES PRESS
NEW YORK

PREFACE.

While much has been written concerning the anti-slavery movement in the United States, the work of historians has been chiefly directed toward the radical movement associated with the name of William Lloyd Garrison. This has often been done at the expense of and sometimes to the total neglect of those who favored gradual emancipation. This inequality of treatment has been accredited to the fact that the Garrisonian abolitionists were exceedingly active and vigorous in their propaganda and not to any preponderance of numbers or larger historical significance. The gradual emancipationists, unlike the followers of Garrison who were restricted to the free states, were found in all parts of the Union. They embraced great numbers of the leaders in politics, business, and education; and while far more numerous in the free than in the slave states they nevertheless included a large and respectable element in Maryland, Virginia, Kentucky, Tennessee and Missouri. It was to be expected that the gradual emancipationists in these border states would act with conservatism. They were themselves sometimes slaveholders and in any event they saw the difficulties and dangers of any sort of emancipation. Their number was, however, too considerable and their activities too noteworthy to warrant the neglect which they have received at the hands of the historians of the anti-slavery movement.

In this volume I have attempted to relate the history of the anti-slavery movement in Kentucky to the year 1850 with special emphasis upon the work of the gradual emancipationists. I intend later to prepare a second volume which will carry the study to 1870; and I hope that the appearance of this work will encourage the promotion of similar studies in the other border states.

I desire to express my obligations to those who have aided me in the preparation of this work. Though but few can be mentioned by name, the services of all are held in grateful remembrance. While most of the work was done at Cornell University, I feel especially indebted to Professor William E. Dodd and to Professor M. W. Jernegan of the University of Chicago. Under their direction my graduate study was begun and my attention directed to the subject of this investigation. To Professor George F. Zook, of The Pennsylvania State College, I am under obligation for reading and criticizing the manuscript. Nor can I fail to mention the many courtesies shown me at the library of the Wisconsin State Historical Society, at the library of the University of Chicago, where the Durrett collection of Kentucky newspapers and manuscripts was placed at my disposal before it had been catalogued or thrown open to the general public, at the library of Cornell University, at the Congressional Library, at Harvard University Library, at the Boston Public Library and at the libraries in Cincinnati. Through the kindness of Miss Sophonisba Breckinridge of the University of Chicago much valuable material was obtained from the Breckinridge papers now deposited in the Library of Congress but not yet available for public use. Above all I am indebted to my wife for valuable assistance rendered me in reading and correcting both manuscript and proof.

In justice to the persons named, I should add that the author alone is responsible for statements of fact and for conclusions. In a few cases, perhaps unwisely, I have disregarded their suggestions.

December 12, 1917.   ASA EARL MARTIN.

CONTENTS.

INTRODUCTION

The portion of Virginia located west of the Appalachian Mountains and known as Kentucky was frequently visited by Indian traders and hunters between 1750 and 1770 and probably from earlier times. The early comers did not remain to make permanent improvements. After hunting and trading in the country for a few months, they either returned to their eastern homes or pushed further westward or southward. The glowing accounts given by them of the beauty and the resources of this distant region awakened much interest in the older communities, and resulted, after repeated failures, in the establishment in Kentucky during the first years of the American Revolution of permanent settlements, which advanced after 1783 with great rapidity.[1] The frontier was pushed back in every direction and by 1792 the increase of population and the development of resources was sufficient to warrant Congress in admitting the district into the Union.[2]

Slavery was introduced into Kentucky with the earliest settlers.[3] While the majority of the pioneers were very poor and consequently non-slaveholders, there was, during the years following the Revolution, an influx of prosperous settlers, particularly from Virginia, who brought a number of slaves with them and engaged in the cultivation of tobacco on a considerable scale.[4] It was not, however, until the Indian danger had been removed and frontier conditions in Kentucky had given place to commercial activity and to planting for profit as well as for subsistence that the number of Negroes materially increased. Their numerical strength can not be definitely determined[5]

[1] Theodore Roosevelt: "Winning of the West," Vol. 3, p. 12f.
[2] United States Statutes At Large, Vol. 1, 1789-99, p. 189.
[3] Draper MSS.: "Life of Daniel Boone," Vol. 3, pp. 351-2. Daniel Boone in a letter to Col. Richard Henderson, April 1, 1775, written in what is now Madison County, said that a party of Indians firing on his company had killed Mr. Tweety and his Negro. Among Boone's accounts there is also an entry recording his purchase of a Negro woman for the sum of 80 pounds (Roosevelt, "Winning of the West," Vol. 3, p. 27). In the records of the various settlements mention is often made of Negroes. (Richard H. Collins: "History of Kentucky," p. 38.) (Lewis Collins: "Historical Sketches," p. 19.)
[4] N. S. Shaler: "Kentucky, A Pioneer Commonwealth," p. 117.
[5] Draper MSS.: Vol. 4, p. 503. In 1777 a census of the town of Harrodsburg gave the slave population as 19 out of a total of 201 inhabitants.

The following table gives a comprehensive view of the white, the slave and the free Negro elements of the population of Kentucky from 1790 to 1850:

YEAR	WHITE	PER CENT.	SLAVE	PER CENT.	FREE NEGRO	PER CENT.
1790	61,133	83.0	12,430	16.9	114	.1
1800	179,873	81.4	40,343	18.2	739	.3
1810	324,237	79.7	80,561	19.8	1,713	.4
1820	434,644	75.9	126,732	23.4	2,759	.7
1830	517,787	75.2	165,213	24.0	4,917	.7
1840	590,253	75.7	182,258	23.3	7,317	.9
1850	761,413	77.5	210,981	21.4	10,011	1.1

previous to 1790, when, according to the first federal census, they constituted 16.9 per cent. of the total population.[6]

The leading slaveholding section in 1790 was the central part of the state, commonly known as the Blue Grass region. During the next three decades slaveholding extended eastward and southeastward to the mountainous districts and quite generally over the western and southern parts of the state. The percentage of the slave population in 1790 varied in the different counties from 8 to 20 per cent. of the total. By 1850 it was equal to that of the white population in several of the counties in the Blue Grass region, while in the mountainous counties along the eastern border it did not exceed 2 or 3 per cent.[7]

Since it is obvious that the growth of slavery in Kentucky must depend upon the system of agriculture, it may be important to notice at this point the various products of the state in the early period. Although no record was made by the census department of the agricultural products in the states before 1840 and little accurate information on the subject is available, some material has been found to indicate the kind and the value of the principal products of farm and factory. In 1789 Lord Dorchester (Sir Guy Carleton), the Governor General of Canada, in a letter to Lord Sidney said that "the cultivated products" of Kentucky were "Indian corn, wheat, rye, barley, oats, etc., and tobacco, which latter article is raised in considerable quantities by slaves, as practiced in Virginia."[8] Furthermore he expressed the opinion that "of all the forms of cultivation of which the colony is susceptible, that which would be at once more profitable to the settlers***would be the rearing of flocks."[9] Henry B. Fearon in his "Sketches of America" gives the value of the exports of Kentucky for 1818 as:[10]

Flour and Wheat	$1,000,000
Pork, Bacon and Lard	350,000
Whiskey	500,000
Tobacco	1,900,000
Cordage, Hemp and Fabrics of Hemp	500,000
Wool and Fabrics of Wool and Cotton	100,000
Cattle	200,000

[6] Draper MSS.: Vol. 4, p. 503. Table note 5.
[7] *Ibid.*
[8] Canadian Archives, 1890, p. 119.
[9] *Ibid.*
[10] Henry B. Fearon: "Sketches of America," p. 238.
See also, Timothy Flint: "History and Geography of the Mississippi Valley," Vol. 1. p. 351; J. L. Allen: "The Blue Grass Region of Kentucky," p. 53.

Horses and Mules............................ $100,000
Salt-petre and Gunpowder.................... 60,000
White and Red Lead......................... 45,000
Soap and Candles........................... 27,000

Total............................$4,782,000

It is noteworthy that cotton does not appear in this list.

In the following table[11] are enumerated for comparison the chief agricultural products in 1840 of the states of Ohio, Kentucky, and Alabama. Ohio is selected as a neighboring free state and Alabama as a representative state of the lower South.

	Ohio	Kentucky	Alabama
Horses and Mules......	430,527	295,853	143,147
Cattle...............	1,217,874	787,098	668,018
Sheep...............	2,028,401	1,008,240	163,243
Swine...............	2,099,746	2,310,533	1,423,873
Wheat, Bushels........	16,571,661	4,803,151	828,052
Barley, Bushels........	212,440	17,491	7,692
Oats, Bushels..........	14,393,103	7,155,974	1,406,353
Rye, Bushels..........	814,205	1,321,373	51,008
Corn, Bushels.........	33,668,144	39,847,120	20,947,004
Potatoes, Bushels......	5,805,021	1,055,085	1,708,356
Sugar, Pounds........	6,363,386	1,377,835	10,143
Tobacco, Pounds.......	5,942,275	53,436,909	273,302
Cotton, Pounds................		691,456	117,138,823

A study of the table shows that by 1840 Kentucky produced a large quantity of tobacco and fairly large quantities of other agricultural staples such as corn, oats and wheat. Cotton was a negligible product in comparison with its production in a state of the lower South. With the exception of the single item of tobacco, the products of Kentucky were strikingly like those of Ohio as to kind and quantity, a fact which undoubtedly had its bearing upon the attitude of the state toward slavery at various periods before 1860. The system of slave labor was bound up only with the production of tobacco in so far as agricultural staples were concerned, since it was hardly to be doubted that the cultivation of wheat, oats, rye, corn, and perhaps of hemp also could be carried on more profitably with free than with slave labor.

---

[11] U. S. Census Report: 1840, Agriculture, Manufactures, etc., pp. 228, 274, 260, 326.

So important was the production of tobacco in Kentucky and so intimately was it connected with the system of slave labor in the state that further description of the industry seems desirable. Though grown in all parts of the country in 1840,[12] tobacco was pre-eminently a border state product and in its production was found the chief employment of the slaves in those states. Notwithstanding this, the Kentucky planters did not generally regard the industry as well adapted to the economic life of the state. The cultivation of tobacco was exhaustive to the soil and required a constant extension of the tobacco fields. This absorption of new land and replacing of white free-holders by Negroes was further extended because of the necessity of providing additional land to give employment to the natural increase of the slaves. These disadvantages were keenly felt in Kentucky where the physical conditions did not favor the plantation system. The soil in the main slave-holding portion of the state was easily tilled and was abundantly productive; the climate was temperate and invigorating. As a result, the system of agriculture was that of the small farm and not that of the vast plantation.

The people of Kentucky early appreciated the fact that the cultivation of tobacco might not be entirely desirable. In Danville, for many years the political and religious center of the state,[13] there existed, between 1786 and 1790, a political club composed of some thirty members, among whom were a number of the officers of the district. Nearly all of them afterwards held important offices of trust and honor in the state and the national governments.[14] The club held regular meetings to discuss and vote upon the issues of the day. At one meeting in 1788, it took under consideration the question "whether the culture of tobacco in the District of Kentucky will be beneficial

---

[12] The number of pounds of tobacco produced by the different states in 1840 was:

Virginia	75,347,106
Kentucky	53,436,909
Tennessee	29,550,432
Maryland	24,816,016
North Carolina	16,772,359
Missouri	9,067,913
Ohio	5,942,273
Connecticut	471,657
Pennsylvania	325,018
Alabama	273,302
Georgia	162,894
Louisiana	119,824
Mississippi	83,471
South Carolina	51,519

U. S. Census: 1840, Agriculture, Manufactures, etc., p. 408.

[13] Thomas Speed: "The Political Club," pp. 19-21. Filson Club Publications, No. 9.

[14] Speed: "The Political Club," pp. 19-22, 38. A full list of the members is given on page 38.

to the citizens of the District," and it was resolved "that it is the opinion of this club that the culture of tobacco will not be beneficial to the citizens of the District of Kentucky."[15]   While the reasons for this decision are not known, it may be argued that the members of the Political Club, most of whom were immigrants from Virginia, had misgivings as to the desirability of developing an extensive system of slave labor in Kentucky, since tobacco was cultivated in the parent state chiefly by slaves. They must have been familiar with Jefferson's "Notes on Virginia," published in 1782, in which he deplored the disastrous effect of slavery on both men and the soil[16] and accordingly they may have felt that they were standing at the parting of the ways.

In conclusion it may be said that, while the introduction of slavery into Kentucky was inevitable in view of the circumstances of settlement, conditions within the state were not particularly favorable to its development.   Adjacent to the free states of the Old Northwest, Kentucky found herself in competition with the more economic system of free labor.   The exhausting nature of tobacco culture was destined to render the planters keenly conscious of the handicap under which their agriculture labored in comparison with the agriculture of the states beyond the Ohio.   Conditions that had operated to bring about emancipation in Pennsylvania and the states to the northward soon exerted a similar influence in Kentucky and the result was an anti-slavery agitation which took the form of a movement for some plan of gradual and compensated emancipation.   Immediate emancipationists and Garrisonian abolitionists were never numerous in Kentucky and the few existing there were almost entirely among the non-slaveholding class.

[15] Speed: "The Political Club," p. 129.
[16] Thomas Jefferson: "Notes on Virginia," pp. 221-230.

THE FIRST ATTACK UPON SLAVERY

CHAPTER I

During the period of the Revolution and the early years of the Republic, sentiment in the country as a whole was unfriendly to the institution of slavery. It was regarded as inconsistent with Christian civilization and out of accord with the great principles of liberty for which the Colonies had contended. Since slavery existed in every state in the Union, the feeling that it was injurious to society was in no sense dependent upon sectional lines. Its existence was lamented by such men as Washington, Jefferson, Monroe, Madison, Franklin, Hamilton, Jay and Adams. There was a general regret that the institution had ever been planted in America and it was hoped that in time it would be abandoned. No effort was made to defend it or to present it as an ideal basis for the political and economic structure of society and at best it was regarded as a necessary evil.[1] It was opposed upon economic grounds by some and upon moral and religious grounds by others and the question, as Jefferson stated it, was whether "the liberties of a nation be secure when we have removed their only firm basis, a conviction in the minds of the people that their liberties are of the gift of God."[2] It is, therefore, not surprising that Jefferson in the constitution which he proposed for the state of Virginia in 1776 inserted a provision that "no person hereafter coming into this country shall be held in slavery under any pretext whatever."[3] His opposition to slavery was expressed again in 1784 in the report to Congress on a plan of government for the Western Territory, which contained a clause prohibiting slavery or involuntary servitude in this territory after the year 1800.[4] Three years later this principle was accepted in the famous Northwest Ordinance.

---

[1] W. F. Poole: "Anti-Slavery Opinion before 1800"; S. B. Weeks: "Anti-Slavery Opinion in the South," publications of the Southern Historical Association, Vol. 2, 1898.

[2] Jefferson: "Notes on Virginia," p. 222.

[3] Writings of Thomas Jefferson: Vol. 2, p. 26.

[4] Writings of Thomas Jefferson: Vol. 3, p. 432. Later in his life Jefferson was forced to abandon his early hope that slavery would soon cease to flourish in America; yet he still believed in its ultimate extinction. In 1814 he said: "The love of justice and the love of country plead equally for the cause of these people." Ibid., Vol. 4, p. 477. He still believed that the hour of emancipation was advancing with the "march of time" and urged continued effort on the part of the friends of freedom.

It was during the Revolutionary period that slavery was introduced into Kentucky and one need not be surprised to find that the newly settled district shared in the opposition described above. The economic and social conditions of the frontier were antagonistic to slavery and favorable to the development of a democratic society. Frontier life tended to produce self reliance, independence, and individuality. It fostered a sense of equality. There was an absence of great wealth, of highly polished society, and of a leisure class. Slaveholding could not be an important element in the social, economic, or political life of such a people and a large percentage of the population did not own slaves. In addition to these pioneers in the Blue Grass region, there were settlers of decided anti-slavery tendencies from New England and other northern states who settled in the northern part of the state. Such was John Filson, the "Yankee Schoolmaster" and the first historian of Kentucky. [5]

While Kentucky remained an integral part of Virginia, there was little opportunity for a general expression of the sentiment of the people as to slavery; but, upon one occasion, their opinion was indirectly voiced in a debate before the Danville Political Club, which, as has been stated, embraced some of the leading men of Kentucky. At one of the meetings, in 1788, the new federal constitution, which had recently been submitted to the states for ratification, was taken under consideration. Sentiment was unanimous against the clause relating to the importation of slaves because it deprived Congress of the power to prohibit the foreign slave trade before 1808. It was the opinion of the members that Congress ought to be given power to cut off the odious traffic at any time it should choose to do so. [6] While this act was not a direct condemnation of slavery, it showed an early desire to check the growth of the institution.

Though the opposition to slavery was general throughout the country, there was, however, little organized sentiment against the institution as such. What there was, seems to have existed in Kentucky as elsewhere, chiefly among the churches.

It was David Rice, the father of Presbyterianism in the West, who took the first conspicuous step toward securing the abolition of slavery in Kentucky. [7] He moved from Virginia in

---

[5] R. H. Collins: "History of Kentucky," Vol. 2, pp. 195, 492.

[6] Speed: "Political Club," p. 151.

[7] R. H. Bishop: "Outline of the Church in Kentucky, containing the Memoirs of David Rice," pp. 114, 95, 385, 417; R. H. Collins: "History of Kentucky," Vol. 1, p. 132f; J. M. Brown: "Political Beginnings of Kentucky," p. 226; Robert Davidson: "History of the Presbyterian Church in Kentucky," pp. 65-71.

1783 and identified his fortunes with those of the new settlement. Besides his active duties as a minister of the Gospel and as the organizer of numerous churches, he was zealously engaged in advancing the cause of education. He established in his house in Lincoln County, in 1784, the first grammar school of the West. He was also the first teacher in Transylvania Seminary, and for years the chairman of its board of trustees. "Father" Rice, as he was commonly known, was recognized for his ability and piety as a leader of the religious and educational thought in the West.[8]

On the eve of the meeting of the convention of 1792 to frame a constitution for Kentucky as a state in the Union, he published, under the signature of "Philanthropos," a pamphlet entitled "Slavery, Inconsistent with Justice and Good Policy"[9] which embraced the doctrine he had long preached. In this he spoke freely of the infringement on personal rights; the want of protection for females; the deprivation of religious and moral instruction; the violent separation of families; the growing danger of servile insurrection; the tendency to sap the foundations of moral and political virtue; the indulging in habits of idleness and vice, especially among the young men; the comparative unproductiveness of slave property; the discouraging of valuable immigration from the eastward; and the probable deterioration of the country. He undertook to answer objections that were commonly raised to emancipation, especially those drawn from the Scriptures, which were being used to justify slavery. In conclusion he proposed that the coming convention should "resolve unconditionally to put an end to slavery in Kentucky."[10] Not content with mere argument, he succeeded in being elected a delegate to the coming convention.[11]

Soon after the assembling of the convention in Danville, in 1792,[12] a special committee, of which Colonel George Nicholas

[8] Davidson: "History of the Presbyterian Church in Kentucky," pp. 65-71.

[9] Bishop: "Outline of the Church in Kentucky," pp. 385ff, gives this pamphlet in full.

[10] *Ibid.*

[11] Lewis Collins: "Historical Sketches of Kentucky," p. 147, gives a list of the delegates to the Convention from the different counties. J. M. Brown: "Political Beginnings of Kentucky," p. 226f, Filson Club Publications. R. H. Collins: "History of Kentucky," Vol. 1, p. 133; Humphrey Marshall: "History of Kentucky," Vol. 1, p. 394.

[12] Marshall: "History of Kentucky," Vol. 1, p. 394; Mann Butler: "History of the Commonwealth of Kentucky," pp. 206-7.

J. T. Morehead in "An Address in Commemoration of the First Settlement of Kentucky" (133-4), at Jonesborough on the 25th of May, 1840, in speaking of the members of the convention of 1792 said: "From the County of Mercer was the Rev. David Rice, a minister of the Presbyterian Church.***He sought a place in the convention, in the hope of being able to infuse into its deliberations a zeal for the gradual extirpation of slavery in Kentucky.*** His learning, his piety, his grave and venerable deportment, and his high rank in the church to which he belonged, gave to his opinions deserved influence, and he supported them in debate with considerable ability."

was the most influential member, was appointed to draft the constitution, which was soon offered for adoption. Apparently no serious differences existed among the delegates except as to recognizing the existence or the perpetuity of slavery.[13]   This question was brought directly before the convention by the ninth article which legalized slavery. After considerable discussion the article was adopted and while it was designed to make the institution as mild and as humane as possible it nevertheless made it virtually perpetual unless there should be a change in the fundamental law. The legislature was denied power to pass laws for the emancipation of slaves without the consent of their owners, nor could it prevent immigrants from bringing in their slaves. On the other hand, the General Assembly was given extensive powers in respect to importation of slaves into the state as merchandise.[14]

It was upon the adoption of this article that the friends and opponents of slavery joined battle. The ablest of those who opposed the definite establishment of slavery in Kentucky was David Rice. During the early days of the convention he delivered an address before that body which was one of the most earnest and forceful productions of the period.[15]   In it he pointed to the anomaly of a "free moral agent, legally deprived of free agency, and obliged to act according to the will of another free agent of the same species; and yet he is accountable to his Creator for the use he makes of his own free agency."[16]

He declared sarcastically that the legislature, in order to be consistent, should make the master accountable for the actions of the slaves in all things here and hereafter.[17]   He

---

[13] Brown: "Political Beginnings of Kentucky," p. 227f.

[14] "The legislature shall have no power to pass laws for the emancipation of slaves without the consent of their owners, previous to such emancipation, and a full equivalent in money for the slaves so emancipated. They shall have no power to prevent emigrants to this State from bringing with them such persons as are deemed slaves by the laws of any one of the United States, so long as any person of the same age or description shall be continued in slavery by the laws of this State. They shall pass laws to permit the owners of slaves to emancipate them, saving the rights of creditors, and preventing them from becoming chargeable to the county in which they reside. They shall have full power to prevent slaves being brought into this State as merchandize. They shall have full power to prevent any slaves being brought into this State from any foreign country, and to prevent those from being brought into this State who have been since the first day of January, one thousand seven hundred and eighty-nine, or hereafter may be, imported into any of the United States from a foreign country. And they shall have full power to pass such laws as may be necessary to oblige the owners of slaves to treat them with humanity, to provide for them necessary clothing and provision, to abstain from all injuries to them, extending to life or limb, and in case of their neglect or refusal to comply with the directions of such laws, to have such slave or slaves sold for the benefit of their owner or owners." William Littell: "Statute Laws of Kentucky," Vol. 1, p. 32; B. P. Poore: "The Federal and State Constitutions," Part 1, p. 653.

[15] This address was printed in pamphlet form soon after the adjournment of the convention under the same title as his pre-convention pamphlet, but under his own name. The pamphlet went through many editions.

[16] David Rice: "Slavery, Inconsistent with Justice and Good Policy," Edition 1792, pp. 5-6.

[17] *Ibid.*, ***, p. 6.

regarded liberty as inalienable by the legislature except for
vicious conduct, and claims to property in slaves as invalid.
"A thousand laws can never make that innocent, which the
Divine Law has made criminal: or give them a right to that
which the Divine Law forbids them to claim."[18] He replied
to the argument that slaveholders would be prevented from
emigrating to Kentucky by saying that five useful citizens
would come for every slaveholder that was lost, and that if
slavery was permitted, free labor would seek other regions.[19]
The alleged unfitness of slaves for freedom was met by the
question, "Shall we continue to maim souls, because a maimed
soul is unfit for society?"[20] But he considered that present
conditions should be taken into account and that gradual
emancipation was the only practical plan. His proposal was
that the constitution should declare against slavery as a matter
of principle, leaving it to the legislature to find the most suitable
means of abolishing it. He suggested, however, that it would
be expedient for that body to "prevent the importation of any
more slaves" and to "enact that all born after such a date should
be born free" and that some system of education be devised for
making useful citizens of the slaves.[21] Emancipation by some
means he regarded as a political necessity, and he closed with
an earnest appeal that the new state might not be stained with
this sin at its birth. "The slavery of the Negroes," he said,
"began in iniquity; a curse has attended it, and a curse will
follow it. National vices will be punished with national calam-
ities. Let us avoid these vices, that we may avoid the punish-
ment which they deserve.***Holding men in slavery is the
national vice of Virginia; and while a part of that state, we were
partakers of the guilt. As a separate state, we are just now
come to the birth; and it depends upon our free choice whether
we shall be born in this sin, or innocent of it. We now have
it in our power to adopt it as our national crime; or to bear a
national testimony against it. I hope the latter will be our
choice; that we shall wash our hands of this guilt; and not
leave it in the power of a future legislature, evermore to stain
our reputation or our conscience with it."[22]

The constitutional provision fixing slavery in the state was
ably supported by Colonel George Nicholas, the most distin-

---

[18] Rice: "Slavery, Inconsistent * * *," p. 14.
[19] *Ibid.*, p. 15.
[20] *Ibid.*, p. 21.
[21] *Ibid.*, p. 21.
[22] *Ibid.*, p. 24.

guished man in the convention and at that time the most eminent lawyer in Kentucky.[23]   After a thorough discussion which lasted for a number of days, the question was put to a vote. This was the only case in which the ayes and noes were recorded in the Journal.   Under the date of Wednesday, April 18, 1792, is the following entry: "A motion was made by Mr. Taylor, of Mercer, and seconded by Mr. Smith, of Bourbon, to expunge the ninth article of the constitution, respecting slavery, which was negatived; and the yeas and nays on the question were ordered to be entered on the Journals."[24]   The result of the vote was: yeas, 16; nays, 26.[25]

Three of the delegates, Wallace of Woodford County, Walton of Nelson County, and Sebastian of Jefferson County, who were generally regarded, prior to the meeting of the convention, as emancipationists, supported the constitution as proposed by the committee.   This change of attitude has been attributed by Brown and others to the influence of Nicholas,[26] although no evidence has been produced to support the contention.   Had they not upheld the constitution, the final result would have been the same, though the pro-slavery majority would have been reduced from ten to four.

If the constitution could be described as the work of any one man, that man would doubtless be Colonel George Nicholas.[27]   In speaking of the political unwisdom of adopting the ninth article a prominent historian of Kentucky makes the

[23] Marshall: "History of Kentucky," Vol. 1, pp. 395, 414; L. Collins: "Historical Sketches of Kentucky," p. 44; Butler: "History of Kentucky," p. 207; Brown: "Political Beginnings of Kentucky," p. 227.   Colonel Nicholas had immigrated from Virginia in 1791, but the fame of his abilities and the record of his public services had preceded him.   As a member of the Virginia Convention which had adopted the federal constitution, he had ably sustained debate against Patrick Henry and George Mason, and deservedly shared with James Madison the credit of carrying the vote that ratified that document.   A list of the delegates to the convention is given in L. Collins: "Historical Sketches of Kentucky," p. 147.
[24] Brown: "Political Beginnings of Kentucky," p. 229.
[25] *Ibid.*, p. 230.   The following table represents the free and the slave population in 1790 of each of the nine counties into which Kentucky was divided at that time and the votes cast in the constitutional convention two years later for and against slavery.

1790	WHITES	SLAVES	SLAVE PER CENT.	VOTES IN CONVENTION	
				PRO-SLAVE	ANTI-SLAVE
Bourbon................	6,929	908	13	2	3
Fayette................	14,626	3,752	25	2	3
Jefferson..............	3,857	903	24	2	3
Lincoln................	5,446	1,094	18	2	0
Madison...............	5,035	739	18	3	2
Mason.................	2,500	229	15	4	1
Mercer................	5,745	1,339	9	2	3
Nelson................	10,032	1,248	23	2	3
Woodford..............	6,963	2,220	12	4	1
Total..............	61,333	12,430	32	5	0
			20	26	16

United States Census: Population, 1870, pp. 31-33; L. Collins: "Historical Sketches of Kentucky," p. 147; Gilbert Imlay: "Western Territory of North America," p. 378 (map).
[26] Brown: "Political Beginnings of Kentucky," p. 230.
[27] Marshall: "History of Kentucky," Vol. 1, p. 414; Butler: "History of Kentucky," p. 207; Brown: "Political Beginnings of Kentucky," p. 228.   Mr. Speed in the "Danville Political Club," p. 162, says that the influence of Nicholas in the convention has been overestimated; that the convention was composed of strong men who thought and acted for themselves.

following comment: "And the unfortunate step was taken under the guidance of a man whose ability and uprightness can not be questioned, whose experience in affairs was large, and whose performances justified confidence. But Nicholas was not yet a Kentuckian. He had not yet learned the ways of the West, nor comprehended where the interests of the new commonwealth were different from what suited or seemed to suit Virginia and her people."[28]

Seven of the forty-five members of the convention were ministers, of whom three, Bailey, Smith, and Garrard, were Baptists; three, Crawford, Swope, and Rice, were Presbyterians; and one, Kavanaugh, was a Methodist.[29] Though David Rice resigned his seat in the convention before the final vote was taken, Harry Innes,[30] elected to take his place, supported the emancipationists. The six ministers voted solidly against slavery, showing that the religious leaders were in accord in this matter, although none of the others seems to have taken as active a part in opposition to it on the floor of the convention as did David Rice.

The constitution of 1792 was not submitted to the people for ratification, but, had it been, there is no reason to doubt that article nine would have been accepted by popular vote. There were not more than 15,000 slaves in the state and the majority of the people, mostly immigrants from Virginia where slavery existed and seemed to be profitable, did not appreciate the importance of the question. The new state had stood at the parting of the ways and the way that was chosen was destined to lead it to the unhappy fate so ably foretold by David Rice.[31]

[28] Brown: "Political Beginnings of Kentucky," p. 231.
[29] Brown: "Political Beginnings of Kentucky," p. 230; Lewis Collins: "Historical Sketches of Kentucky," p. 147.
[30] Brown: "Political Beginnings of Kentucky," pp. 228-29.
[31] For attitude of the churches of Kentucky toward slavery before 1792, see the following chapter, pp. 19ff.

ANTI-SLAVERY IN KENTUCKY
1792–1800

CHAPTER II

The constitution of 1792 had scarcely gone into effect when it was assailed on all sides.[1] There was dissatisfaction with the method of electing the governor and the state senators.[2] There were objections to the limitations placed upon local government and to the arbitrary powers given the sheriff.[3] Still another demand for constitutional reform came from the anti-slavery element, which was encouraged by the strong fight in 1792 and soon went forward with renewed efforts.[4]

As was to be expected, the anti-slavery element found ready expression through the religious organizations of the state. The Baptists, the Presbyterians, and the Methodists, the leading denominations in Kentucky, were the only denominations to take any considerable part in the slavery controversy before 1850. The Friends, whose opposition to slavery is proverbial, although not so numerous in Kentucky as in the adjacent states, contributed indirectly to the cause of anti-slavery. The Roman Catholics, the Episcopalians, the Disciples (Christians), and the Cumberland Presbyterians did not figure largely in the slavery agitation.

[1] For a number of years after the adoption of the constitution of 1792, the slave code of Virginia continued to be used in Kentucky. It was gradually superseded, however, by special laws, the first of which, regulating all dealings with and the method and procedure of the trial of slaves, were passed during the first session of the legislature. Littell: Vol. 1, pp. 120, 157-8. Two years later, provisions were made for the regulation of the importation and the emancipation of slaves (*Ibid.*, p. 246) and finally, in 1798, the several acts concerning slaves, free Negroes, Mulattoes, and Indians, together with a number of additional enactments, were consolidated into one code, which did not differ materially from the codes of Virginia and the other slave States. (*Ibid.*, Vol. II, pp. 113-23). Although severe in many respects, its provisions were generally interpreted and applied very liberally. This was especially true of the law regulating voluntary emancipation, first passed in 1794, by which any person, by his last will or testament, or any other instrument in writing that was properly attested and approved in the county court by two witnesses was permitted to emancipate his slave or slaves. The court was given full power to demand bond and sufficient security of the emancipator for the maintenance of any slave that might be aged or infirm either in body or in mind in order to prevent his becoming a charge to the county. (*Ibid.*, p. 246f; Vol. II, pp. 119-20). This large discretionary power was exercised with great moderation and the provisions of the act liberally construed by the courts. The Supreme Court of Kentucky in 1829 decided that a slave might be emancipated by any instrument in writing; it was not even necessary that it be sealed and recorded, although it might be if the holder wished it. (2 J. J. Marshall, pp. 223ff). This decision was reaffirmed the following year. (4 J. J. Marshall, p. 104f.)

[2] Carl Schurz: "Life of Henry Clay," Vol. 1, p. 27; Butler: "History of Kentucky," p. 280; The Mirror, Feb. 10, 1798.

[3] R. H. Collins: "History of Kentucky," p. 61; The Mirror, Feb. 10, 1798.

[4] Butler: "History of Kentucky," p. 280; Schurz: "Life of Henry Clay," Vol. 1, p. 27; The Mirror, March 24, 1798.

As early as 1788, the Baptist church took a stand on the anti-slavery question.[5]   At the annual meeting in Goochland County, in this year, the subject was first introduced in the Baptist General Committee of Virginia, which embraced at this time the district of Kentucky. After being discussed at some length, the question was finally deferred till the next annual meeting, in order to give the members more time to deliberate, and to consult with the ministers and the churches in the various parts of the state. At this next meeting, which assembled at Richmond, it was resolved, "That slavery is a violent deprivation of the rights of nature, and inconsistent with a Republican Government, and therefore we recommend it to our brethren, to make use of every legal measure to extirpate this horrid evil from the land, and pray Almighty God that our honorable legislature may have it in their power to proclaim the Great Jubilee, consistent with the principles of good policy."[6] This expression of sentiment is significant not only because the church took a strong and advanced position on the question, but also because it was one of the first explicit declarations in favor of the. abolition of slavery issued by any religious society in the South.

This attitude was reflected by the Baptists of the District of Kentucky when, in 1789, the Baptist Church at Rolling Fork, in Nelson County, propounded to the Salem Association, of which it was a member, the query, "Is it lawful in the sight of God for a member of Christ's Church to keep his fellow creatures in perpetual slavery?" The Association declined to answer the question on the ground that it was "improper to enter into so important and critical a matter at present." Thereupon, the Rolling Fork Church, by an almost unanimous vote, withdrew from the Association.[7]   At about the same time the church at Lick Creek, one of the strongest in the state, became divided on the question of slavery and was denied a seat in that Association until the difficulty should be settled.[8] At its annual meeting in 1791, the Elkhorn Association appointed a committee to draw up a declaration on the subject of "Religious Liberty and Perpetual Slavery," and the following year

---

[5] In the absence of a central organization to prescribe rules for the government of the entire body of members, the churches were grouped into associations through which certain general objects were accomplished. As it was customary for the associations to express opinions on matters of general interest, it is through them that we may expect to discover the attitude of the churches of this denomination toward the institution of slavery.
[6] R. B. Semple: "History of the Virginia Baptists," p. 79; J. H. Spencer: "History of the Kentucky Baptists," Vol. 1, p. 183.
[7] Spencer: "History of the Kentucky Baptists," Vol. 1, p. 184, Vol. 2, pp. 47, 48, 49.
[8] *Ibid.*, Vol. 1, p. 184.

adopted the report of the committee, pronouncing slavery inconsistent with the principles of the Christian religion. Inasmuch, however, as the individual churches disapproved of the act, the Association recalled the memorial at a special meeting in December of the same year, a meeting probably assembled for that purpose.[9] About the same time, John Sutton and Carter Tarrant organized in Woodford County a Baptist congregation avowedly opposed to slavery under the name of the New Hope Church. This, Taylor, in his "History of the Ten Churches," pronounces the first emancipation church in America.[10]

For several years the question of slavery continued to agitate the individual churches of Kentucky, but the associations assumed an attitude of non-interference and took no action on the matter. In many of the churches emancipation parties were formed, whose adherents declared slaveholding contrary to the principles of their religion and refused to commune with those practicing it. Because the Salem Association refused to pronounce slavery an evil, Mill Creek Church in Jefferson County withdrew in 1794. Under the leadership of Joshua Carmen and Josiah Dodge, the dissatisfied members of Cox's Creek, Cedar Creek, and Lick Creek Churches formed an independent church, whose members refused to commune with slaveholders.[11] Carmen and Dodge were soon joined by the venerable William Hickman, one of the pioneers of Kentucky and probably the most influential Baptist preacher in the state before 1800, likewise by John Sutton, Carter Tarrant, Donald Holmes, David Barrow, Jacob Griggs, George Smith, and other ministers.[12] Many ministers openly preached emancipation from the pulpits, sometimes even in the presence of slaves. For this they were bitterly assailed, since it was maintained that the promulgation of such doctrines would tend to cause insubordination among the slaves and thereby disturb the peace of society.

In the Methodist Episcopal Church the anti-slavery sentiment was very pronounced. Its General Conference declared in 1780 that slavery was "contrary to the law of God, man, nature, and hurtful to society; contrary to the dictates of con-

---

[9] Spencer: "History of the Kentucky Baptists," Vol. 1, p. 184.
[10] John Taylor: "History of the Ten Churches, 1823," pp. 79-81. See also Spencer: "History of the Kentucky Baptists," Vol. 1, p. 186.
[11] Spencer: "History of the Kentucky Baptists," Vol. 1, pp. 163, 184, 187; Vol. II, pp. 97, 107; David Benedict: "History of the Baptist Denomination," Vol. II, p. 246.
[12] Spencer: "History of the Kentucky Baptists," Vol. 1, p. 185, Vol. II, pp. 152, 186, 188; Taylor: "History of the Ten Churches," pp. 79-81.

science, and pure religion, and doing that which we would not others would do unto us and ours."[13]   The Conference of 1784, which organized the new independent church in America, not only concurred in this opinion but by stringent regulations attempted to limit and control slave-holding within the church. A provision was incorporated in the discipline which required every slaveholder within the society, within twelve months after notice to "legally execute and record an instrument whereby he emancipates and sets free every slave in his possession."[14]   Slaves of a certain age were to be set free within a certain period, in such a way as to provide a gradual emancipation.   These rules were to apply only in so far as they were consistent with the laws of the states in which the slaveholder resided, and the Virginia brethren, in particular, were given two years in which to consider the rules.[15]   While the Conferences of 1796 and 1800, largely as a result of the opposition of the southern churches, where legal obstruction to manumission prevented the enforcement of the strong rules regarding slavery, somewhat relaxed the discipline of the church in this respect, the continuing interest of the Methodists in furthering emancipation can not be doubted.[16]   The ministers in Kentucky not only attempted to avoid all connection with slavery themselves but zealously endeavored to enforce the enactments of the General Conference on the subject.[17]

The Presbyterian Church, though pronounced in its opposition to slavery, was more cautious than either the Methodists or the Baptists.   Its General Assembly, in 1789, not only expressed its disapproval of slavery but recommended that "meas-

---

[13] A. H. Redford: "History of Methodism in Kentucky," Vol. 1, pp. 254-59; L. C. Matlack: "History of American Slavery and Methodism," pp. 14-31.

[14] The Conference of December 24, 1784, at Baltimore, Tigert, Bound Minutes, pp. 195.

[15] Tigert, p. 217.   In 1784 the Conference adopted the following resolution: "We view it as contrary to the Golden Law of God, on which hang all the law and the prophets, and the inalienable rights of mankind, as well as every principle of the Revolution, to hold in deepest debasement, in a more abject slavery than is perhaps to be found in any part of the world except America, so many souls that are capable of the image of God."

[16] "Journal of the General Conferences," Vol. 1, pp. 40-41; L. C. Matlack: "The Anti-Slavery Struggle and the Methodist Episcopal Church," pp. 58-74.
While the Conference of 1800 negatived a proposition to exclude all slaveholders from the church, the ministers were instructed to consider the subject "with deep attention" and to communicate to the Conference "any important thought upon the subject" that might occur to them.   The Annual Conferences were directed to draw up addresses for the gradual emancipation of slaves to the legislatures of those States in which no general laws had been passed for that purpose; and they were to appoint committees for conducting the business. All officers of the church and traveling preachers were to assist in securing signatures to these addresses.   This plan was to be continued from year to year until the desired end had been accomplished.   (Journal of the General Conferences, Vol. 1, pp. 40-41). The Methodist Episcopal Church was thus virtually organized into an agency for anti-slavery agitation.

[17] H. C. Northcott: "Biography of Rev. Benjamin Northcott" (1770-1854), pp. 88-89.

ures consistent with the interests of civil society" be taken "to procure eventually the final abolition of slavery in America."[18]

In Kentucky, as elsewhere, the anti-slavery element in the church displayed considerable activity during the early years of the state.

The Presbytery of Transylvania, which embraced the entire state of Kentucky, resolved in 1794 that slaves belonging to the members of that body should be taught to read the Scriptures and should be prepared for freedom.[19] Two years later it earnestly recommended that the people under its care "emancipate such of their slaves as they may think fit subjects for liberty, and that they take every possible measure, by teaching their young slaves to read, and giving them such other instruction as may be in their power, to prepare them for freedom."[20]

At this early date, the Presbytery was much disturbed by the opposition on the part of a considerable number of the members not only to the institution of slavery but to communion with slaveholders. The controversy became so serious that the matter was brought before the General Assembly of the church in 1795. That body appointed a committee composed of David Rice and Dr. Muir, ministers, and Robert Patterson, an elder, to draft a letter to the Presbytery on the subject. After considerable discussion, their report was adopted. The letter begins by stating that the General Assembly "hear with concern from your Commissioners that differences of opinion with respect to holding Christian Communion with those possessed of slaves agitate the mind of some among you and threaten divisions which may have the most ruinous tendency." The Presbytery was asked to use forbearance and moderation until the General Assembly should see fit to take a more decided stand on the question.[21] They were referred to the previous recommendation that the slaves be educated in such a way as to be prepared for a better enjoyment of freedom and that reasonable measures be taken to procure the final abolition of slavery in America.[22] Regardless of this act of the General Assembly, the sub-

---

[18] S. G. Baird: "A Collection of the Acts, Etc., of the Supreme Judicatory of the Presbyterian Church," pp. 806-7.
 The action of the Synod of New York and Pennsylvania in 1787 on the question of slavery was adopted by the General Assembly of the Presbyterian Church two years later. In 1795 the action of the assembly of 1789 was reaffirmed and some rather drastic regulations adopted concerning manstealing.
[19] John Robinson: "The Presbyterian Church and Slavery," p. 123; Davidson: "History of the Presbyterian Church in Kentucky," p. 336. The Presbytery of Transylvania was formed in 1786 by the Synod of New York and Philadelphia.
[20] Robinson: "The Presbyterian Church and Slavery," p. 124.
[21] Baird: "A Collection of the Acts, Etc., of the Supreme Judicatory of the Presbyterian Church," pp. 807-808.
[22] The subject of slavery came before the General Assembly in 1793 and again in 1795, when the decision of that body on the subject in 1789 was reaffirmed. (Robinson: "The Presbyterian Church and Slavery," pp. 17-18.)

ject was frequently brought before the Presbytery and on one occasion, 1796, the following resolutions were adopted: "That although the Presbytery are fully convinced of the great evil of slavery, yet they view the final remedy as alone belonging to the civil powers; and also do not think that they have sufficient authority from the word of God to make it a term of church communion. They, therefore, leave it to the conscience of the brethren to act as they may think proper; earnestly recommending to the people under their care to emancipate such of their slaves as they may think fit subjects of liberty; and that they also take every possible measure, by teaching their young slaves to read and giving them such other instruction as may be in their power, to prepare them for the enjoyment of liberty, an event which they contemplate with the greatest pleasure, and which they hope, will be accomplished as soon as the nature of things will admit."[23] In 1797, the Presbytery again declared slavery to be a great moral evil, but, while they acknowledged that there might be exceptions, they were unable, even though they discussed the subject for many years, to answer the question, "Who are not guilty of moral evil in holding slaves?"[24]

In 1800, the West Lexington Presbytery in a letter to the Synod of Virginia spoke of slavery as a subject "likely to occasion much trouble and division in the churches in this country." It stated, also, that it was the opinion of a large majority of the members of the Presbyterian church in Kentucky that slaveholding should exclude from church privileges, but it hesitated to decide till directed by superior judicatories.[25] This Presbytery in 1802 prohibited church sessions from excluding slaveholders from communion until such exclusion should be sanctioned by the higher authorities.[26]

The ministers of the church seem to have been in general staunch emancipationists and a very large majority of the elders and members were equally opposed to the continuance of slavery.[27] The most conspicuous leader in the Presbyterian church during these years was the Rev. David Rice, whose activity in behalf of emancipation in the constitutional convention of 1792 has been reviewed in the preceding chapter. He was

[23] Davidson: "History of the Presbyterian Church in Kentucky," p. 336; Robinson: "The Presbyterian Church and Slavery," p. 123.
[24] Davidson: "History of the Presbyterian Church in Kentucky," p. 337.
[25] *Ibid.*, p. 337. The West Lexington Presbytery was formed in 1799.
[26] *Ibid.*, p. 337. By 1802, the number of Presbyterians in Kentucky had so multiplied as to call for the organization of a Synod. Accordingly the Synod of Kentucky was formed, which was composed of three Presbyteries and thirty-seven ministers.
[27] Robinson: "The Presbyterian Church and Slavery," p. 123.

an implacable foe of slavery, never overlooking an opportunity to use his influence against the institution. To David Rice must be given much of the credit for the advanced position taken by the Presbyterians of Kentucky.[28]

In view of the prominent part played by the religious denominations in the life of the frontier, the significance of the attitude of the churches toward slavery can hardly be overestimated. The opposition to the constitution of 1792 and the effort to provide compensated emancipation in 1799 must find their explanation in part in the attitude of the members of the frontier churches. During the years immediately following the constitutional convention of 1792, special efforts were made by David Rice and other anti-slavery leaders to gather their scattered forces into some kind of permanent organization in order that the various branches of their work might be carried on in a systematic and efficient way. This difficulty had been met in the States along the Atlantic Coast by the formation of abolition societies,[29] of which there were twelve in 1791. As a rule, their membership was very small and their work restricted to their individual localities. The increased opposition to the slave trade and the failure of Congress to legislate against it led them to widen the scope of their work. Accordingly delegates from the various local societies met in Philadelphia in 1794 and perfected a permanent national organization under the name of the "American Convention of Delegates of Abolition Societies."[30]

The Kentucky anti-slavery workers followed the plans of the eastern societies. During the early part of 1795 they began, through the Rev. David Rice, a correspondence with William Rogers, a member of one of the abolition societies in Philadelphia, concerning the organization of similar societies in Kentucky. In his reply Mr. Rogers stated that the Philadelphia society was "much pleased with your endeavors in promoting a similar

---

[28] Bishop: "Outline of the Church in Kentucky, Containing the Memoirs of David Rice," p. 83.   Rice's dying testimony in 1816 gave the final emphasis to his condemnation of slavery, a feeling which he shared with many of his fellow clergy.   "I have too much participated in the criminal and the great neglect of the souls of slaves. Though we live at the expense of those unfortunate creatures, yet we withhold from them a great part of the means of instruction and grace—many, indeed, deprive them of all, so far as they can.   This added to that of depriving them of the inalienable rights of liberty, is the crying sin of our country; and for this I believe our country is now bleeding at a thousand veins."

[29] Before 1830 the term abolition was used to designate every plan for abolishing slavery, including gradual compensated emancipation. After this time, due to the Garrisonian or modern abolition movement, it was used to apply only to immediate, uncompensated emancipation.

[30] "Minutes of the Proceedings of the First Meeting of the American Convention, 1794," Pamphlet; M. S. Locke: "Anti-Slavery in America, 1619-1808," p. 101; A. D. Adams: "Anti-Slavery in America, 1808-1831," p. 154.   There were only nine societies in the American Convention in 1794.   In 1818 a new constitution was adopted and the name changed to "The American Convention for Promoting the Abolition of Slavery and Improving the Condition of the African Race."

institution in Kentucky, which, should it take place, will of course receive every possible aid from the society in this city."[31]

The Kentucky societies were organized as proposed, but almost nothing more is known about them. In the minutes of the American Convention of Delegates of Abolition Societies in 1797, the Kentucky societies were referred to a number of times, although they were not represented in the convention. They appear, however, to have had some correspondence with the convention.[32] A correspondent in The Knoxville Gazette (Tennessee), January 23, 1797, in a call for a meeting of all those interested in the organization of an abolition society, mentioned the existence of two such societies in Kentucky, one in Philadelphia, one in Baltimore, one in Richmond, and one in Winchester (Virginia). The work of these societies was declared to be to relieve "such persons as are illegally held in bondage; to effect their relief by legal means alone without any intention to injure the rights of individuals, not to take negroes from their legal masters and set them free as some have vainly imagined; but by lawful means to vindicate the cause of such of the human race as are lawfully entitled to freedom either by mixed blood or by any cause."[33] More liberal emancipation laws were advocated as well as the education of slaves as a means of "preparing them for freedom."[34]

Nothing further has been found concerning the early Kentucky societies. They were doubtless originated through the influence of the Rev. David Rice for the purpose of advancing the cause of gradual emancipation, which was being extensively advocated in the state at that time, and their disappearance may be connected with the failure of the movement in the constitutional convention of 1799. They bear the distinction of having been the first abolition organizations west of the Appalachian Mountains, preceding by eighteen years those in both Ohio and Tennessee.[35]

The eleventh article of the constitution of 1792 provided for a vote at the election of 1797, on the question of calling a convention to amend that instrument or to adopt a new one.

---

[31] Draper MSS., Hist. Miscel., 1.
[32] "Minutes of the Proceedings of the Fourth Convention of Delegates, 1797," Pamphlet. Societies from New York, New Jersey, Pennsylvania, Maryland, and Virginia were represented in this convention and societies from Delaware, Rhode Island, and Kentucky were referred to, pp. 37, 41.
[33] The Knoxville Gazette, January 23, 1797.
[34] *Ibid.*
[35] Adams: "Anti-Slavery in America, 1808-1831," pp. 264-267, gives a list of abolition societies and the date of organization of each. The Kentucky societies were not known to her. No reference to them has been found in any secondary work.

If the vote in 1797 should be favorable, another was to be taken in 1798.[36] In both years more votes were cast for the convention than against it, and although there was some doubt as to whether or not "a majority of all the citizens in the state voting for representatives" had voted in the affirmative,[37] the legislature, being "ripe for a convention,"[38] ordered the election of delegates.

In a pamphlet entitled "No Convention," which John Breckinridge[39] published, over the pen name of Algernon Sidney shortly before the election of 1798, he declares, "The emancipation of our slaves is said to be one of the objects for which the people wish to call a convention; and the better organization, or total destruction of the Senate, the other.

"It must be acknowledged that the first reflects an encomium upon the wisdom, humanity and justice of our countrymen, that cannot be too much appreciated or too warmly applauded. It discovers the philosophy of the human mind marching on boldly to oppose tyranny and prejudice, and indicates an approaching era when slavery shall be driven from our enviable country. But if a renovation in this particular be the object in view, you have surely mistaken the price necessary to carry so important a work into execution, as well as to organize or make any change in your constitution at all.***Your slaves ought to be free; but let us not liberate others at the probable expense of our own freedom."[40] Though he attached considerable importance, in this pamphlet, to the slavery issue, his opposition to the convention was based mainly on the demand for the abolition of the Senate.[41]

It is not apparent what may have been the relative importance attached by voters to these two issues in 1797, but it is clear that as the contests over the convention progressed the emancipation issue attracted increasing attention. Sidney and

---

[36] Littell: "Statute Laws of Kentucky," Vol. 1, p. 29.
[37] Marshall: "History of Kentucky," Vol. 2, pp. 257-258; R. H. Collins: "History of Kentucky," Vol. 2, p. 61; Butler: "History of Kentucky," pp. 280-281; The Mirror, February 10, 24, March 28, 1798.
In 1797, 5,446 of a total of 9,811 votes and in 1798, 8,804 of a total of 11,853 votes were cast for the convention.
[38] Samuel Hopkins to John Breckinridge, December 8, 1798. Breckinridge Papers.
[39] John Breckinridge (1760-1806), a Virginian by birth, was a member of one of the most influential Kentucky families. In 1798, as a member of the Kentucky Legislature, in collaboration with Thomas Jefferson, he drew up and himself introduced the famous "Kentucky Resolutions." From 1801 to 1805 he represented Kentucky in the United States Senate and from 1805 until his death in 1806 he was Attorney General in Jefferson's cabinet.
The Breckinridge Papers, from which considerable material for this and other chapters was obtained, contains the papers of John Breckinridge, William Breckinridge, Robert J. Breckinridge, John Cabell Breckinridge and other members of the family. The author was given permission to examine this valuable collection, which is deposited in the Congressional Library, but which has not yet been opened for public use by the owner, Miss Sophonisba P. Breckinridge, of the University of Chicago.
[40] Breckinridge Papers, 1798, pamphlet undated.
[41] Ibid.

his arguments were bitterly assailed in a hand bill, signed "Keiling,"[42] which in turn was answered by Sidney in a most scathing article in the Kentucky Gazette.[43] A lively exchange of hand bills and newspaper articles ensued, in which a number of people took part.[44] One of the hand bills, signed "Junius" and addressed to "The Electors of Franklin County," enthusiastically advocates a convention as a means to the reorganization of the Senate and to the securing of other reforms. The author manifests no desire for the abolition of slavery, but he admits that that subject was attracting more and more attention.[45] Another advocate of the convention said, "The man of landed property is told that agrarian laws will be passed; and the slaveholder is alarmed by the fear of immediate emancipation." This he attributed to the enemies of the convention and added that no citizen had "brought forward a proposition for emancipation." He asserted also that no one desired "an immediate liberation of the slaves," but that many did favor a gradual compensated emancipation. He could see no occasion for alarm on the question, however, since any constitutional convention in Kentucky would be composed largely of slaveholders who, in case they should decide upon some plan of emancipation, could be depended upon to protect the slaveholders from monetary losses.[46]

Breckinridge, however, was less certain of the slaveholders' safety. In a letter to Governor Shelby, March 11, 1798, he displayed considerable uneasiness as a result of the wide-spread discussion by the general public and press of a "speedy emancipation of slaves upon some principle." He says further, "If they can by one experiment emancipate our slaves; the same principle pursued, will enable them at a second experiment to extinguish our land titles; both are held by rights equally sound."[47]

In view of his subsequent career, the connection of Henry Clay with the anti-slavery movement of this period deserves special consideration. It is probable that he received here the impressions that were to determine his course throughout the controversy. In 1798, at the age of twenty-one, he published over the signature "Scaevola" a series of articles addressed to

[42] Breckinridge Papers, 1798, undated.
[43] Kentucky Gazette, May 9, 1798.
[44] A number of these hand-bills are to be found in the Breckinridge Papers for 1798.
[45] Breckinridge Papers, dated May 1, 1798.
[46] Stewart's Kentucky Herald, April 17, 1798. This article was signed "Voter."
[47] John Breckinridge to Gov. Shelby, March 11, 1798, Breckinridge Papers for 1798.

the "Electors of Fayette County,"[48] in which he discussed at length the importance of the slavery issue in the coming convention.[49]   In the number for April 25, he asserted that the convention was opposed by many because it was supported by the anti-slavery party.   He pointed out forcefully the reasonableness and the advantages of gradual emancipation and declared that if the convention did not wish to abolish slavery it should at least remove the prohibiting clause from the constitution so that the legislature could take up the subject any time it saw fit to do so.   The article closed with the following arraignment of slavery: "All America acknowledges the existence of slavery to be an evil which, while it deprives the slave of the best gifts of Heaven, in the end injures the master, too, by laying waste his lands, enabling him to live indolently, and thus contracting all the vices generated by a state of idleness.   If it be this enormous evil the sooner we attempt its destruction the better. It is a subject which has been so generally canvassed by the public that it is unnecessary to repeat all the reasons which urge to a conventional interference."[50]

The result of these discussions was a larger majority for the convention in, 1798 than in 1797.[51]   How far this may be an expression of anti-slavery strength it is impossible to say, but doubtless all anti-slavery men who voted favored the convention.

When we come to the choice of delegates the anti-slavery sentiment emerges more clearly.   In some counties, if we may trust statements made long afterwards, and by pronounced anti-slavery men, it became the chief issue, and candidates pledged themselves, if elected, to support or to oppose a gradual emancipation clause in the constitution.[52]   In others, the question was whether or not the owners of slaves should be compensated in case of gradual emancipation.   It appears that the country people were becoming united against the town people, who generally supported emancipation.[53]   In this situation the leaders in Fayette County, the political center of the state, and one of the principal slave-holding communities in it, laid plans "for the

---

[48] Calvin Colton: "Works of Henry Clay," Vol. 1, pp. 209, 214; Schurz: "Life of Henry Clay," Vol. 1, p. 27.
    Henry Clay emigrated from Virginia to Kentucky in 1797.
[49] Colton: "Works of Henry Clay," Vol. 1, p. 209.
[50] The Kentucky Gazette, April 25, 1798.
[51] In 1797 for the convention 5,446 out of 9,814 votes were cast.
    In 1798 for the convention 8,804 out of 11,513 votes were cast.
[52] William Birney: "James G. Birney and His Times," p. 16; Speech of Robert J. Breckinridge in Reply to Speech of Robert Wickliffe, October 12, 1840, Breckinridge Papers. Robert J. Breckinridge was a son of John Breckinridge.
[53] George Nicholas to John Breckinridge, January 20, 1798.   Breckinridge Papers for 1798.

most independent and principled men amongst us to step forward and prevent mischief."[54] A meeting was called for January 26, 1799, at Bryant Station, whose purpose was to formulate a common policy and to nominate candidates to the convention. With the avowed object of furnishing an example to other counties by enlisting the interest and securing the attendance of leading men, delegates were invited from the Militia Companies and the religious societies of the county.[55] Thus was formed a body commonly known as Bryant (Bryan's) Station Convention, which "decided the destinies of Kentucky for that era."[56] Five subjects were proposed for the consideration of the convention: 1, "no emancipation either immediate or gradual;" 2, representation according to population; 3, a legislature of two houses; 4, the courts; 5, the compact with Virginia to be retained in the new constitution.[57]

The convention proved to be well attended[58] and included the leading men in the county among whom were John Breckinridge, George Nicholas, and Daniel Logan. After nominating candidates, among them John Breckinridge, it drew up "a Declaration to be made by Convention Candidates," which provided that no man ought to be voted for as a member to that convention who would not subscribe to five declarations, one of which was as follows: "I do declare that in case I am elected to the Convention, I will be decidedly opposed to an emancipation of the slaves, either immediate or gradual without paying to the owners thereof their full value in money, previous to such emancipation."[59] While this declaration manifests no opposition to compensated emancipation it is fairly certain that the men back of it were antagonistic to any sort of emancipation. Since the anti-slavery forces were strong in Fayette County, it is not improbable that the political leaders were forced to assume this conciliatory attitude. The declaration seems to have been a compromise and was so regarded in many sections of the state. While the Bryant Station Convention was often referred to both

---

[54] Samuel Hopkins to John Breckinridge, December 8, 1798. Breckinridge Papers for 1798.

[55] Stewart's Kentucky Herald, March 12, 1799. See also Breckinridge Papers for 1799.

[56] Speech of Robert J. Breckinridge ***, 1840, p. 7; Daniel Logan to John Breckinridge, January 25, 1799, Breckinridge Papers for 1799. A hand-bill (Breckinridge Papers), signed "Voter" and addressed to the "Inhabitants of Fayette County" describes in detail the meeting of "The Bryant Station Convention."

[57] Speech of Robert J. Breckinridge ***, 1840, p. 7. See also handbill, *Ibid.*

[58] Stewart's Kentucky Herald, March 12, 1799. The attendance was estimated at between 300 and 400.

[59] Speech of Robert J. Breckinridge ***, pp. 7-8.

as an anti-slavery and as a pro-slavery body,[60] the information
at hand seems to show that it was a moderately pro-slavery convention dominated by men who were more interested in preventing radical action against slavery than in perpetuating the institution.

In the election of delegates to the constitutional convention
a few weeks later, the Bryant Station candidates were successful
and the leaders in Fayette County, particularly John Breckinridge and George Nicholas, were active in the selection of delegates elsewhere in the state.   Efforts were made to bring the
right men forward and these efforts appear to have met with a
favorable response.[61]

The cause of the pro-slavery party was doubtless assisted
by the passage in June and July, 1798, of the Alien and Sedition
Acts, which in Kentucky as elsewhere aroused great opposition
to the federal administration and resulted in November in the
passage of the famous "Kentucky Resolutions."   The importance
of and the general interest in these measures affected the choice of
delegates to the constitutional convention by bringing forward
trusted leaders who had been temporarily set aside because of
their pro-slavery inclinations.   Local issues were now sub-
ordinated to the desire to present a solid front to the aggressions of the national government.   When in the midst of this
excitement the elections for delegates to the convention were
held, the conservative pro-slavery element was found to be in
the majority.[63]

---

[60] See Breckinridge Papers for 1799; especially James Hopkins to John Breckinridge,
January 27, 1799, and George Nicholas to John Breckinridge, February 16, 1799. See also
Speech of Robert J. Breckinridge***, pp. 7f.
   The writer referred to above in Stewart's Kentucky Herald for March 12, 1799,
said: "When you consider that the very Gentlemen that differed from you as to the expediency of calling a Convention, and made every exertion to thwart your wishes are now the
warm supporters of the project from Bryan's Station."

[61] Samuel Hopkins, of Christian County, in a letter to John Breckinridge, February
4, 1799 (Breckinridge Papers, 1799), in a reply to a letter from Breckinridge inquiring about
the sentiment in that county and asking him to announce Hopkins' candidacy there stated
that he had complied with the request; however, he feared that his opponent, a Mr. Ewing,
would be elected.   He further stated that "the importance of the present era ought to be truly
Estimated by every citizen—this convention business, I like it not.—I hate experiments upon
government."   In a letter to Breckinridge dated July 15, 1799, he stated that he had been
defeated in the convention election.   He said, however, "I feel rejoiced that the disorganizers
are ousted in the late elections."   Breckinridge had also considerable correspondence with
his political friends in Hardin County.   In a reply to one of his letters, John McIntyre said
that the convention elections "ought to draw the attention of every man who has the good
of his country at heart—at so critical a moment.***Our liberties and property are likely to be
exposed to ignorant and designing men."   (Breckinridge Papers, February 10, 1799.)   See
also Ben Helm to John Breckinridge, February 17, 1799, and W. E. Boxwell (Harrison County)
to John Breckinridge, May 12, 1799.   (Breckinridge Papers for 1799.)

[63] In speaking of this election William Lewis in a letter to John Breckinridge, July 18,
1799 (Breckinridge Papers for 1799), said: "I am pleased to hear that your convention will
not effect an emancipation at this time, as it would be a wretched piece of policy in excluding
all wealthy emigrants possessing that property from seeking an asylum in the State.   They
are certainly the most desirable emigrants, on account not only of the wealth they introduce,
but their condition and polite manners—it is from those that your character as a State is to be
formed—exclude this class from your citizens and what will the bottom be?   A crude un-
digested mass."   See also Birney: "James G. Birney and His Times," pp. 21-22.

The Convention assembled July 22, 1799. Considerable time was devoted to slavery.[64] The question of emancipation was raised during the early days of the session and, in general, the plans discussed, although differing in many particulars, provided for a slow and gradual emancipation. A certain date was to be fixed. All born before that date were to be slaves for life and all born after it were to be free at a specified age. It does not appear that any one believed in or advocated immediate emancipation.[65] The proposal to insert in the constitution a clause providing for gradual emancipation was finally decided in the negative. A proposal to place the power of providing for general emancipation in the hands of the legislature was then taken under consideration. This matter had been extensively discussed during the election of delegates and some of the anti-slavery men, including Henry Clay, were desirous of having the power of removing slavery placed in the hands of the legislature if it should prove impossible to adopt a constitutional provision for its ultimate extinction.[66] No change was made in the constitution in this respect. The power to extinguish slavery was not granted to the legislature, although Robert J. Breckinridge forty years later maintained that it was the intention of the convention to do this.[67] The language of Article VII of the Constitution of 1799 is substantially the same as that of Article IX of the Constitution of 1792. The legislature could pass a law for the emancipation of slaves but only with the consent of the owner and with full compensation in money.[68]

---

[64] A few scattered printed reports including a manuscript copy of the constitution are in the Breckinridge Papers for 1799.

[65] Breckinridge Papers for 1799. Henry Clay in a speech in the U. S. Senate, February 7, 1839 (Annals of Congress, 1839, Vol. 7, p. 354), said: "Forty years ago the question was agitated in the State of Kentucky of a gradual emancipation of the slaves within its limits.*** No one was rash enough to think of throwing loose upon the community, ignorant and unprepared, the untutored slaves of the State."

[66] The Kentucky Gazette, April 25, 1798. M. J. Howard during the early days of the convention sent a manuscript copy of the constitution to John Breckinridge for criticism. In a letter which accompanied it (Breckinridge Papers, undated), he said in regard to the above proposal, "As whatever might be here said, restricting or not restricting the Legislature, with regard to emancipation, would probably have but little effect, as the Body of the People have at all times, an indefeasible and inalienable Right to alter or abolish their Constitution of Civil Government, whenever they, or a majority of them, shall think fit, or necessary for their welfare, or benefit."

[67] Speech of Robert J. Breckinridge ***, p. 8. Mr. Breckinridge further asserted that a majority of the members of the convention adhered to the declarations adopted by the Bryant Station Convention and that they not only intended to give the Legislature a limited power to provide for general emancipation, but did give it full power to emancipate the post nati with or without compensation. Although Mr. Breckinridge had access to his father's papers and had met during his boyhood many members of the convention, his interpretation of the slave clause in the constitution whether right or wrong was not that given it by either the legislature or the people generally during the years following.

[68] The clause in the proposed constitution dealing with the importation of slaves caused considerable discussion. Some wished to allow free importations, while others urged strict constitutional restrictions. A third class desired to place the entire matter in the hands of the legislature. In this as in other points a compromise was agreed upon, by which the provision in the constitution of 1792 for a limited legislative control was adopted with an additional provision regarding the trial of slaves for felony.

Similarly the constitutional provisions of 1792 in regard to bringing slaves into the state were repeated in the constitution of 1799.

The exact strength of the anti-slavery element in the convention of 1799 is not known.[69]   Henry Clay once said, in this connection, that "The proposition in Kentucky for gradual emancipation, did not prevail; but it was sustained by a large and respectable minority."[70]   And Robert J. Breckinridge in the pamphlet published in 1840 asserted that slavery was ingrafted on the constitution by "no great majority" and only "after a most violent conflict."[71]   These statements are well sustained by the literature of the period.

---

[69] Mr. Birney in his "James G. Birney and His Times," p. 21, says: "If the convention could have been held in May, 1798, immediately after the election, Kentucky would have been made a free state and the causes of the civil war destroyed in the germ." This conclusion was based on the number of so-called anti-slavery votes in favor of the convention in the elections of 1797 and 1798.   But since a number of important questions, of which slavery was only one, were involved at that time, it does not follow that the anti-slavery element alone forced the call for the convention.   The defeat of emancipation he attributed to the fact that local issues were eliminated by the national questions growing out of the passage by Congress of the Alien and Sedition Laws.   Though there is no doubt that the anti-slavery strength was greatly weakened by these measures, nothing has been found to indicate even the probability that the majority of the population in either 1798 or 1799 favored emancipation.

[70] Colton: "Works of Henry Clay," Vol. 1, pp. 216-217.

[71] "Speech of Robert J. Breckinridge ***," p. 7. By 1800 slavery had been abolished or plans of gradual emancipation adopted in the Northwest Territory and in all the states north of the Mason and Dixon Line, with the exception of New York and New Jersey, which followed in 1804.

ANTI-SLAVERY IN KENTUCKY
1800–1830

CHAPTER III

The emancipationists were indeed defeated in the constitutional convention of 1799 but they by no means accepted
their defeat as final. On the contrary, they made attempts
almost every year to secure the passage of a bill ordering that the
sense of the people be taken on calling a new convention.[1]
These bills frequently passed the House. Although they were
designed to secure only the gradual, not the immediate, abolition of slavery,[2] the pro-slavery men viewed with such uneasiness and alarm every attempt on the part of the anti-slavery
minority to reopen the question in any form that the bills were
always defeated in the Senate. Niles, in his Weekly Register,
summed up the situation in these words: "In Kentucky, I am
told by several gentlemen of high standing, there is so strong
an opposition to slavery, that the chief slave-holders have long
feared to call a convention to alter the constitution, though
much desired, lest measures should be adopted that might
lead to gradual emancipation." He then predicted that before
many years Kentucky, Tennessee, and Missouri "would follow
the lead of Pennsylvania and cease to be slaveholding states as
well from principle as from interest."[3]

Slavery was brought before the legislature in many other
ways. Bills intended to encourage voluntary emancipation,
to ameliorate the condition of the slave, and to secure the enactment of more rigid importation laws were repeatedly introduced. The advocates of these measures declared openly
that the purpose of such legislation was to prepare the state for
gradual emancipation through a change in the constitution.[4]

The question of slavery was brought before the people of
Kentucky in 1819 and 1820 in connection with the discussions
in Congress concerning the admission of Missouri into the

---

[1] Col. W. F. Evans, in a speech in the House of Representatives of Kentucky, in 1838
said: "From an examination of the Journal you will discover that the Bill has been introduced almost every year since the year 1802." (Maysville Eagle, February 10, 1838). See
also Shelbyville Examiner, January 5, 1833.

[2] Kentucky Reporter, February 17, 1823; Nov. 24, 1823; Nov. 22, 1824; Western
Luminary, August 29, 1828; Genius of Universal Emancipation, August 30, 1828; The Argus,
December 25, 1817; Maysville Eagle, December 16, 1827.

[3] Niles' Weekly Register, Vol. 18, p. 27 (1820).

[4] Kentucky Reporter, November 22, 1824; Argus, November 17, 1817.

Union.   As in other sections of the country, the subject received wide attention.   While the people of the state generally followed Henry Clay in his demand for the admission of Missouri, there were numerous expressions of opinion and in a few instances resolutions adopted by mass meetings to the contrary.   The fact that the controversy had no considerable influence upon the anti-slavery movement in Kentucky, but was usually treated as a political question, appeared clearly in the resolutions passed by the Kentucky legislature, which refrained "from expressing an opinion either in favor of or against the principles of slavery," but which was intent upon "preserving the State sovereignties in their present rights."[5]

It can not be said that the churches contributed much to the cause of emancipation in the first quarter of the century. The years 1800-1830 have been characterized by students of the anti-slavery movement as the period of stagnation and this was unquestionably true in so far as the attitude of the churches toward slavery was concerned.   Conservative treatment of questions arising from slaveholding was the rule and in this way the churches bear testimony to the fact that the liberalism of the Revolutionary period was rapidly declining.

The action of the Methodist General Conferences of 1804 and 1808 is much less pronounced in its opposition to slavery than that of the preceding Conferences.[6]   The Conference of 1804 abandoned the plan adopted in 1800 of memorializing state legislatures, and three southern states, North Carolina, South Carolina, and Georgia, were expressly exempted from the rules

---

[5] Niles' Weekly Register, Vol. 17, p. 344.   The prevailing opinion was that expressed by the Louisville Public Advertiser, December 6, 1819, when it said: "It appears that measures have been taken in New Jersey and the principal Eastern cities to prevent the introduction of slavery into Missouri.   Though we have never been the advocate of slavery in any form, we are sorry to discover that questions are to be urged, perhaps principles enforced in Congress which belong exclusively to the polity of the several States and the rejection or admission of which should be left to the State or States concerned.   Missouri has obtained the requisite population—she demands the right of self government—to be admitted into the Union with all the privileges and immunities of her sister, Alabama.* * * Neither the principles of humanity nor the letter nor spirit of the Constitution can, in our opinion, justify our Eastern brethren in the course they are now pursuing toward the people of Missouri.   We cannot believe they have adopted this course from selfish or sordid motives.   They cannot doubt the attachment of the Western people to the Union, and we trust they do not anticipate any dangerous innovation upon their rights or pursuits should we eventually predominate in the councils of the Nation.   We must, therefore, attribute what we deem an improper interference in the affairs of Missouri to the want of information on the subject of slavery, as it really exists." The Western Monitor, January 18, 1820, said: "The people of the Missouri claim, and we think justly, the privilege of being admitted into the Union on an equal footing with the other States, and of engrafting into their Constitution such provisions as they may choose; unrestrained except by the necessity of rendering it republican and consistent with the Constitution of the United States.* * * We deprecate as much as any of our Eastern brethren the existence of the evil which has been entailed upon us.   But we deny the possibility of suddenly removing it by legislative acts.   It is not now a question of whether it should be established in Missouri. It is there already and we hesitate not to say Congress cannot eradicate it.* * * We are decidedly of the opinion that Congress has no constitutional right to prescribe the conditions mentioned as we are equally well convinced that no good could possibly result from exercising the right if they possessed it."

[6] See *supra*, pp. 20, 21.

as to slavery. The Conference of 1808 went further. It voted to strike from the discipline all but the first two paragraphs of the section dealing with slavery. This removed for all time every syllable respecting slave-holding among private members. It must be said, however, that this action was due in no small degree to the numerous difficulties encountered by the General Conference in enforcing its decrees in the southern states where statutory enactments often conflicted with the rules of the General Conference. In some states even voluntary emancipation could be accomplished only by special action on the part of the legislature.[7] The Conference of 1824 amended the section on slavery for the last time until 1860, but the changes were unimportant; and by 1828 the unwillingness of the central authority of the church to take any action was so great that, although it still condemned slavery as an institution, it tabled a resolution providing a method of dealing with the inhumanity of members toward their Negro servants. Reaction could go no further.[8]

Notwithstanding the reluctance of the General Conference to undertake the regulation of a matter fraught with so much danger to the integrity of the church, the Methodists of Kentucky appear to have maintained a commendable opposition to the domestic slave trade, concerning which the General Conference in 1808 instructed the Annual Conferences to "form their own regulations"[9], and likewise to slaveholding on the part of the officials of the church. In answer to the query, "What method shall be taken with those members of our society that shall enter into the slave trade?"the Western Conference, which embraced the region west of the Appalachian Mountains, in 1808, instructed the circuit preachers to summon before the quarterly meeting all persons charged with buying or selling slaves with speculative motives and if the Conference should find upon examination that the charges were sustained the persons were to be expelled from the society.

---

[7] The attitude of the General Conference toward action by the church on the subject of slavery is given by the Conference of 1816 as follows: "We most sincerely believe, and declare it as our opinion, that slavery is a moral evil. But as the laws of our country do not admit of emancipation without a special act of the legislature, in some places, nor admit of the slave so liberated to enjoy freedom, we cannot adopt any rule by which we can compel our members to liberate their slaves; and as the nature of the cases in buying and selling are various and complex, we do not think it possible to devise any rule sufficiently specific to meet them. But to go so far as we can, consistent with the laws of our country and the nature of things, to do away with the evil, and remove the curse from the Church of God." (Journal of the General Conferences, Vol. 1, p. 170.)

[8] This summary is taken largely from a manuscript thesis prepared by Professor J. N. Norwood of Alfred University on "The Slavery Schism in the Methodist Episcopal Church. A Study of Slavery and Ecclesiastical Politics." Cornell University Library.

[9] Journal of the General Conferences, Vol. 1, pp. 44, 60, 93, 170.

This action is representative of the attitude of the Methodists toward the domestic slave trade throughout the period.[10]

In Kentucky there was no relaxation from the rule forbidding ministers to hold slaves. Peter Cartwright, for fifty years a presiding elder in this region, testified that "In Kentucky our rules of discipline on slavery were pretty generally enforced, and especially on our preachers, traveling and local. Whenever a traveling preacher became the owner of a slave or slaves, he was required to record a bill of emancipation, or pledge himself to do so; otherwise he would forfeit his ministerial office. And under no circumstances could a local preacher be ordained a deacon or an elder if he was a slaveholder, unless he gave the church satisfactory assurances that he would emancipate at a proper time."[11]

The course of the Presbyterian Church with respect to slavery in Kentucky was not substantially different from that of the Methodist Episcopal Church. The General Assembly of the Presbyterian Church gradually receded from the position adopted in 1795,[12] until, in 1816, it merely pronounced slavery a "mournful evil" and "a gross violation of the most precious and sacred rights of human nature." After that, it became increasingly evident that the denomination was to rely upon words rather than deeds.[13] The successive General Assemblies pointed with pride to former utterances against slavery and apparently considered them sufficient to satisfy the most zealous reformer while the enforcement of existing regulations became more and more lax as slavery took a firmer grip upon the southern states and as hostile legislation made their enforcement more difficult. There were, however, occasional exceptions. Thus in 1809 the session of the Concord Church (Kentucky) suspended a member for exposing for sale at public auction a Negro boy, and upon appeal to the Synod of Kentucky the act was affirmed.[14]

---

[10] Peter Cartwright: "Fifty Years a Presiding Elder," p. 53f. See also Bishop Asbury's Journal, Vol. 3, p. 290; Redford: "History of Methodism in Kentucky," Vol. 2, p. 37.
[11] "Autobiography of Peter Cartwright, The Backwoods Preacher," p. 195. See also, Northcott: "Biography of Benjamin Northcott," p. 89. In a few communities in Kentucky attempts were made to enforce rigidly all the rules of the church regarding slavery. The most important instance was that of the Hartford Circuit (North Central Kentucky), which was continually agitated by the subject from 1804 to 1825. (Redford: "History of Methodism in Kentucky," Vol. 1, p. 260f.)
[12] See *supra*, pp. 21-24.
[13] Baird: "Collection of Acts, Etc. *** of the Presbyterian Church," pp. 809ff. The General Assembly in 1816 also directed slaveholders "to continue and increase their exertions to effect a total abolition of slavery," with "no greater delay than a regard to the public welfare demands," and recommended that if a "Christian professor in our communion shall sell a slave who is also in communion with our Church" without the consent of the slave, the seller should be suspended till he had repented and made reparation.
[14] Robinson: "Presbyterian Church and Slavery," p. 53. The Synod of Kentucky was established in 1802.

The period is noteworthy in respect to the awakened interest in the education of the slaves, in which the Presbyterians played a considerable part. As early as 1809, the Synod of Kentucky directed the Presbyterians to take such action "as to them might seem most prudent" to secure the religious instruction of the slaves and also the humane and Christian treatment of them.[15] It does not appear that much was accomplished for a few years after this action was taken; but, in 1825, a renewed interest in the welfare of the slaves was displayed in the Synod[16] and the matter was also frequently mentioned in the Western Luminary, the Presbyterian paper of the state. Thereupon, many ministers for the first time held special meetings for the slaves and organized schools for their religious instruction.[17] This was thought to be necessary both for an appreciation of the Christian religion and as a preparation for freedom. In the following year (1826) fifteen Presbyterian schools for the people of color were reported to the annual meeting.[18] From this date until the end of the slavery period the Presbyterians of the state displayed an ever-increasing interest in the general welfare of the slave population.

The records of the Baptist churches of Kentucky revealed to a far greater extent the local contests that were being waged by certain bold spirits in behalf of anti-slavery. This was to be expected in view of the absence of a centralized government in the Baptist church and in view of the greater opportunity thus afforded local controversies to find expression in the associations. We have seen that at a very early day there were dissensions among the Kentucky Baptists[19] and these dissensions presently became so acute that a number of associations endeavored to prevent the discussion of the question of slavery in the pulpit.[20] In this the associations were assuming the conservative part played by the central authorities in the Methodist Episcopal and Presbyterian churches.

The Elkhorn Association in 1805 resolved that "this Association judges it improper for ministers, churches or Associations

---

[15] Robinson: "Presbyterian Church and Slavery," p. 53.
[16] Davidson: "History of the Presbyterian Church in Kentucky," p. 338.
[17] *Ibid.* See also, John Breckinridge to Robert J. Breckinridge, December 11, 1827 (Breckinridge Papers for 1827). He states that it is his wish that an acre of ground be set aside on his tract for the African Church.
[18] Davidson: "History of the Presbyterian Church in Kentucky," p. 338. See also the Genius of Universal Emancipation, Vol. 7, pp. 158, 140; Vol. 8, pp. 47, 172, 173, and the files of the Western Luminary for that period.
[19] See *supra*, pp. 19ff.
[20] Spencer: "History of the Kentucky Baptists," Vol. 1, p. 184; Vol. 2, pp. 17, 27, 120, 235. The most notable instances were those in the Elkhorn, Bracken, Cumberland, and North District Associations.

to meddle with emancipation from slavery, or any other political subject; and as such we advise ministers and churches to
have nothing to do therewith in their religious capacities."[21]
Similarly the Cumberland Association in 1815 in answering
the query, "Is it right to uphold hereditary and perpetual
slavery?" made the following reply: "We conceive that all
nations, by nature, have a right to equal freedom. But as we
are involved, in our nation, with hereditary slavery, we think
it would be best to wait for the dispensation of Providence, and
pray to God for the happy year of their deliverance to commence."[22]

The acts of these associations did not check the agitation
as had been expected, but only tended to increase and inten-
sify it. In October, 1805, the Bracken Association brought
five charges before the North District Association against the
Rev. David Barrow, the ablest preacher in the body, which
pertained to his sentiments on the subject of slavery. The
North District Association, however, accepted his explanations
and apologies.[23]   This action was not satisfactory to a number
of the churches that had determined to secure his expulsion.
Consequently the matter came before the Association again in
October, 1806, when he was again charged with "preaching the
doctrines of emancipation to the hurt and injury of the brother-
hood."[24]   Mr. Barrow refused to alter either his mode of
preaching or his attitude toward slavery, whereupon he was
publicly expelled from the Association, and a committee was
appointed to bring the matter before the church at Mount
Sterling, of which he was a member.[25]   This action was annulled
and revoked in the following year after three churches and two

---

[21] Spencer: "History of the Kentucky Baptists," Vol. 2, p. 17.

[22] *Ibid.*, Vol. 2, p. 235.

[23] The anti-slavery agitation in the Baptist Church in Kentucky is discussed in Rev.
David Benedict's "History of the Baptist Denomination" (1813), Vol. 2, pp. 231-2, 236, 245ff.
Benedict spent several months during 1810 and 1811 visiting the various churches and associations of Kentucky.   The subject is more fully discussed by the Rev. David Barrow in a pamphlet published in 1808, entitled, "Involuntary, Absolute, Hereditary Slavery Examined on the
Principles of Nature, Reason, Justice and Scripture," in which he attempted to vindicate his
course in respect to slavery.   This pamphlet of fifty pages is written in a dignified style and
shows the author to have been a man by no means deficient in ability, either natural or acquired.   A copy of this exceedingly rare and valuable pamphlet is in the Cornell University
Library.   On the title page is found the interesting announcement that "This pamphlet is
not to be sold, but given away."   It contains perhaps the fullest materials regarding anti-
slavery in the Baptist Churches of Kentucky down to 1808.   Spencer, in his "History of the
Kentucky Baptists," relies largely on these two sources for his material.

[24] David Barrow: "Involuntary, Absolute, Hereditary Slavery Examined on the
Principles of Nature, Reason, Justice and Scripture."   See also Spencer: "History of the
Kentucky Baptists," Vol. 2, p. 120.

[25] Barrow: "Involuntary, Absolute, Hereditary Slavery ***," pamphlet.   See also Spencer: "History of the Kentucky Baptists," Vol. 1, p. 186; Vol. 2, p. 120.

ministers had withdrawn from the Association; but the seceders refused to renew their former relations.[26]

The expulsion of Barrow resulted in the withdrawal of ministers and churches from nearly every association in Kentucky and in the formation of Emancipation Baptist churches, which either excluded slaveholders or denied them the right of communion.[27] Under the leadership of David Barrow and Carter Tarrant, an association was formed embracing part of these churches in the north central part of the state. The first meeting of this new association was held in August, 1807, with eleven ministers and nineteen laymen in attendance.[28] Another meeting was held the following month, when a permanent organization was effected under the name of The Baptized Licking Locust Association, Friends of Humanity.[29]

The purpose of this Association can best be learned from the consideration of eleven queries discussed at this meeting. The query, "Can any person be admitted a member of this meeting, whose practice appears friendly to perpetual slavery?" was answered in the negative. To the query, "Is there any case in which persons holding slaves may be admitted to membership in the church of Christ?" the answer was, "No; except in the following, viz.—1st. In the case of a person holding young slaves, and recording a deed of their emancipation at such an age as the church to which they offer may agree to. 2nd. In the case of persons who have purchased in their ignorance and are willing that the church shall say when the slave or slaves shall be free. 3rd. In the case of women, whose husbands are opposed to emancipation. 4th. In the case of a widow who has it not in her power to liberate them. 5th. In the case of idiots, old age, or any debility of body that prevents such slave from procuring a sufficient support."[30] The answer to another query declared that no member was to purchase any slave or slaves except with a view to ransoming them from perpetual slavery, and then only after the approval of the church had been obtained. The association then declared that their ideas of

[26] Barrow: "Involuntary, Absolute, Hereditary Slavery***," pamphlet. Spencer: "History of the Kentucky Baptists," Vol. 2, p. 120.
[27] Barrow: "Involuntary, Absolute, Hereditary Slavery***," pamphlet. Benedict: "History of the Baptist Denomination," Vol. 2, p. 245.
[28] Benedict: "History of the Baptist Denomination," Vol. 2, p. 247. See also Spencer: "History of the Kentucky Baptists," Vol. 1, p. 186. It is a significant fact that Barrow's pamphlet was dated August 27, 1807, although it did not appear in print until the following year.
[29] Benedict: "History of the Baptist Denomination," Vol. 2, p. 247. See also Spencer: "History of the Kentucky Baptists," Vol. 1, p. 186. This association received its name from the Licking Locust Church in the northern part of the state, which was considered the mother church among the emancipation churches of Kentucky.
[30] Benedict: "History of the Baptist Denomination," Vol. 2, p. 247.

slavery had occasioned no alteration in their view of the doctrine of the Gospel.[31]

The emancipating Baptists or the Friends of Humanity, as they were commonly called, had, previous to the formation of the association, consistently refused to commune with slaveholders. They had opposed slavery both in principle and in practice, as being a "sinful and abominable system, fraught with peculiar evils and miseries which every good man ought to abandon and bear his testimony against." They endeavored to effect in the most prudent and advantageous manner for both slaves and their owners the general and complete emancipation of the Negro race in America.[32]

We have no means at present of knowing the number of preachers or churches that went into the organization in 1807. Benedict estimates their strength at the time of the organization of the society at twelve ministers, twelve churches, and three hundred members.[33]

Notwithstanding the zeal for anti-slavery which characterized the organization of the Friends of Humanity, the dozen years of their existence exhibited the same relaxation that was noticeable in the large religious bodies. At their second meeting during the latter part of 1807 at the New Hope Meeting House, one of the first emancipating Baptist churches in the state, of which Carter Tarrant was pastor, they resolved "that the present mode of association or confederation of churches in their relation to slavery is unscriptural and ought to be laid aside."[34] Thereupon a number of the members acting independently of the churches proceeded to organize an anti-slavery society called the Kentucky Abolition Society.[35] This organization did not replace the Friends of Humanity but merely took over the anti-slavery work of the association. The churches as before refused to commune with slaveholders.[36]

Through David Barrow, the Friends of Humanity, in 1810, began a correspondence with the object of uniting the emancipating churches of Kentucky with the Miami Baptist Association of Ohio, which also refused to commune with slaveholders. Their overtures were rejected on the ground that the Kentucky

---

[31] Benedict: "History of the Baptist Denomination," Vol. 2, pp. 247-248.
[32] Benedict: "History of the Baptist Denomination," Vol. 2, pp. 245-246, 248, 229, 234; Z. F. Smith: "History of Kentucky," p. 368.
[33] Benedict: "History of the Baptist Denomination," Vol. 2, p. 545.
[34] Ibid., Vol. 2, p. 248.
[35] See below, pp. 42ff.
[36] Benedict: "History of the Baptist Denomination," Vol. 2, p. 248. See also Spencer: "History of the Kentucky Baptists," Vol. 1, pp. 186-189.

emancipators had compromised their position by admitting slaveholders to the communion table under certain conditions.[37] Two years later, Benedict said that the "zeal of the Emancipators has in some measure abated, and of course they are less opposed; and it is hardly probable that any lasting effect will be produced by their means. Their leading maxims are approved of by many who have not united with them, but who still hold slaves with many scruples respecting its propriety."[38] In 1816, they met at Lawrence Creek meeting house in Mason County under the name of the Association of Baptists, Friends of Humanity. Six churches were represented. By this time, a manifest tendency to "open communion" and other signs of decay were exhibited. The organization kept up a feeble existence until a few months after the death of Barrow, in 1819, when it was dissolved.[39] From this date until the division of the church in 1845 into the Northern and Southern branches, the Kentucky Associations maintained the same attitude that they had held previously, namely, that of non-interference in the question of slavery, regarding it as a political issue outside of the jurisdiction of the church.

It is difficult to determine the exact influence of the emancipating Baptists on the anti-slavery movement in the Baptist church and on the movement in the state as a whole. While their activites greatly disturbed the Baptist churches in Kentucky for a period of more than thirty years, they kept the evils of slavery before the people and doubtless contributed to the cause of emancipation. In any event they furnished an interesting protest against the position adopted by the regular Baptist associations.

A number of prominent men were associated with the emancipating churches at different times during their existence. Revs. James Garrard, afterwards governor of the state, Ambrose Dudley, and William Hickman for a time actively supported the movement.[40] Carter Tarrant, one of the most active and influential of the emancipators, wrote a history of the Association, which was published shortly before his death in 1815.[41] But by far the most conspicuous anti-slavery leader in the Baptist Church, and one who did more than any other person to .perfect the organization of the scattered eman-

[37] A. H. Dunlevy: "History of the Miami Baptist Association," p. 49.
[38] Benedict: "History of the Baptist Denomination," Vol. 2, pp. 249-250.
[39] Spencer: "History of the Kentucky Baptists," Vol. 1, p. 186.
[40] Spencer: "History of the Kentucky Baptists," Vol. 1, p. 187.
[41] *Ibid.*, Vol. 1, pp. 189-190.

cipation churches and to hold them together in the society of Friends of Humanity, was the Rev. David Barrow.[42] From 1808 until his death in 1819, he was also actively associated with the Kentucky Abolition Society, serving for a number of years as its president. Perhaps no minister of the Baptist Church in Kentucky enjoyed the confidence and esteem of his brethren and of the people generally in a higher degree than did Mr. Barrow. They frequently spoke of him as the "wise man." He was by far the most distinguished and the ablest preacher among the emancipating Baptists and without any exception the most gifted writer among the early Baptist ministers of Kentucky.[43]

In summarizing the attitude of the churches of Kentucky toward slavery in the first quarter of the century it is to be observed that the churches reflected very clearly the changing point of view. As slavery became more firmly rooted in the social, economic and political life of the people, opposition became less popular and seemed to offer less hope of success. To assume that the existence or non-existence of slavery was a political and not a religious matter was therefore a safe and reasonable position. It was perhaps more easily assumed because many of those who opposed this policy, despairing of overcoming it and desiring to free themselves from the evils of a slave society, moved into the free territory north of the Ohio.[44] Thus the radical element in the churches was weeded out.

We have seen that one of the results of the movement conducted by the emancipating Baptists was the formation in 1808 of the Kentucky Abolition Society, the first distinctly anti-slavery organization in the state after the dissolution of the early anti-slavery societies in 1797.[45] The Kentucky Abolition Society, while composed largely of members of the Baptized Licking Locust Association, Friends of Humanity, embraced also a considerable number of anti-slavery advocates from other religious denominations of the state. At their first meeting a constitution was adopted and a permanent organization

---

[41] Barrow was a native of Virginia and a Revolutionary soldier. In 1798 he removed to Montgomery County, Kentucky, where he spent the remainder of his life.

[43] Benedict: "History of the Baptist Denomination," Vol. 2, pp. 245-251, 225. See also Spencer: "History of the Kentucky Baptists," Vol. 1, pp. 193-197.

[44] Benedict: "History of the Baptist Denomination," Vol. 2, p. 261; Dunlevy: "History of the Miami Baptist Association" (Ohio), p. 132, 159; Birney: "James G. Birney and His Times," p. 164; Bishop: "Outline of the Church in Kentucky," p. 144. Bishop speaks of six Presbyterian congregations under the leadership of the Rev. Armstrong and Fulton who had moved into Indiana territory in order to free themselves from the evils of slavery. In a number of instances Methodist and Baptist congregations, together with their ministers, for similar reasons moved from Kentucky.

[45] The Baptized Licking Locust Association, Friends of Humanity, though a religious body, did the work of an ordinary anti-slavery society and might be properly termed one.

effected. The purposes and work of the society which every member pledged himself to further were grouped under the following heads:[46]

1. To pursue such measures as would tend to the final constitutional abolition of slavery.

2. To appoint persons to prepare sermons, orations, and speeches on slavery which were to be delivered at given times and to publish such of them as the annual meeting might desire.

3. To look after the interests of free Negroes and mulattoes and to inculcate morality, industry, and economy among them. This was to be accomplished largely by means of education.

4. To ameliorate the condition of slaves by every means in their power according to the constitutional laws of the state.

5. To seek for justice in favor of such Negroes and mulattoes as were held in bondage contrary to the constitutional laws of the commonwealth.

6. To seek to secure the constitutional abolition of the domestic slave trade.[47]

The range of activities thus set forth was a wide one; while an aggressive spirit was displayed, it is important to note that it was not a radical one. This position was clearly set forth in the constitution as follows: "Slavery is a system of oppression pregnant with moral, national and domestic evils, ruinous to national tranquility, honor and enjoyment, and which every good man wishes to be abolished, could such abolition take place upon a plan which would be honorable to the state, safe to the citizen and salutary to the slaves."[48]

The permanent plan of organization provided for auxiliary branches or local chapters to be formed in different parts of the state. Each of these was to send delegates to the annual meeting on the basis of its membership. The organization of both the state and the local societies was, as a rule, very simple. It provided for a president, vice-president, secretary, and treasurer as regular officers and usually one or more committees. Annual meetings of the state society were to be held, at which the interests of the organization as a whole were to be considered. Memorials and petitions were to be sent to the officials of the

---

[46] In the Abolition Intelligencer and Missionary Magazine, Vol. 1, p. 81, is given a history of the organization and growth of the Kentucky Abolition Society to 1816. For the organization of the Society, see also Benedict: "History of the Baptist Denomination," Vol. 2, p. 248.
[47] Abolition Intelligencer***, Vol. 1, No. 6, p. 81. The Constitution is published in full in this number. Birney: "James G. Birney and His Times," p. 24.
[48] Abolition Intelligencer***, Vol. 1, p. 81.

state and nation when it should be deemed advisable; addresses giving information on the subject of slavery were to be published from time to time and the general objects of the society were to be furthered in every possible way. The auxiliary branches were also to hold regular meetings, some as often as once a month, to promote the objects of the state society in that vicinity as well as the objects of the local chapter; these objects differed in the different parts of the State, and a few instances have been found in which a local society even sent addresses to the State legislature or to Congress.[49]

The number of members and the number of branches comprising the Kentucky Abolition Society in 1808 or the years immediately following are not known. Most of the ministers associated with the Friends of Humanity became members of the new organization and influenced many of the members of their churches to do likewise.[50] The membership was augmented by others who had not been connected with the Baptist church but were ready to assist in every way possible in securing the abolition of slavery.[51]

The efforts of the Kentucky Abolition Society soon attracted considerable attention and incurred severe criticism. The members were repeatedly accused, as the Friends of Humanity had been before them, of talking against slavery and slaveholders in the hearing of, and even to, "multitudes of ignorant Negroes," who might "pervert the most proper reasonings to improper purposes."[52] The society was not discouraged by this opposition. It issued a circular in which its aims were set forth and the objections answered,[53] and thereafter for several years, other circulars reviewing the progress of its work and outlining its plans for the future appeared.

The annual meeting of 1815 displayed an unusual amount of activity. A number of auxiliary branches had recently been established in various parts of Kentucky[54] and the constitution

---

[49] Abolition Intelligencer ***, Vol. 1, No. 6, p. 81; Genius of Universal Emancipation, Vol. 7, No. 165, p. 194.

[50] The Friends of Humanity numbered about 300 in 1808.

[51] Draper MSS., Hist. Miscel. 1. It appears from the manuscript letter of William Rogers, of Philadelphia, March 31, 1795, to the Rev. David Rice, that the Baptists of Kentucky refused to affiliate in any great numbers with the societies that were formed during the latter part of the century. That movement was originated by members of the Presbyterian Church and received most of its support from that denomination, while the movement of 1808 began in the Baptist Church as a result of the peculiar circumstances which have been described.

[52] Benedict: "History of the Baptist Denomination," Vol. 2, p. 246.

[53] Abolition Intelligencer ***, Vol. 1, p. 84. In this circular it was stated that, "We, as an infant Abolition Society in this State, have been ungenerously represented as a dangerous body of citizens forming combinations against the government, raising money for our own emolument, blending the church and the world together ***."

[54] Abolition Intelligencer ***, Vol. 1, No. 6; Genius of Universal Emancipation, Vol. 1, p. 156.

of 1808 was now amended to meet the needs of the expanding order, but without altering the avowed purpose "to bring about a constitutional and legal abolition of slavery in this Commonwealth."[55] A memorial was sent to the legislature of Kentucky describing the nature and the purposes of the organization and asking for an act of incorporation. The petition was brought before the house of representatives by Mr. Daniels, who urged that it be granted.[56] No action, however, appears to have been taken on the matter. A memorial signed by David Barrow as president and Moses White as secretary was sent also to the House of Representatives of the United States setting forth the deplorable condition of the free people of color. It asked that a suitable territory be laid off as an asylum for all Negroes and mulattoes emancipated or to be emancipated within the United States and that such financial assistance be granted them as their needs might demand.[57] Upon this an adverse report was made the following year by the Committee on Public Lands.[58]

In 1821, the society, which had kept up a correspondence with like societies in other parts of the country,[59] resolved to widen the scope of its activities. The small number of papers which would allow the opponents of slavery to set before the people the arguments against the system was one of the greatest difficulties that the anti-slavery workers generally had to contend with, since the columns of the regular newspapers, especially in the states south of the Mason and Dixon Line, were as a rule closed to all anti-slavery discussions. The Kentucky Abolition Society, therefore, determined to establish at Shelbyville a semi-monthly anti-slavery paper under the editorship of the Rev. John Finley Crowe. By way of prospectus, proposals enumerating the principles of the society, with extracts from its constitution, were sent to various periodicals for publication.[60] The first number of the paper,

---

[55] Genius of Universal Emancipation, Vol. 1, p. 156. Lundy in this number said that he had been informed that there were but six or seven members of the society in 1815. The language of the preamble to the Constitution adopted at that date proves the statement to be incorrect. The six or seven members might have been confused with the number of auxiliary branches or with the number in attendance at the annual meeting, which was composed of delegates from the local societies. The Constitution says in part, "It is not possible for these different little societies in their detached situation to unite their efforts against the great will with the same good effect without some general medium of union."

[56] Western Monitor, December 15, 1815.

[57] American State Papers, Miscel. Vol. 2, No. 395, p. 278.

[58] Ibid.

[59] Edward Needles: "Historical Memoirs of the Pennsylvania Society," pp. 58, 80; "Minutes of the Proceedings of the American Convention *** for 1812," p. 17; for 1818, p. 41; The Abolition Intelligencer ***, September, 1822; Genius of Universal Emancipation, Vol. 2, pp. 61-62.

[60] These proposals were printed in full in the Indiana Gazette (Corydon, Indiana), November 29, 1821, and in Lundy's Genius of Universal Emancipation (Greenville, Tennessee), March, 1822. See also A. E. Martin: "Pioneer Anti-Slavery Press," in the March number of the Mississippi Valley Historical Review, 1916, pp. 525ff.

which was called the Abolition Intelligencer and Missionary Magazine, appeared in May, 1822,[61] as a monthly instead of a semi-monthly, as stated in the proposals.[62]

Each number of the Abolition Intelligencer and Missionary Magazine contained sixteen pages, the first eight of which were devoted wholly to a discussion of slavery and the last eight to missions. The historical value of such a paper can hardly be overestimated. It was a repository for all plans for the abolition of slavery, for all laws, opinions, arguments, essays, speeches, reviews, statistics, congressional proceedings, notices of books and pamphlets, colonization efforts, political movements, —in short, for everything relating to slavery.[63]

There were just two anti-slavery papers published in the United States at that time, one, the Abolition Intelligencer and Missionary Magazine, the other, Lundy's Genius of Universal Emancipation. It is worthy of notice that both of these papers were published west of the Appalachian Mountains. This is true of every anti-slavery paper published before 1826.[64]

Since the Abolition Intelligencer and Missionary Magazine was not so well supported as had been anticipated, as the state society, which had less than 200 members at that time, was unable to give any substantial aid, it had to be discontinued. The twelfth and last number was issued in April, 1823, when the paid subscribers numbered fewer than 500.[65] If it had been possible to continue the paper till after Lundy's removal from

---

[61] Lundy announced in the Genius of Universal Emancipation for April, 1822, that "the work was expected to have been commenced before this time, but it is painful to learn that it does not, as yet, meet with the encouragement that would be likely to defray the expenses of publication***. The Society, I am told, have resolved to put the work in operation, very shortly; and that it may prosper, should be the wish of every philanthropic and humane mind. Those who are expected to have the editorial management of the paper, are well qualified for a discharge of the duties that will devolve upon them. Some of them, with whom I have had the pleasure of personal acquaintance, are men of talent, and excellent character, and it is to be presumed that it will be ably conducted."

[62] Abolition Intelligencer***, May, 1822. Only twelve numbers of this paper were issued, nine of which are in the Wisconsin State Historical Society Library at Madison, Wisconsin. See also Martin: "Pioneer Anti-Slavery Press."

The first number of the paper contained a full and explicit enumeration of the objects of the society and of the paper. Among other things they desired to prepare the public mind for the gradual constitutional abolition of slavery, to convince the people that that institution was a national, an individual, and a moral evil, hostile to the spirit of the government, ruinous to the prosperity of the nation, destructive to social happiness, and subversive to the great principles of morality.

[63] Abolition Intelligencer***, May, 1822. See also Martin: "Pioneer Anti-Slavery Press," p. 526.

[64] Following is a list of the anti-slavery papers published before 1827, which avowed the extinction of slavery as one, if not the chief, of their objects. (Martin: "Pioneer Anti-Slavery Press," p. 526f.)

The Philanthropist, Ohio, 1817-19.
The Manumission Intelligencer, Tennessee, 1819.
The Emancipator, Tennessee, 1820.
The Genius of Universal Emancipation, Ohio, 1821; Tennessee, 1822-24; Maryland, 1824-30.
The Abolition Intelligencer and Missionary Magazine, Kentucky, 1822-23.
The African Observer, Pennsylvania, 1826.
The Genius of Universal Emancipation was the only anti-slavery paper published before 1826 that had an existence of more than two years.

[65] Abolition Intelligencer***, March, 1823.

Tennessee to Baltimore in 1824, the Abolition Intelligencer and Missionary Magazine might have received enough subscribers from the anti-slavery strongholds of east Tennessee and Ohio to have made the publication profitable or at least self-supporting. To what extent the discontinuance of the Abolition Intelligencer and Missionary Magazine and the subsequent decline of the Kentucky Abolition Society may be attributed to the active opposition which that periodical excited, it is impossible to say. Articles condemning the Intelligencer as seditious, and even threats of violence against the editor were not unknown,[66] and the pulpit joined the press in denouncing the society for publishing it. In 1827, Lundy said that there were still eight societies in Kentucky, with a membership of 200,[67] but he did not mention the Kentucky Abolition Society, which probably had gone out of existence. The local societies also soon disappeared or were transferred into colonization societies.[68]

The abolition societies in Kentucky, though small in numbers, nevertheless performed a valuable and necessary service. They kept alive anti-slavery discussion by a continued agitation of the subject; they strenuously opposed and materially checked the internal slave trade by pointing out the horrors of the system; they defended the free Negro before the law and labored to better his condition by raising his standard of life; they endeavored to ameliorate the condition of the slaves and to prevent the separation of families. Though it is true that they did not wholly succeed in any one of these undertakings, yet it must be said that they succeeded in part in all of them. In this the Kentucky societies did not differ materially from those in other sections of the country during the same period. All were conservative, for the most part advocating gradual constitutional abolition. To be sure, there were already individuals in both the free and the slave states favoring immediate emancipation, but they were not numerous. In 1808 David Barrow said that he did not know of one among the Kentucky anti-slavery workers who advocated an immediate general emancipation; "those who have considered the subject know that it is a matter of very great importance and that it will require time to prepare those sons

[66] Abolition Intelligencer***, August, 1822; June, 1822; quoted from the Compiler, July 1822, quoted from the Columbian.
[67] Genius of Universal Emancipation, October 13, 1827.
[68] The Colonization Society will be discussed in Chapter 7.

and daughters of wretchedness to receive the blessings of liberty as well as to remove the prejudices."[69]

The strong sectional feeling growing out of the slavery controversy, which was to play such an important part in our history, was not very pronounced during these years, especially before 1820. Slavery had been too recently abolished in the northern states—in New York not until 1827—for a strong radical feeling to be developed there, and in the South it was by no means universally regarded as indispensable to the economic interests, although in the cotton states it was making rapid strides in that direction. The Missouri contest and the struggle over the state constitutions of Illinois and Indiana aroused individuals, societies, and legislatures to the importance of the question and emphasized a divergency of sectional interests, which were forcibly expressed when the legislature of Ohio passed a resolution in 1824 favoring the emancipation and colonization of the adult children of slaves at the expense of the national government. This proposal was endorsed by the legislatures of at least six northern states including Pennsylvania, while it was attacked by all the states of the lower South.[70] But in the border states, where slavery was poorly adapted to the economic life of the people, sectionalism was as yet less evident and the question of emancipation probably was still more generally discussed than in any other part of the country.[71]

---

[69] Barrow: "Involuntary, Absolute, Hereditary Slavery * * *," p. 24.
[70] Ames: "State Documents on Federal Relations," No. 5, p. 11 (with citations); J. B. McMaster: "History of the United States," Vol. 5, p. 204.
[71] Lundy in the Genius of Universal Emancipation, October 13, 1827, makes the following classification of the abolition societies of the United States:

FREE STATES	SOCIETIES	MEMBERS
Massachusetts		
Rhode Island		300
New York		
Pennsylvania	16	900
Ohio	4	300
Total	24	1,500
SLAVE STATES		
Delaware	2	75
Maryland	11	500
District of Columbia	2	100
Virginia	8	250
Kentucky	8	200
Tennessee	25	1,000
North Carolina	50	3,000
Total	106	5,125
GRAND TOTAL	130	6,625

In the FREE STATES table, "Massachusetts" has 4 societies.

THE COLONIZATION MOVEMENT IN KENTUCKY
1816–1850

CHAPTER IV

One of the problems confronting the anti-slavery agitators in all parts of the country was the free Negro, who constituted a considerable element of our population prior to the Civil War.[1]   His condition was well described by Henry Clay in 1829, when he said: "Of all the descriptions of our population, and of either portion of the African race, the free people of color are, by far, as a class, the most corrupt, depraved and abandoned.*** They are not slaves, and yet they are not free.   The laws, it is true, proclaim them free; but prejudices, more powerful than any law, deny them the privileges of freemen.   They occupy a middle station between the free white population and the slaves of the United States, and the tendency of their habits is to corrupt both."[2]   In the North as well as in the South, the free Negro was deemed an undesirable member of society,[3] and many slaveholders who recognized slavery as a great evil were convinced that general emancipation without a removal of the freed slaves would be yet worse, and must result in insurrection, murder, and every form of outrage.

This peculiar position which the free Negro occupied in relation to the slave, to the abolition movement, and to the white

---

[1] The free Negro population of the United States from 1790 to 1840 was: 1790, 59,511; 1800, 110,072; 1810, 186,446; 1820, 226,775; 1830, 319,467; 1840, 386,265.   About 45 per cent. of these lived in the slave States.   In 1830 there were 4,816 free Negroes in Kentucky.

[2] Speech of Henry Clay before the American Colonization Society in 1829, African Repository, Vol. 6, p. 12.

[3] The Negro codes in the northern states were in many cases as strict as, and in some instances more strict than those in the southern states.   In general in the slave states the free Negro was restricted in his freedom by the following limitations: General exclusion from the elective franchise, denial of the right of locomotion, denial of the right of petition, exclusion from the army and militia, exclusion from all participation in the administration of justice, and limitations as to education.   There were also laws in most of the states forbidding or restricting the importation of free Negroes.   Such laws were passed in Kentucky in 1807 (Littell: "Statute Laws of Kentucky," Vol. 3, p. 499).
In 1833, Niles in his Weekly Register, Vol. 45, pp. 167-168, makes the following comment upon the condition of the free Negro: "There are many and great inducements in the free States,*** to rid themselves of a surplus free colored population.   These are not of the best class of colored persons.   They know enough to feel that they are degraded, and to be almost without a hope of bettering their condition; and hence they become careless of the future."   He quoted at length from the Prison Discipline Society, for 1827, which showed a very large per cent. of Negro criminals in all the northern states.   The proportion of the different states varied from one-third in New Jersey, where they constituted one-thirteenth of the population, to one-third in Connecticut, where they represented one-thirty-fourth of the total population.

population centered upon him a great deal of attention, especially from those friends of emancipation who felt that the success of their efforts depended to a large extent upon the ability of the Negro to reap the advantages of freedom and who naturally looked to the free Negro to furnish this example to the world. The attitude of the anti-slavery societies toward this element of the population was set forth clearly in the address of the American Convention of Delegates for the Promotion of the Abolition of Slavery and Improving the Condition of the African Race to the free Negroes in 1818.   In part it is as follows: "Vain will be the desire on the part of the friends of abolition, to behold their labors crowned with success, unless those colored people who have obtained their freedom, should evince by their morality and orderly deportment, that they are deserving the rank and station which they have obtained in society; unavailing will be the most strenuous exertions of humane philanthropists in your behalf, if you should not be found to second their endeavors, by a course of conduct corresponding with the expectations and the wishes of your friends*** so to order and regulate your conduct and deportment in the world and amongst men, that your example may exhibit a standing refutation of the charge, that you are unworthy of freedom***. Finally, be sober; be watchful over every part of your conduct, keeping constantly in view, that the freedom of many thousands of your colour, who still remain in slavery, will be hastened and promoted by your leading a life of virtue and sobriety."[4]   This same sentiment is expressed in the numerous addresses issued by anti-slavery societies as well as in their constitutions, where it was inserted as one of the fundamental objects of the organizations.   Nearly every society had a special department or a committee whose duty it was to look after the interests of the free Negroes, to see that their rights were not abused, and to raise their standards of morality.

It was with a view to finding a solution for this difficult problem that the American Colonization Society for the Free People of Color was founded at Washington in 1816.   While it is with the history of colonization in Kentucky that this chapter is particularly concerned, it will be necessary to turn attention briefly to the history of the above society into which the local anti-slavery societies of the state were at length absorbed and with which the colonization societies there were affiliated.[5]

---

    4 "An Address to the Free People of Colour ***," by the American Convention of Delegates for the Promotion of the Abolition of Slavery, 1818.
    5 See *supra*, p. 47.

The objects of the Society were stated in its constitution and in the numerous addresses issued by the society. The annual meeting in 1826 "Resolved, That its only object is, what has been at all times avowed, the removal to the Coast of Africa, with their own consent, of such people of colour within the United States, as are already free, and of such others, as the humanity of the individuals, and the laws of the different states, may hereafter liberate."[6]   And Henry Clay, president of the society, three years later said in this connection:"From its origin, and throughout the whole period of its existence, it has constantly disclaimed all intention whatever of interfering, in the smallest degree, with the rights of property, or the object of emancipation, gradual or immediate.*** It hopes, indeed, that if it shall demonstrate the practicability of the successful removal to Africa, of free persons of colour, with their consent, the cause of emancipation, either by states or by individuals, may be incidentally advanced."[7]

While this policy of the society was generally approved, as was to be expected, it met with greater success in the border states than elsewhere. In the lower South, indeed, the society was always viewed with some suspicion,[8] and pro-slavery leaders generally came to consider it a scheme looking towards eventual emancipation.[9]   On the other hand the leading anti-slavery organization, The American Convention of Delegates for the Promotion of the Abolition of Slavery and Improving the Condition of the African Race, withheld all support on the ground that the society was doing nothing to further the ends that the convention had in view.[10]   Nevertheless, the American Colonization Society did not lack for distinguished and influential supporters. Justice Bushrod Washington was its first president and John Marshall, James Madison, James Monroe, and Henry Clay were among his successors.

The legislatures of Virginia, Maryland, and Georgia endorsed its request, to which the national government acceded in 1821, that Liberia be purchased for its use.   In short, it drew adherents from many quarters.   Some hoped to rid the state of the

---

[6] African Repository, Vol. 1, pp. 335-6; Niles' Weekly Register, Vol. 45, p. 167.
[7] African Repository, Vol. 6, p. 13.   His entire speech before the Colonization Society in 1829, of which he was President, is given in this number.
[8] Birney: "James G. Birney and His Times," pp. 118-119.
[9] Register of Debates, 19th Congress, 2d Session, p. 328.   Senator Hayne, of South Carolina, in discussing in Congress, in 1827, the making of an appropriation for the American Colonization Society, said: "Are not the members and agents of this society everywhere (even while disclaiming such intentions), making proclamations that the end of their schemes is universal emancipation? *** Does not every Southern man know that wherever the Colonization Society has invaded our country a spirit of hostility to our institutions has immediately sprung up?"
[10] "Minutes of the American Convention***, 1818," pp. 30, 38, 47-54, 65f.

undesirable free Negroes. Others saw in the society an aid to the eventual extinction of slavery through voluntary emancipa-- tion and transportation of the freedmen to Africa. The society was, therefore, admirably adapted to the sentiment of the border states. To the extent that it promised even indirectly to advance the cause of emancipation it could command the support of the anti-slavery element while its program of removal for the free Negro would commend it to pro-slavery and anti-slavery men alike.

While the colonization idea was generally approved in Kentucky, as in other sections of the country, the membership of and number of auxiliary societies increased very slowly for a number of years after the founding of the original society at Washington in 1816. The first auxiliary society was not established in Kentucky until 1823, and the second not until 1827.[11] We have seen, however, that the abolition societies described above adopted colonization as one of their objects in 1823 and gradually gave it increasing prominence, until in the late twenties they had become in reality colonization societies. There is abundant evidence, that, in effecting this change, the abolition societies were reflecting a growing body of public opinion. As early as 1823 the Presbyterian Synod of Kentucky had approved the work of the American Colonization Society and appointed a special committee to further its objects in the state.[12] At about the same time the Kentucky newspapers took up the scheme and devoted increasing attention to it. Their attitude was well illustrated by an article on voluntary emancipation and colonization, published by the Commentator in 1825. In part it is as follows: "This voluntary mode of putting an end to slavery, will we hope find increasing proselytes. It violates no rights real or imaginary; it inflicts injury on no interests or feelings; it displays a spirit worthy of the freest people in the world and it proves by demonstration that while we are tenacious on the subject of our own freedom we are desirous of extending its blessings to all classes of the human race even by the sacrifice of some of our interests."[13] The plan also received the hearty support of the religious papers, especially the Western Luminary and the Presbyterian Herald, both of which published colonization arti-

[11] Adams: "Anti-Slavery in America," p. 106.

[12] Davidson: "History of the Presbyterian Church in Kentucky," pp. 337-8. The General Assembly of the Presbyterian Church had taken similar action in 1818.

[13] The Commentator, August 12, 1825.

cles and notices in practically every number. In 1827, the General Assembly of the state passed a joint resolution endorsing colonization,[14] and similar action was taken two years later with only two dissenting votes. At the latter date the Kentucky representatives in Congress were asked to use their influence to secure an appropriation of money for the purpose of furthering the interests of the society.[15]

The effect of these influences is not difficult to trace. The number of societies increased from two in 1827 to five in 1829 when they were united in the Kentucky Colonization Society,[16] which in turn became an auxiliary to the American Colonization Society. The following year four agents were appointed to devote all their time traveling in the state for the purpose of disseminating information concerning the society and for the establishment of auxiliaries.[17]

The energetic canvass thus instituted in the interest of colonization soon bore fruit. In a letter to the Kentucky Reporter in 1830, astonishment was expressed by a correspondent at the ardor with which men of all ranks entered into the movement and the opinion was expressed that 10,000 members could be secured to the society in the course of the next three or four years. The writer also stated that numerous individuals had expressed their willingness to surrender their Negroes at any time that the society might be ready to receive them.[18] The African Repository in commenting on the work of the various colonization societies in the United States in 1830 said: "Probably in no state of the Union has the scheme of African Colonization found more decided friends or met with more general approbation than in Kentucky."[19] The governing bodies of the Presbyterian,[20] the Methodists,[21] and the Baptist[22] churches of Kentucky repeatedly approved colonization and at different times made special efforts to promote its interests. It is therefore not surprising that by 1832 the number of societies in Kentucky had increased

[14] The Spirit of Seventy-Six, March 22, 1827; The Western Luminary, June 24, 1827.
[15] Niles' Weekly Register, Vol. 35, p. 387.
[16] Adams: "Anti-Slavery in America," p. 106. See also, African Repository, Vol. 3, p. 27; Vol. 7, p. 94; Vol. 8, p. 91; Vol. 9, pp. 194, 216.
[17] The Kentuckian, June 1, 1829; African Repository, Vol. 4, p. 351; Vol. 5, pp. 27-291 Vol. 6, p. 82.
[18] The Kentucky Reporter, 1830, quoted in the African Repository, Vol. 5, pp. 27-29.
[19] African Repository, Vol. 6, p. 80.
[20] Davidson: "History of the Presbyterian Church in Kentucky," p. 337. See also Western Luminary, March 5, 1834, Western Presbyterian Herald, Nov. 21, 1837.
[21] A. H. Redford: "Western Cavaliers," pp. 71, 125, 149, 398. The National General Conference approved the colonization idea in 1828. (Journal of the General Conference, Vol. 1, p. 357; Vol. 2, p. 59. See also African Repository, Vol. 3, p. 120; Vol. 4, p. 126; Vol. 6, p. 83.)
[22] The (Baptist) Cross, February 6, 1834.

to 31.[23]   Some of these moreover were county organizations composed of several local societies.

The reason for this general approbation lay, as has been suggested, in the double appeal made by colonization.   In its constitution of 1829, the Kentucky Colonization Society had declared that its purpose was to relieve the Commonwealth "from the serious inconvenience resulting from the existence among us, of a rapidly increasing number of free persons of colour, who are not subject to the restraints of slavery."[24]   With this purpose even pro-slavery men could sympathize.   Conservative anti-slavery men, on the other hand, could not overlook the declaration that "The late disposition to voluntary emancipation is so increasing that no law is necessary to free us from slavery, provided there is an asylum accessible to the liberated."[25]

And it appears, therefore, that in Kentucky, at least, the anti-slavery feature of the colonization scheme was not merely passive.   The state and local societies were to some extent centers of anti-slavery thought, since in the numerous addresses before them, which were usually published in the current newspapers, as well as in the African Repository, the institution of slavery was attacked upon moral, economic, and political grounds.   The tendency, or rather the desire, of the Kentucky masters to give up their slaves for the purpose of freeing and removing them to Liberia was repeatedly referred to. Thus Robert J. Breckinridge, in 1831, said that colonization took for granted the fact that slavery was a great moral and political evil "and (the society) cherished the hope and the belief also, that the successful prosecution of its objects would offer powerful motives and exert a persuasive influence in favor of emancipation.   And it is with this indirect effect of the society that the largest advantage is to result to America."[26]   J. C. Young, the president of Centre College at Danville, Kentucky,

---

[23] Adams: "Anti-Slavery in America," p. 106.
      Female colonization societies were organized in Louisville, Lexington and elsewhere in the state.   They were exceedingly active and rendered valuable service in obtaining funds for the society.
      The growth of societies to promote colonization was by no means confined to Kentucky.   The American Colonization Society, at the end of its first decade (1826), had 62 auxiliary branches.   By 1832 they had increased to 228 and of these 92 were in the free states and 136 in the slave states.   Only 22 were found in the lower South, and of the 114 in the border states, 34 were in Virginia and 31 in Kentucky.

[24] "Proceedings of the Kentucky Colonization Society for 1831," Pamphlet.   See also African Repository, Vol. 4, p. 351.

[25] "Proceedings of the Kentucky Colonization Society for 1831." Ibid.

[26] Speech before the Kentucky Colonization Society in the African Repository, Vol. 7, p. 176.   A correspondent in the Western Luminary, August 29, 1827, in an article signed "Harper," declared that slavery was ruining Kentucky and that the state must soon suffer the consequences.   He said, "Renationalize the blacks.   Send them back to their country, beginning first with those that are, and shall become free—and then progress by slow degrees with the residue.   The colony in Liberia is a star in the east which points out the mode of relief."

stated, before the Kentucky Colonization Society in 1832, his belief that colonization would greatly advance both the immediate and the permanent prosperity of the country and that it would eventually end in escape from slavery.[27] Similarly the Danville Colonization Society in a petition to the legislature of Kentucky in 1831 said in this connection: "Within the last ten years these degraded people have nearly doubled their numbers, * * * . Two-thirds of this increase has been produced by emancipation from the slave class, and the same spirit which produced that result is still abroad among us, and is every day acquiring increased potency over the minds of men. The work of emancipation is still going on, and will go on, with increased rapidity."[28] In 1835 the Hon. Joseph R. Underwood, later United States Senator, expressed the opinion that this sentiment would continue to increase until it pervaded and influenced a majority of the slaveholders of the state. He said further that these opinions were based upon certain facts, which he enumerated and discussed at some length, among which were: 1. Slave labor was more expensive than free and consequently in the states where there were no slaves the products could be sold cheaper than where they were raised by slaves. 2. Communities that had no slaves surpassed those that had, in almost everything that rendered life comfortable. 3. Many valuable citizens were leaving the state for no other reason than the existence of slavery in it.[29] The influence of Henry Clay, too, must have been very great, as his opinion on this as on other questions carried with it a great deal of force. As president of the American Colonization Society he declared: "If I could only be made instrumental in ridding of this foul blot (slavery) that revered state that gave me birth, or that not less beloved state which kindly adopted me as her son, I should not exchange the proud satisfaction that I should enjoy for all the honor of all the triumphs ever decreed to the most successful conqueror."[30] That Clay and thousands of his fellow citizens regarded slavery as an evil and

[27] African Repository, Vol. 9, p. 59.
[28] African Repository, Vol. 7, p. 211. The liberal enforcement of the emancipation laws of the State was discussed in the Spirit of Seventy-Six, January 31, 1827, and in the Maysville Eagle, February 14, 1838.
[29] Hon. Joseph R. Underwood: "Address before the Kentucky Colonization Society in 1835," Pamphlet, p. 20.
In the report of the managers of the Kentucky Colonization Society, at its annual meeting in 1830, the following statements were made: "Experience has taught that slaves add nothing to our national wealth. Where they exist labor is not only high, but badly performed; and the communities growing up around us who are clear of this evil flourish over us, and by their cheapness of labor and more abundant industry are making us tributary." (African Repository, Vol. 6, p. 81.)
[30] "Annual Report of the American Colonization Society," Pamphlet, 1827.

as antagonistic to the economic interests of the state and that they believed that colonization would either accomplish eventually the extinction of slavery or contribute largely toward that end are evident to any one cognizant of the facts. The problem before them was an exceedingly complicated one, and its solution a difficult and uncertain task. While such opinions as the above were freely voiced it is clear that the position of the Kentucky Colonization Society, reiterated in its numerous reports, in numerous speeches, and in the newspapers[31] throughout the state, must have enjoyed a large measure of support among the conservative classes of the state. Thus the Louisville Journal, one of the most influential papers in Kentucky, declared ".We look upon colonization as the only plan consistent with individual rights and the peace and happiness and the prosperity of the nation which has been or can be devised for the abrogation of slavery in the Southern states. * * * Its object is not to pronounce the negro free and equal to the white but to endeavor to make him so—not simply to break the chains from his limbs, but to place him in a position to deserve and enjoy freedom."[32]

While a majority of those affiliated with the movement in Kentucky appear to have had this attitude toward the work, there were some who wished merely to remove the free Negroes from the state and who were opposed to any anti-slavery tendencies on the part of the colonization society. A good representative of this class was the Hon. Robert Wickliffe, whom Cassius M. Clay frequently compared to McDuffie of South Carolina, because of his radical pro-slavery views. Wickliffe was at one time a member of the colonization society of Kentucky. In an address before the Female Colonization Society of Lexington, he made the statement that the society was not designed to interfere in any way between master and slave, whereupon Robert J. Breckinridge arose and flatly contradicted the statement, and further said that if the ultimate aim of the society was not to emancipate the slaves, he would wash his hands of it. Others expressed the same opinion, and shortly afterwards Wickliffe severed his connection with the society forever.[33] The Louisville Public Advertiser, a Democratic and anti-Clay paper, also strongly opposed colonization. An editorial of 1830

---

[31] The newspapers of the state were almost unanimous in their support of colonization and permitted it to be discussed freely in their columns. A few, however, doubted the practicability of the plan and one, the Louisville Public Advertiser, openly opposed it.
[32] The Louisville Journal, September 15, 1836.
[33] Robert Wickliffe: "Reply to Robert J. Breckinridge," 1840, Pamphlet, p. 44.

said: "We think that it is high time for the people of the state to begin to scrutinize with severity the course and conduct of the 'Heaven directed Genius' (Henry Clay) on this subject. Under pretense of raising funds to transport the free people of colour to Liberia, hundreds of associations have been formed and appeal after appeal has been made to the sympathies of the public, the real object of which was to prepare the public mind for the effort we are now told will be made by the 'Heaven directed Genius' to induce the Kentuckians to undertake the great work of emancipation. We have always viewed the project of colonizing the people of colour in Liberia as deceptive and pernicious and only intended to cover the real designs of its leading advocates—that of emancipating slaves and leaving them among us, some to fall victims to folly and vice and others to be amalgamated—united by ties of blood with the sons and daughters of their political champions."[34]

Whatever their intentions, the Kentucky colonization societies were never able to accomplish a great deal in the way either of ridding the state of the free colored population or of lessening to any great extent the number of slaves, but a small beginning was made which it was hoped would tend toward a final solution of the problem. There were many instances of willingness on the part of masters to free their slaves for transportation to Africa,[35] but the lack of funds appears to have greatly hampered the work. The Louisville Branch of the Kentucky Colonization Society, which appeared to be more active than any other in the state, raised $805.25 in 1832[36] and $3,000 in 1839.[37] In 1833 the Kentucky Colonization Society collected $1,137.67[38] and in 1836 it turned over to the American Colonization Society $1,000.[39] These sums were obviously inadequate to accomplish much in view of the cost of transportation which was estimated at from twenty to thirty-five dollars for each individual.[40]

---

[34] Louisville Public Advertiser, April 19, 1830. This was the strongest and most radical pro-slavery paper in the state.
[35] Niles' Weekly Register, Vol. 48, p. 42; Vol. 49, p. 195; The Commonwealth, February 20, 1839, stated that there were a number of large slaveholders in the state who were ready to liberate their slaves whenever the Kentucky Colonization Society was prepared to transport them to Africa.
[36] African Repository, Vol. 9, p. 28.
[37] Ibid., Vol. 15, p. 154.
[38] Louisville Herald, March 4, 1833.
[39] African Repository, Vol. 12, p. 269. In 1833 the students of Andover Theological Seminary, at the suggestion of R. S. Finley, the agent of the Kentucky Colonization Society, pledged themselves to raise in six months a sum sufficient to effect the emancipation of 100 slaves in Kentucky. (Advocate of Popular Rights, September 21, 1833).
[40] The Hon. Daniel Mayer in an "Address Before the Kentucky Colonization Society" in 1831 estimated the cost of transportation to Africa at $20.00 for each individual. (Pamphlet.) This estimate is probably too low. The Hon. Joseph R. Underwood in an "Address before the Kentucky Colonization Society in 1835" placed the average cost at $35.00.

It is probably true that the leaders of the movement had, never expected to rely upon small sums collected in this way. After demonstrating the practicability of colonization they had looked for governmental help. As early as 1830 the Kentucky Colonization Society sent a memorial to Congress, in which slavery was condemned and the government was asked to assume the same attitude toward the free Negro that it held toward the American Indian and to provide means for his transportation and colonization either in the unsettled section of our own country or in Liberia.[41] The following year a petition was sent to the legislature of Kentucky asking for an appropriation of money for the purpose of transporting to Liberia all free colored persons willing to go. It was suggested that an annual tax of ten cents be levied on every slave in the state as a means of raising this fund. A bill embodying this suggestion was introduced by Representative Green, but it failed of passage.[42] That this action was a disappointment to the society may be gathered from the speech of Robert J. Breckinridge, delivered in the same year when he said: "It is generally known that the original members of the American Colonization Society anticipated, that at some future period, the general government and some if not all of the state governments would co-operate in their exertions for the removal of an evil which was obviously national in all its aspects, and which no private exertions were adequate to extinguish."[43] And Henry Clay said in this connection in 1837: "The Society was formed to demonstrate the practicability of colonization in Africa, and, if it were unhappily dissolved tomorrow, that great purpose of its founders will have been completely accomplished. No one can now doubt that, with the application of adequate means, such as the governments of the several states of the Union could supply, almost without an effort, the colonization of the descendants of the African race may be effected to any desirable extent. The founders of the Society never imagined that, depending as it does upon spontaneous contributions from the good and the benevolent irregularly made, without an established revenue, and without power, the Society alone was competent to colonize all the free

[41] African Repository, Vol. 5, p. 347. The rules of the society require the holding of the annual meetings during the sessions of the legislature. For further attempts to influence the legislature see Breckinridge Papers for 1830 and 1831 and especially H. Wingate to R. J. Breckinridge, Dec. 1, 1830; Dr. S. Marshall to R. J. Breckinridge, December, 1831.
[42] Lexington Observer, September 16, 1831. African Repository, Vol. 7, pp. 148, 212. A great number of plans were proposed and discussed from time to time for raising funds for carrying out the plans of the society, but none of them met with the approval of the legislature.
[43] African Repository, Vol. 14, p. 17.

persons of colour in the United States. They hoped, and the Society still hopes, that, seeing what has been done, and can be done, governments may think fit to take hold of the principle, and carry it out as far as they may deem right, with their ample powers and abundant resources. * * * Great national enterprises are not to be speedily executed, like those of individuals, in the short span of the life of one person. * * * Near two centuries elapsed, during which her (Africa's) sons were constantly transported to the shores of the New World, doomed to a state of bondage. A period of similar extent may possibly be necessary to restore their descendants to the parent country, with all the blessings of law and liberty, religion and civilization. A sudden and instantaneous separation of the two races, if it were possible, would be good for neither nor for either country."[44]

In view of the shortage of funds it is not surprising that the number of free Negroes transported from Kentucky to Africa was in fact very small.[45] The efforts of the society, however, were not relaxed. In 1844, an agitation was started for the establishment of a separate colony in Africa to be known as "Kentucky in Liberia"[46] and to be modeled after "Maryland in Liberia" which had been established the previous year.[47] In 1845 the Rev. A. M. Cowan, the agent of the American Colonization Society in Kentucky, began a campaign to raise $5,000 to be used in purchasing a suitable tract of land on which the free colored people of Kentucky might be settled.[48] The newspapers, the religious denominations, and various other organizations entered actively into the campaign, and as a result the money was raised before the end of the year. Acting under instructions from the American Colonization Society, Governor Roberts of Liberia laid off a tract of land forty miles square on the north side of the St. Paul River for that purpose.[49]

Special inducements were offered to attract the free Negroes and to make them contented and prosperous after their arrival. The emigrants were to enjoy all the advantages of the government

---

[44] African Repository, Vol. 14, p. 18. Speech before the American Colonization Society 1837.
[45] Ninety-six slaves from Kentucky were sent to Liberia, in 1833, and others were sent from time to time during the thirties, but the average was probably less than that for 1833. Louisville Public Advertiser, March 27, 1833. Among the emigrants for 1833 were eleven slaves freed by Robert J. Breckinridge and turned over to the Colonization Society together with considerable money and supplies for their maintenance after their arrival in Africa. African Repository, Vol. 20, p. 310.
[47] Ibid., Vol. 19, p. 341.
[48] Ibid., Vol. 21, p. 380; The Frankfort Commonwealth, September 30, 1845; Niles' Weekly Register, Vol. 69, p. 102.
[49] African Repository, Vol. 21, p. 283.

of Liberia and all the privileges that they would enjoy in any settlement in the Commonwealth.[50]   Those who were unable to pay their own expenses were to be provided for by funds raised in Kentucky and they were to be supported for six months after their arrival.[51]   Each head of a family or single adult was promised a building lot in the town with five acres adjoining or if he settled two miles out of town fifty acres, or three miles from town one hundred acres of land.[52]

A vessel was chartered to sail in November, 1845, with about 200 emigrants for the new settlement, but the ship did not sail until February, 1846, and then with only thirty-five emigrants from Kentucky, although there was a large number from other states in the Mississippi Valley.[53]   Of the thirty-five emigrants from Kentucky, twenty were men, six were women, and nine were children.   Only two were free Negroes.   Twelve were church members, two of them ministers.   There were three carpenters, one blacksmith, and one shoemaker.[54]

The American Colonization Society granted the Kentucky Colonization Society permission to use all the money raised in the state for the transportation of emigrants from Kentucky,[55] and a special effort was made to induce the state legislature to make an appropriation to defray the expenses of transportation but without success.[56]   The Presbyterian Synod of Kentucky pledged $500 toward the purchase of a ship to run as a regular packet between New Orleans and Liberia to carry emigrants and provisions from the Mississippi Valley.[57]   The Rev. Mr. Cowan called a convention of the free Negroes of Kentucky in order to induce a greater emigration to Liberia.   Lexington, Louisville, and Danville were each to send one Negro representative to the settlement in Africa at the expense of the society.   After one year's residence in the colony these representatives were to return and report to the free Negroes of the state.[58]   As was planned the representatives were sent to Liberia, but no record has been found of either their return or the contemplated report.

---

[50] African Repository, Vol. 21, p. 283.
[51] Ibid.; Niles' Weekly Register, Vol. 68, p. 362.
[52] Presbyterian Herald, January 15, 1846.
[53] Ibid.; African Repository, Vol. 23, p. 65.   The number of Negroes emigrating from Kentucky to Liberia during the following years was: 1840, 12; 1841, 20; 1843, 14; 1844, 21; 1845, 36; 1846, 35.
[54] Ibid.
[55] African Repository, Vol. 22, p. 304.
[56] Ibid., Vol. 22, p. 38.
[57] The Liberator, October 24, 1845.
[58] Niles' Weekly Register, Vol. 72, p. 323.

There was considerable discussion in Kentucky about this time of the advisability of compelling all free Negroes to emigrate to Africa and upon at least one occasion, in 1845, a mass meeting was held in Fayette County and resolutions to that effect adopted and forwarded to the legislature. It was proposed that they be given free passage and provisions for the voyage.[59] No action appears to have been taken by the legislature on the subject.

African colonization continued to be discussed in Kentucky until the end of the Civil War and confidence in the feasibility of the plan was never lost. In an address before the Kentucky Colonization Society in 1847 Judge Bullock said: "It is a remarkable fact, that whilst the colonization society has carefully avoided all interference with the relations of master and slaves, it has done more to promote emancipation than all the abolition societies in the country. * * * The emancipation which it promotes and encourages is real emancipation."[60] John A. McClung, one of the leading citizens of the state, speaking before the society in the following year, declared that slavery was merely temporary in all but the cotton states; that it was gradually receding in a southern direction and that while it would thus eventually be extinguished in Kentucky the black population would remain unless removed by means of colonization. This he maintained could be easily accomplished without much loss to the community or suffering to the Negro.[61] As late as 1848 Senator Underwood of Kentucky, a slaveholder of large views and much sagacity, said in the United States Senate in a discussion on the great territorial bill: "I am no advocate of the institution of negro slavery. I believe its existence in Kentucky to be prejudicial to the best interests of the white population, and if I had the power to colonize and remove every slave within the borders of my state, I would cheerfully do it." After expressing his belief in the practicability of colonization he proposed the following plan: "Let a future date be fixed, after which every slave child born shall be the property of the state, for the purpose of colonization. Place our children when weaned in the hands of those who will raise them—females till they are eighteen and males to twenty-

[59] Anti-Slavery Bugle, October 3, 1845.
[60] African Repository, Vol. 23, p. 109.
[61] African Repository, Vol. 24, pp. 133-149.

five and upon their reaching those ages send them to Africa."[62]
He expressed the belief that those to whom the children were
bound would be willing, in consideration of their services, to
pay their transportation to Africa.   The departure of the females as they reached womanhood would put an end to the
birth of slaves within the state and consequently, he declared,
the extirpation of slavery would be just as "certain as
the laws of nature," and, although the process would extend
over a considerable number of years, that would be to the advantage of both races.[63]

While the colonization movement in Kentucky did not
accomplish much in removing the free Negroes, it indirectly
performed a valuable service by keeping emancipation constantly before the people.   The anti-slavery workers of the
state generally allied themselves with the colonization movement
because it seemed to be fairly practicable and because it stood
a better chance of success than any other plan.   Furthermore,
with the coming of radical abolitionism in the North during
the thirties many friends of emancipation in the border states
were forced to support the colonization movement as their
only means of attacking slavery, since in 1836 the anti-slavery
societies were completely displaced by the colonization societies.
This, however, was not a significant change, save as it affected
a few radical individuals in Kentucky.   On the whole the anti-
slavery societies there had, during their entire existence,
held nearly the same views about slavery and the necessity by
gradual means of extinguishing it as those of the colonization
society.

    [62] The Presbyterian Herald, September 21, 1848. An interesting proposal for the
colonization of the Kentucky Negroes in Texas is found in the Crittenden Papers, S. S. Nicholas
to Lee Crittenden, January 7, 1844.
    [63] The Presbyterian Herald, September 21, 1848. Also quoted in The Examiner,
November 1, 1848.
    This is only one of numerous plans that were proposed from time to time.   Most
of them were concerned only with African colonization although a few desired to colonize the
Negro in Mexico, the West Indies or the western part of the United States.   From this date
until the beginning of the Civil War, these colonization discussions continued unabated as did
the work of the Colonization Society.

ANTI-SLAVERY SOCIETIES AND THE ADVENT OF GARRISONIAN ABOLITION, 1830–1840

CHAPTER V

Probably no period in the history of the United States has been more characterized by the spirit of reform than that of the second quarter of the Nineteenth Century. All the social, moral, and religious influences of the community seemed to be gathered into a movement designed to annihilate the wickedness of man and introduce economic and social well-being. Transcendentalism, idealism, and humanitarianism were dominant in the philosophy of the time. Religious and social reforms of every kind, genuine and sham, were eagerly taken up and propagated with great enthusiasm. New sects arose with strange doctrines. The Mormons made many converts while the Millerites proclaimed and awaited with confidence the advent of the millennium. A vigorous assault was made on Masonry by a powerful political party formed on the basis of this idea alone. The temperance movement won notable victories. The agitation for woman's rights was begun and able champions of the cause appeared. Peace societies were organized. The transportation of the mails on Sunday was one of the debated topics of the day. Theatres, lotteries, the treatment of the Indian by the general government, all came under the most searching review. The environment seemed to be favorable to the rapid and rank growth of reforms and crusades, many of them utterly impracticable, but all of them pushed with the greatest devotion and enthusiam.

Immediate abolition, when it appeared in the free states, was only one of the liberal and humanitarian ideas that were sweeping over the country, and in some of the slave states, especially those along the northern border, the subject of gradual emancipation was freely discussed. The struggle in the constitutional convention of Virginia, in 1829, and in the two succeeding legislatures, where the plan for the gradual abolition of slavery was defeated by a very small majority, is an evidence of the sentiment that prevailed in the border states during those years.

In Kentucky, anti-slavery agitation assumed more prominence than at any time since the struggle of 1798-99 over the constitutional convention. The new interest was not confined to the colonization society and its auxiliaries discussed in the preceding chapter. Men of all grades in society and of all creeds and of all political parties enlisted in the cause. In the volumes of the Genius of Universal Emancipation for 1828, 1829, and 1830, Benjamin Lundy repeatedly asserted that the spirit of emancipation was gaining ground in Kentucky. He especially noted as deserving the support of every friend of the cause[1] the efforts of the Western Luminary, the first religious newspaper published in the Southwest. This paper was a Presbyterian journal established in 1823 under the able editorship of Thomas T. Skillman,[2] who from the beginning had attacked the system of slavery fearlessly and continued to do so until his death in 1833. In 113 numbers of the Western Luminary covering the period from 1828 to 1833, ninety-one colonization and anti-slavery articles are found, many of them published in long series and dealing with various phases of the matter.[3] They were ably written and were copied by many of the Kentucky newspapers as well as by newspapers in other sections of the country. The Russellville Messenger was likewise active in its opposition to slavery.[4] Anti-slavery sentiment was by no means confined to the editors of these sheets. The unusual activity and the character of the anti-slavery leaders in the state caused many other newspapers to throw open their columns to a discussion of the subject.

The movement against slavery in Kentucky was due to economic as well as humanitarian reasons, but the fact remains that the idea of gradual emancipation was making headway in the early thirties. A slaveholder of Kentucky in a communication to the African Repository in 1829 wrote as follows: "I think I hazard nothing in saying that a large portion of us, who are even slaveholders ourselves, are looking forward with pleasing anticipation to that period when slavery shall no longer be a blot

---

[1] Genius of Universal Emancipation, April, 1830.

[2] This paper was founded by John Breckinridge, but his connection with it ended in 1826. William Breckinridge was associated with Skillman in this work for a number of years after 1826.

[3] An incomplete file of this paper is in the library of the University of Chicago. William Lloyd Garrison in the Liberator, December 3, 1831, spoke in the highest terms of the fearless attack that the Western Luminary was making on slavery.

[4] In the Genius of Universal Emancipation, for April, 1830, Lundy said in this connection: "Several of the newspapers of Kentucky continue to advocate the abolition of slavery, in that state, with a freedom and boldness calculated to inspire the hope that the day of political and moral redemption is drawing near." The papers referred to were The Western Luminary, The Russellville Messenger, and The Kentucky Reporter.

upon the escutcheon of our Republican Institutions."[5] A correspondent in the Western Luminary expressed a similar sentiment in the following year, when he said that the people of Kentucky felt that slavery was a "burden; a yoke which is growing heavier. The holders are becoming more weary than the slaves. They are looking around for relief with great anxiety."[6] An editorial in the Western Luminary a little later stated that the subject of slavery, which a few years before had been regarded as an "interdicted topic, a subject too delicate to bear even the most calm and dispassionate discussion, was beginning to be viewed now in a more rational manner, by the citizens of our state generally. It has become a popular topic in our religious and political journals, the private circles, and the legislative halls. For one we acknowledge we are glad it is so. We are not of those who think the concealment of a public evil from the view of the community can be attended with any beneficial consequences. If then it be a great national evil among us—and who does not feel our present system of slavery to be such an evil—do not the plainest dictates of common sense teach us that the subject, unpleasant and humiliating as it is, should be understood by the community, in all its bearings? Ignorance under some circumstances may be productive of incalculable evil, but can certainly accomplish no good."[7]

A writer in the Louisville Herald, in 1833, said that a mild and candid discussion of slavery was not only permitted but even invited by the public sentiment.[8] And the editor of the Cincinnati Chronicle after an extensive trip through Kentucky in 1832 stated that "in traveling through no inconsiderable portion of the State of Kentucky, and mingling with both town and country population, I could not but remark the change within the last few years, in public sentiment, upon the question of slavery.* * * There is moreover a growing sentiment among the holders of slaves, that neither the pecuniary interest, the comfort nor the personal safety of the white population, is enhanced by slavery.* * * Something it must be owned has been gained toward the cause of general emancipation and the removal of the slaves of this country, when such sentiments

---

[5] African Repository, Vol. 5, p. 174.

[6] Genius of Universal Emancipation, July, 1830, quoted from the Western Luminary.

[7] Western Luminary, December 21, 1831. A correspondent in the Western Presbyterian Herald, November 30, 1837, in speaking of the anti-slavery sentiment in 1830 said in reference to the Virginia Convention of 1829: "Had a convention been called in Kentucky about the same time I believe it might have been successful."

[8] Genius of Universal Emancipation, June, 1833, quoted from the Louisville Herald.

and such opinions are held and openly avowed among those upon whom slavery has been entailed for generations."[9]   And the Rev. J. F. Clarke, who lived in Kentucky from 1833 to 1840, writing many years later, asserted that "The sentiment in Kentucky, in those days, among all the better class of people, was that slavery was a wrong and an evil, and that it ought to be abolished. It was also believed that Kentucky would, when the time came for altering the Constitution, insert a clause in the new Constitution that would allow slavery to be abolished. * * *   I learned my anti-slavery lessons from slavery itself and from the slaveholders around me. * * *   The majority were on the side of those who contended that slavery was an evil and a wrong. Nobody in the state thought that there was anything improper or dangerous in having the subject fully discussed."[10]   It would appear that Rev. Mr. Clarke's reminiscences are not altogether trustworthy on this point, since they were written during the latter part of his life and many years after this period. In the main, however, though overdrawn, they are correct. As early as 1828 a gentleman from Kentucky in a letter to Benjamin Lundy said that the sentiment and feelings of the people of the state were not so hostile to slavery as formerly and that only a few men in the entire state attempted to defend the institution on either moral or economic grounds.[11]   It is hardly necesssary to say that public sentiment was not united in respect to the anti-slavery agitation. As the movement developed protests were made in the legislature and in the newspapers against emancipation sermons and anti-slavery discussions as tending to cause insurrection and tumult among the slaves such as had recently occurred in Virginia.[12]   It was frequently maintained that the conditions were not favorable for abolition or for a free discussion of the subject. Such arguments, however, were generally unavailing.

The arguments for gradual emancipation in this period rested in part upon ethical and religious grounds but chiefly upon economic considerations. Questions were raised as to the moral relations between master and slave, as to the consistency of slavery with the principles of democratic government, and as to its consistency with the principles of Christianity. Far more

[9] The Cincinnati Chronicle, quoted in the Genius of Universal Emancipation, April, 1833.

[10] J. F. Clarke: "Anti-Slavery Days," pp. 22, 25.

[11] Genius of Universal Emancipation, Vol. 7, August 30, 1828.

[12] The Commonwealth, December 13, 1831, quoted from the speech of Elisha Smith, of Rockcastle County, in the House of Representatives of Kentucky, December, 1831.

influential, however, was the argument based upon the fact that the system of slave labor was not adapted to the real economic needs of the state.[13] Reference was frequently made to the prosperity of the states north of the Ohio River and particularly to Ohio. In a speech in the Kentucky Senate in 1828 on a bill more effectively to prevent the importation of slaves, Mr. Green, of Lincoln County, said, "Let us look to the state of Ohio, with her rapidly increasing population of freemen, her roads and canals, and all her other internal improvements.***Why is it that she is outstripping Kentucky? Not because she has a milder or more salubrious climate, for her winters are longer and her growing season shorter. Not because her soil is more fertile, for she can show no large body of lands equal to the rich land of Kentucky. Yet her citizens are able to undersell you in every market. Upon what other principle can this be explained, but on this: that free labor is cheaper than slave labor—a principle well understood by every person who has the slightest acquaintance with practical economy."[14]

And there was much to support the contention. In 1800, the inhabitants of Ohio numbered only 45,365, while Kentucky had a population of 220,955. By 1830 the population of Ohio had increased to 937,903 while that of Kentucky was only 687,917.[15] The industries and public works of Ohio had increased

[13] The Kentuckian, December 18, 25, 1828; January 8, 22, 29; February 5, 12, 1829.
[14] The Spirit of Seventy-Six, January 31, 1828. This same sentiment was expressed forcefully by a correspondent in the Louisville Herald, May 16, 1833, in these words: "They (slaves) have done grievous harm already, by hindering our growth, keeping us far behind our sister states, impoverishing our soil, corrupting our morals and manners.***We believe that slavery in our state is unprofitable and ruinous, to say nothing of other objections; and as a question of political economy we assert that it imposes upon us a heavy and ever increasing tax which must be taken off or sooner or later beggary and decay must be our portion. It is madness to try to wink these things out of sight, it is folly to pretend to deny them. All experience and observation, the history and the present condition of Virginia and Maryland speak with a trumpet voice. The latter has already begun to take measures to regenerate its sinking fortunes.***Though blessed with a fruitful soil, with many natural advantages, they see and acknowledge that their lands have every year been growing poorer, that they are slowly but certainly sinking in political importance."
A long series of articles dealing with this phase of the subject was printed in the Louisville Herald, 1833. Those of especial importance are in the numbers for January 16, February 12, 13, and May 28. See also editorial in the Shelbyville Examiner, May 4, 1833.
[15] The following tables give the per cent. of increase and the positive growth of three border states, Kentucky, Tennessee and Missouri, and of three free states, Ohio, Indiana and Illinois.

PER CENT. INCREASE

	1790–1800	1800–10	1810–20	1820–30	1830–40	1840–50
Kentucky	199	84	38	21	13	26
Tennessee	195	147	61	61	21	20
Missouri	..	..	219	110	173	77
Ohio	..	408	152	61	62	30
Indiana	..	347	500	133	99	44
Illinois	..	..	349	185	202	78

POSITIVE GROWTH (THOUSANDS)

	147	185	157	123	91	202
Kentucky	147	185	157	123	91	202
Tennessee	69	156	161	259	147	173
Missouri	..	20	45	73	243	298
Ohio	45	185	350	356	581	460
Indiana	5	18	122	195	342	302
Illinois	..	12	42	102	318	375

(Abstract of Twelfth Census, pp. 34-36)

accordingly. The agricultural products of the two states did not differ materially, but it was asserted that the farmers of Ohio could outsell the Kentucky farmers in all the eastern markets.[16] It was even shown that Ohio tobacco, the great staple of Kentucky, could be sold in Baltimore cheaper than tobacco produced by slave labor in Maryland.[17]

It might have been expected as a result of these extensive inquiries into the rightfulness and the economic utility of slavery that positive plans looking toward gradual emancipation would be brought forward. As a result of the large number of slaves in the state and their unpreparedness for freedom, it was generally believed that any plan that might be adopted must be necessarily only gradually put into operation and extend over a large number of years. With this end in view numerous plans and proposals were made during the early thirties and among them was a plan for the liberation of the offspring of slaves and the formation of societies of slaveholders to effect that purpose.

The first step in this direction was the circulation, in 1831,[18] of petitions signed by prominent men from different parts of the state and setting out the following purpose: "Several citizens, slaveholders, under a full conviction that there are insurmountable obstacles to the general emancipation of the present generation of slaves, but equally convinced of the necessity and practicability of emancipating their future offspring, and desirous that a society be formed for the purpose of investigating and impressing these truths on the public mind, as well by example as by precept; by placing themselves immediately by mutual voluntary arrangement, under a well regulated system of gradual emancipation; such a system as they would recommend to their fellow citizens for adoption as the law of the land. In this view it is proposed to all slaveholders of every religion, opinion, or country who are willing to abolish slavery by the gradual emancipation of the coming generation and who are willing, as a pledge of their

---

[16] C. M. Clay: "A Review of the Late Canvass, 1840," Pamphlet, p. 14; Lexington Observer, Oct. 21, 1831; Speech of May Squire Turner in the House of Representatives of Kentucky; Western Luminary, March 5, 1834, August 29, 1827. Also African Repository, Vol. 10, p. 45; Speech of James G. Birney, proposing Gradual Emancipation; The Cross (Ky.), February 6, 1834; Address of the Hon. J. T. Morehead before the Kentucky Colonization Society in 1840. Ogden in his "Letters from the West" (R. G. Thwaites: "Early Western Travels," Vol. 1, pp. 80, 112) in 1821 attributed the increase of population and the industrial superiority of Ohio over Kentucky to the existence of slavery in the latter. Other references on this subject are: Louisville Herald, January 11, 1833, February 12, May 16, May 28, 1833; Genius of Universal Emancipation, July, 1833, p. 63, quoted from Western Luminary; African Repository, Vol. 6, p. 9, Speech of Henry Clay before the American Colonization Society in 1836.

[17] Clay: "Review of the Late Canvass," Pamphlet, p. 14.

[18] For further evidence that many slaveholders were inclining, in 1830-34, toward a system of gradual emancipation, see Western Luminary, March 5, 1834; African Repository, Vol. 5, p. 174; Vol. 10, p. 43; Birney: "James G. Birney and His Times," pp. 99ff; Hon. Daniel Mayer, "Proceedings of the Kentucky Colonization Society, 1831," Pamphlet, p. 21.

sincerity, to emancipate all slaves born their property hereafter, when they shall severally arrive at an age to be fixed on by compact, to form themselves into societies having these great and glorious objects in view."[19] It was intended, upon the addition of fifty names to these petitions, to call a meeting for the purpose of organizing a state society to carry out the plan.

The undertaking did not prosper to the degree that had been anticipated. Although they might be in sympathy with the gradual extinction of slavery, slaveholders generally were not willing to make personal sacrifices of their property in slaves unless they had some assurance that the system would be abolished throughout the state by constitutional means in the near future. Others believed that nothing effective or permanent could be accomplished by this plan, and still others thought that some method of compensated emancipation would and should be adopted by the state or nation. The friends of Henry Clay refused to take any part in the movement, until after the presidential election of 1832, and they discouraged others from doing so.[20] The required number of subscribers to the petitions was soon obtained, but leadership was lacking and the movement was temporarily abandoned.[21]

The revival of this plan and its successful execution are to be credited to James G. Birney, a native of Kentucky, and at this time a slaveholder of Huntsville, Alabama. Birney had become interested in colonization of free Negroes about 1830, but continued to hold slaves without any thought of making war upon slavery as an institution. According to his own statement he could not remember a time when he thought slavery right, but he confined his efforts to preventing importations, abolishing slave markets, and securing kind treatment for slaves.[22] He never bought a slave in the market, and sold those he owned only when he found that there was no other way of securing their kind treatment, being himself dependent upon an overseer. Birney was at this time a good representative of many of the south-

[19] *Western Luminary*, February 16, 1831. Quoted also in the *Liberator*, March 26, 1831. Similar notices appeared in a number of Kentucky papers.

[20] Birney: "James G. Birney and His Times," p. 133.

[21] Among those of reputations who identified themselves with the movement were Rev. John C. Young, Rev. J. D. Paxon, Judge John Green, Daniel Yeiser, William Armstrong, James McDowell, Thomas T. Skillman, and Robert J. Breckinridge.
The Western Luminary, March 26, 1831; The Liberator, April 16, 30, 1831. In this last number Garrison said that 36 names had been added to the charter members and that "There is some hope, therefore, that many children of the present generation of slaves in Kentucky may escape the doom of their parents."

[22] Birney: "James G. Birney and His Times," pp. 44, 46, 104, 111-114.

ern slaveholders who were convinced that slavery was an evil but did not clearly see a way to abolish it.[23]

In the summer of 1832 Birney unexpectedly received from the American Colonization Society an appointment, which he accepted, as its agent for the states of Alabama, Mississippi, Louisiana, and Tennessee.[24] In the autumn of that year he proceeded to organize colonization societies and to lecture in the principal cities in these states.[25] As a result of this work he became a thorough student of slavery and acquired an increased interest in the Negro, but he soon saw the hopelessness of colonization as a remedy for slavery, and in 1833 he gave up the work and removed to his native state.[26]

Birney had displayed from the beginning an interest in the movement in Kentucky to provide for the liberation of the offspring of slaves and had written a number of letters to the leaders, particularly to Thomas Skillman, approving the plan and urging them to renewed efforts. Upon his return to Kentucky, in 1833, he entered into the slavery controversy with all his energy. Before leaving Alabama he had written to the early signers of the petition, urging them to issue a call for a convention at Lexington to carry out the plan.[27] In compliance with his wishes a call was issued for December, 1833, but some of the signers now avowed a change of opinion and others declined to attend the meeting. Some had doubts, and others thought the convention ill-timed. As a result only nine persons, all slaveholders, were present, but a formal organization was nevertheless effected,[28] under the name of "The Kentucky Society for the Relief of the State from Slavery." The society was connected with no other organization. The members pledged themselves to emancipate all slaves born their property thereafter on their reaching the age of twenty-five years, and their offspring with them. This, the only pledge required, was given by the members in honor and with good feeling. There was no plan for coercion and any member might withdraw who felt disposed to do so. Through the influence of Birney the membership was thrown open to all classes in the community.[29] By the end of 1834, sixty or seventy men had subscribed to the pledge required by the

---

[23] Birney: "James G. Birney and His Times," pp. 24, 34, 38, 40.
[24] *Ibid.*, pp. 110-130.
[25] *Ibid.*
[26] *Ibid.*, pp. 130-140.
[27] *Ibid.*, p. 132. See also The Liberator, June 23, 1832.
[28] Birney: "James G. Birney and His Times," pp. 133-134.
[29] Western Luminary, March 5, 1834; "Address of J. G. Birney in the Court House at Lexington, explanatory of the principles, etc., of The Kentucky Society for the Relief of the State from Slavery." This was quoted also in the African Repository, Vol. 10, pp. 43-46.

society, and a number of auxiliary branches had been organized, but soon after this the society suffered another relapse which ended à few months later in its dissolution. A contributing cause was the rise of the radical abolitionists in the North and the association of James G. Birney with their activities in Kentucky.

An account of the formation of a similar society under the name of "The Ashmun Association," having as its object the gradual and voluntary emancipation of the slaves of the state, is found in the Lexington Observer, February 24, 1832. The constitution is quoted in full, the preamble of which is as follows: "And whereas the Colonization Society has to do with those only who are already free or are freed for the special purpose of being transported to their native country; And whereas great difference of opinion exists among the politicians of our country in relation to the constitutional rights of the States to pass laws for the universal emancipation; And whereas the policy of sudden and universal emancipation, and especially for those who are emancipated to remain among us, is doubted by many; And whereas we presume that no objection can be urged against individual efforts or a combination of individual efforts for their gradual emancipation and transportation which neither have for their object nor do in any respect increase the existing evil. We, therefore, citizens of the Commonwealth of Kentucky agree to form ourselves into an association according and subject to the following resolutions."[30] The most important provision of the constitution of this society was this: "We promise and agree that each and every male and female child of color to which we have the right of property as a slave, that have been or shall be born after the day and date written after our names, respectively, shall be born free, according to the following stipulations and provisions, to wit: That the said child or children shall be held and considered as bound to us who claim and hold the legal right to it or them as apprentices or wards to our orders and discretion until the age of twenty-five if male and twenty if female, at the expiration of which period we will permit him, her or them to be sent by the Colonization Society to Africa, or if the said society have not the means sufficient for the transportation thither we will either furnish them ourselves or hire the said wards to the lowest bidder in relation to the time for the purpose of raising them * * * ."[31] Annual meetings of the

[30] Lexington Observer, February 24, 1832. Any connection with the colonization or anti-slavery societies was disavowed.
[31] Lexington Observer, February 24, 1832.

society were to be held each year in Frankfort and efforts were to be made to form auxiliary societies in each county in the state. The constitution of the society together with a memorial signed by the members was sent to the legislature of Kentucky in 1832, setting forth the purposes of the order and praying that "such laws be passed as will render effectual the purposes of the Association."[32] The society at its organization contained about fifty members, all of whom appear to have been slaveholders.[33] A correspondent in the Lexington Observer the following month in commenting upon the society made this criticism of it: "The plan is too weak and ineffectual to accomplish much; for not many I apprehend, who own large numbers of slaves will join the society. Secondly it is too unequal; for a few would bear all the burthen of the great work and all reap the benefits."[34] Nothing further has been found concerniEg this society. In all probability no meeting was held after 1833.

The societies of the early thirties are significant in that they were composed of slaveholders who regarded slavery not only as morally wrong but as hostile to the best interests of the state. Although their numerical strength was never great, the character of the men associated with them caused the undertaking to be seriously considered. The anti-slavery sentiment that existed at any given time or place can not be judged solely by the number of members of such societies in the slave states. Regardless of their program such organizations were regarded with suspicion and consequently many of the anti-slavery sympathizers and workers refused to join with them. Nor would the political leaders affiliate with them lest they should thereby counteract their own or their party's success. The fact that the anti-slavery societies of Kentucky at no time embraced in their membership more than one out of every two thousand voters, while the anti-slavery forces at all times previous to the Civil War represented a strong minority in the legislature and at the polls substantiates this point.

Another type of anti-slavery organization commonly spoken of as Modern Abolitionism, or Garrisonian Abolitionism, which embraced immediate, unconditional emancipation on the soil, came into existence about 1830. While previous to this

---

[32] Lexington Observer, February 24, 1832.
[33] Niles' Weekly Register, Vol. 42, p. 300.
[34] The Lexington Observer, March 2, 1832. The writer proposed a plan for levying a tax of 1 per cent. upon slave property to be used for the transportation of free Negroes and manumitted slaves to Africa.

date these doctrines had been advocated by a number of men,[35] yet, owing to the state of public opinion both in the North and in the South on the subject of slavery, they had attracted no special attention. In the meantime, however, the South, on account of the extensive development of cotton planting and consequently of slavery, was becoming more and more reconciled to the existence of the institution, while the opposite conditions prevailed in the North, where the economic aspect of the question was disappearing and the moral aspect was demanding and receiving increased attention.

This was the state of affairs in the country when William Lloyd Garrison identified himself with the movement about 1830. He was a remarkable man and his special abilities enabled him to take advantage of the achievements of the past thirty years and to utilize them to the fullest extent. He added a new interest and forcefulness to the movement. There was no mistaking his purposes when he declared in the first number of the Liberator that he would "be as harsh as truth, and as uncompromising as justice. * * * I am in earnest; I will not equivocate; I will not excuse; I will not retreat a single inch and I will be heard."[36] This uncompromising program adopted and pursued by him immediately aroused the opposition of the South as well as that of a very large element in the North, and at the same time fired his followers with enthusiasm and determination. The movement spread rapidly into all sections of the North.

The American Anti-Slavery Society advocating immediate emancipation was organized in 1833. Two years later it embraced 225 auxiliary branches. But this was not accomplished without strenuous opposition, which often resulted in riots and mob violence.[38]

The sentiment in the slave states was of course even more pronounced in its opposition to abolition propaganda, than in

---

[35] Birney: "James G. Birney and His Times," p. 169. Adams: "Anti-Slavery in America," pp. 59-62, 80.
The most important were Charles Osborne, George Bourne, John Rankin, and James Duncan.
[36] The Liberator, January 1, 1831.
[37] Clarke: "Anti-Slavery Days," p. 36; Birney: "James G. Birney and His Times," p. 142.
[38] Clarke: "Anti-Slavery Days," p. 36; Birney: "James G. Birney and His Times," p. 197.
There were mobs all over the North, wherever anti-slavery missionaries went. July 4, 1834, a mob in New York City sacked the house of Louis Tappan. At the same time, the school houses and churches of colored people were attacked and damaged. August 31, 1834, there was a riot in Philadelphia, which continued for three nights. Forty-four houses of Negroes were damaged or destroyed. Many blacks were beaten and cruelly injured and some were killed. In the year 1835 Rev. Samuel J. May was mobbed five times in the state of Vermont. October 21, 1835, there was a riot in Utica, N. Y., and another on the same day in the city of Boston, where the meeting of the Women's Anti-Slavery Society was broken up, and Garrison was carried through the streets with a rope around his body.

the North although in Kentucky the fears and suspicions of the people were not so early or so generally aroused on the subject as in other sections of the South.[39] From the beginning of the Modern Abolition movement, however, the question constantly demanded and received more and more attention, especially after the abolitionists had begun an active participation in the internal affairs of the state.[40]

Soon after the dissolution of the gradual emancipation society, James G. Birney, one of the most active and influential members of that body, espoused the cause of immediate abolition. On the 19th of March, 1835, a year frequently referred to by the writers on slavery as the "mob year," he was instrumental in organizing at Danville the Kentucky Anti-Slavery Society, auxiliary to the American Anti-Slavery Society. The new organization, which was composed of forty charter members, all of whom were non-slaveholders, although a number of them had only recently manumitted their slaves, elected Professor Buchanan of Centre College as president.[41]

The subject of immediate abolition was freely discussed in Danville for some time. Mr. Birney held a number of public debates with the Rev. J. C. Young. Little or no opposition was encountered at first, but the movement did not prosper as he had anticipated. In a letter to Gerrit Smith, March 21, 1835, Birney made the following comment on the prospects of the society: "Immediate emancipation will have to be sustained here by the comparatively poor and humble. The aristocracy, created and sustained by slavery, will be ugly enemies—aye, and they will be so almost to our extermination."[42]

Shortly after the organization of the society, Birney issued proposals for the publication at Danville of an abolition paper, The Philanthropist, the first number of which was to appear the 1st of August.[43] No sooner had the principles of the society and of The Philanthropist and their connection with the Ameri-

[39] The Commonwealth, for December 26, 1838, declared that Kentucky had been passive while the southern states had been raising a great outcry, believing "that time and reflection would bring back those misguided and wicked disturbers of her repose to a sense of justice and propriety."
[40] As early as April 24, 1835, the Louisville Public Advertiser, one of the strongest pro-slavery papers in the state, made the following protest against northern interference in the domestic affairs of Kentucky: "Pamphlets and periodicals are published in the North and circulated in the South with a view to stir up servile war—and these publications are followed by attempts to prepare the public mind to refuse aid to the South in the event of an insurrection. The truth is, all this clamor against slavery—all the attempts that have been made to stir up a servile war, have originated in the public hostility of Northern politicians to the people of the slaveholding States."
[41] Birney: "James G. Birney and His Times," pp. 156-157. See also The Liberator, May 16, 1835; Amos Dresser: "Narrative of Amos Dresser," p. 5.
[42] Birney: "James G. Birney and his Times," p. 157.
[43] Ibid., p. 179.

can Anti-Slavery Society become known than opposition to the undertaking was expressed in all parts of the state. Mass meetings were held and resolutions adopted in which the citizens present pledged themselves to prevent the publication of The Philanthropist "peaceably if we can, forcibly if we must." Threats of violence were made against any and all men who should countenance the paper or aid in its circulation. A mass meeting at Danville appointed an executive committee of thirty-three persons to address to Mr. Birney a letter of remonstrance and to "take such other steps as might be necessary."[44] In this letter, dated July 12, occurs the following significant passage: "We address you now in the calmness and candor that should characterize law-abiding men, as willing to avoid violence as they are willing to meet extremity, and advise you of the peril that must and inevitably will attend the execution of your purpose. We propose to you to postpone the setting up of your press and the publication of your paper until application can be had to the Legislature, who will by a positive law set rules for your observance, or, by a refusal to act, admonish us of our duty. We admonish you, sir, as citizens of the same neighborhood, as members of the same society in which you live and move, and for whose harmony and quiet we feel the most sincere solicitude, to beware how you make an experiment here which no American slaveholding community has found itself able to bear."[45]

Mr. Birney flatly refused to accede to this proposition[46] whereupon the committee bought out the printer and threatened to use violence against anyone who should engage himself to assist in this undertaking.[47] Encouraged by the Postmaster General, Amos Kendall, the postmaster at Danville, declared his intention of excluding the publication from the mails.[48] By the middle of September it had become manifest to Mr. Birney that an anti-slavery paper could not be published at Danville.[49] Shortly afterward he moved to Cincinnati, Ohio, where he entered even more actively into anti-slavery work.[50] His departure marked the disappearance of the Kentucky Anti-Slavery Society.

[44] Birney: "James G. Birney and His Times," p. 180.
[45] Birney: "James G. Birney and His Times," pp. 180-181. This letter was written by a Whig member of Congress.
[46] *Ibid.*, p. 181.
[47] *Ibid.*, p. 182.
[48] *Ibid.*, p. 184.
[49] *Ibid.*, p. 183.
[50] See "Narrative of the Late Riotous Proceedings against the Liberty of the Press in Cincinnati by the Executive Committee of the Ohio Anti-Slavery Society," Pamphlet. At Cincinnati he began the publication of The Philanthropist. After a few numbers, however, had been issued the printing establishment was destroyed by a mob and he was again forced to move in order to continue the publication of the paper.

Brief as was its existence the organization and activities of this society produced a profound impression upon the people, of Kentucky. Modern abolition had become a real issue and all classes, regardless of creed or party, joined in its condemnation. Determined to check the spread of the doctrine, they organized secret societies in various parts of the state with the avowed object of protecting the constitutional rights of the people from the encroachments of the North. Sectional jealousy, which had not been pronounced in Kentucky previous to this date, seemed now to be in process of formation.

From the point of view of the historian the effect of Garrisonian abolition upon the anti-slavery sentiment in Kentucky must be regarded as particularly significant. While substantial progress toward emancipation was being made in the early thirties the reaction against immediate abolition stayed all progress toward gradual emancipation and caused the state to range itself alongside the other slaveholding states in resistance to aggression from without. Some evidence of this is found in the attitude of the churches and of the religious press.

In 1835 the annual conference of the Methodist Episcopal church in Kentucky adopted resolutions, in which it arraigned the abolitionists and the anti-slavery associations by whose acts "the peace and quiet of a large portion of the nation are disturbed, and their common interest, laws and safety placed in jeopardy."[51]

An extract from an editorial in the Baptist Banner (Kentucky) for the same year indicates the reasons for this opposition. "There has been considerable excitement of late in the southern and western portions of our country, in relation to the efforts of certain meddling individuals to effect the abolition of slavery. We do not know that it may be the purview of a religious periodical to notice these movements. But as the agitators of this subject make religion a cloak to subserve their ends, it becomes its professors everywhere to condemn it. We will not pretend to discuss the question of slavery. That it is an evil—a curse, we admit and deplore. But while we admit this, we condemn as irreligious and as tending to the worst consequences the course pursued by the abolitionists. * * * It is

⁵¹ Redford: "Western Cavaliers," p. 149. The Methodist General Conference which met at Cincinnati, Ohio, in 1836, passed a resolution bitterly opposing modern abolitionism. They further disclaimed any right, wish or intention to interfere in the civil and political relations between master and slave as they existed in the slaveholding states. The opinion of the Conference was expressed against any further agitation of the subject in the General Conference. Journals of the General Conferences.

not to the master but to the slave they speak. They use every endeavor to put their incendiary publications into the hands of the slave to arouse him to a sense of his wrongs and to excite him to a vindication of his rights. * * * Tell us not that Christianity favors such things. There were slaves in the days of the Saviour and He was not an abolitionist. * * * The apostles said, 'Be obedient to your masters.' * * * Taking this as our rule of judgment when we see men whose acts are calculated to excite the slaves to the worst and most horrid deeds of rapine and bloodshed we can not call them misguided philanthropists or enthusiastic Christians; but revolutionists and assassins."[52]

The Western Presbyterian Herald in reviewing the principles advocated by the abolitionists said: "These sentiments are plainly subversive to all government, and are too deeply dangerous, corrupting and revolutionary to be promulgated under the sanction of any society which cherishes the expectation of receiving a portion of the public favor and of doing good to any portion of mankind. * * * Freedom of speech is to be distinguished from licentiousness. No man has a moral right to use the power of speech in defiance of reason and revelation, or to disseminate through the press doctrines as obnoxious to the interests of society as those which characterized the French Revolution, and which disgrace the worst infidel school of the day."[53]

There seems to have been a uniform impression among the great majority of the citizens of the state, that the abolition movement was wrong as it stood related to the political fabric, but the exact character of the wrong was not so well defined in the public mind as to enable the people to see how a remedy could be applied to arrest and control the mischief that appeared

---

[52] Baptist Banner, October 3, 1835. See also September 19, 1835. In 1835, at Nashville, Tennessee, a vigilance committee, composed of sixty members, twenty-seven of whom were church members, including one ordained minister and a number of deacons of the various churches, tried and publicly whipped Amos Dresser, a young theological student, on the charge of circulating anti-slavery literature. He was engaged in selling the "Cottage" Bible during his vacation. Being a member of an anti-slavery society in Ohio, he had thoughtlessly carried some of its publications with him and these were found in his possession. Nashville Banner, August 12, 1835; Amos Dresser: "Narrative of Amos Dresser," pp. 1-6.
[53] Western Presbyterian Herald, September 28, 1837. The Commonwealth for August 29, 1835, gives the following explanation for the attitude of the South toward the abolitionists: "In times of great excitement strong measures most usually prevail and the abolitionists have been told of a doom which awaits them should they dare penetrate beyond the limits of the slave states. That death, instant and terrible, will await tampering with the slaves is certain. Can the South be blamed for this? Assuredly not. Self-protection is the law of nature which will assert its supremacy at every hazard. So long as the domestic relations continue to bind man to man—so long as the security in the possession of property is esteemed an essential right, men will protect the one from invasion and the other from plunder. That slavery is an evil, no people know better than those people who own slaves. They know, too, what are the depths of its roots—what would be the consequences of its instant abolition." For further references on this subject see the numbers for April 18, November 14 and December 26, 1838.

to be growing out of this agitation. Any examination of the
newspapers and the literature during the years between 1830
and 1840 shows conclusively that the people of Kentucky were
practically unanimous in their opposition to modern abolitionism. The activities of the abolitionists and the abuses heaped
upon them by the papers in all parts of the country naturally
culminated in mob violence, as has been noted. The papers
in Kentucky, as elsewhere, were exceedingly severe in their denunciations and in many instances made threats that might
easily be construed as sanctioning radical action though they
consistently opposed mob violence.[54]   In 1837 the Louisville
Journal declared that the abolitionists could be defeated only
by "moderation, truth, tolerance—that these are the only
means to disarm them of their fanatical doctrines and that violence, outrage and persecution will infallibly inflame their zeal,
enlarge their numbers and increase the power of their dangerous
doctrines."[55]   The Western Presbyterian Herald, a paper that
strongly condemned abolition, voiced the attitude of the Kentucky press when it said: "The liberty of the press should be
sustained; mob violence should be discountenanced, not for the
sake of abolitionism, nor in fact for the sake of any other cause
good or bad, but for the sake of truth and righteousness and for
the great principle of civil and political liberty."[56]

---

[54] Western Presbyterian Herald, November 30, 1837. An editorial in this number
stated that the papers in Kentucky had opposed mob violence in dealing with the abolitionists.
The papers were unanimous in their condemnation of the action of the mob at Alton, Ill.,
some of which characterized the act as murder. See Clarke: "Anti-Slavery Days," p. 25;
Philanthropist, November 21, 28, 1837.

[55] Louisville Journal, November 11, 1837.

[56] Western Presbyterian Herald, January 25, 1838. Maysville Eagle, November 18,
1837, took a similar view.

THE KENTUCKY CHURCHES AND SLAVERY
1830-1850

CHAPTER VI

The sentiment in favor of the abolition of slavery, which was general during the early thirties, found expression, as has been seen above, through the colonization and anti-slavery societies. But the outstanding features of the history of the anti-slavery movement in Kentucky between 1830 and 1850 are the attitude of the churches toward slavery, the passage of the non-importation law in 1833, the effort to secure its repeal, and the final effort and the failure to effect emancipation in the constitutional convention of 1849. The present chapter will be devoted to a discussion of the attitude of the churches toward slavery during this period.[1]

The duty of looking after the spiritual welfare of the slaves devolved upon the churches. There were few churches in the South that did not have Negro communicants; and in some instances the colored members outnumbered the white.[2]

The Methodists and the Baptists, the principal denominations in the South, always paid a great deal of attention to the religious welfare of slaves. Consequently, the Negro was attracted to those churches. Their doctrines he comprehended easily, and the emotional character of the service appealed to him. In the Methodist church, ministers were appointed each year to devote their entire time to missionary work among the slaves, thus securing a powerful hold on them.[3]

The Methodists of Kentucky appear to have been as diligent in the enforcement of the rules laid down by the General

---

[1] See *supra*, pp. 20-24, 34-42.
[2] Spencer: "History of the Kentucky Baptists," Vol. 1, p. 742; Vol. 2, p. 158. Of the 697 members of the Louisville Baptist Church in 1841, 559 were colored. (*Ibid.*, Vol. 2, p. 21). In 1861 the Elkhorn Association (Baptists) had 7,760 members, of whom 5,089 were colored. See also J. G. Birney: "American Churches the Bulwark of American Slavery," p. 24; Collins: "Historical Sketches of Kentucky," p. 131. The slave membership of the Methodist Church in Kentucky was 8 per cent in 1790 and 23 per cent. in 1845.
[3] H. N. McTyeire: "History of Methodism," p. 584. The following announcement was published in "The Directory of the City of Lexington, Kentucky," for 1838-39, p. 85: "Divine service at eleven o'clock and at candle light every Sunday. This church is under the care of the Rev. Isaiah Whitaker, Missionary to the people of color." See also, Matlack: "History of American Slavery and Methodism," p. 32; Birney: "American Churches the Bulwark of American Slavery," p. 2. According to Birney there were in the United States in 1840 about 2,700,000 slaves of whom about 200,000 were church members, divided among the denominations about as follows: Baptist, 80,000; Methodist, 80,000; and other denominations, 40,000, most of whom were Presbyterians.

Conferences on the subject of slavery as those in any other section of the South. During the latter part of the eighteenth and the early years of the nineteenth centuries, the anti-slavery element was especially active in the Methodist church.[4] This activity, however, as a result of the increased importance of slavery and the passage of hostile legislation by many of the southern states, became less and less pronounced during the first half of the nineteenth century. This changed attitude is very evident in the action of the General Conference of the church, which was held at Cincinnati, Ohio, in 1836, when by a vote of 120 to 14 the Conference disclaimed any intention to interfere with the civil and the political relations of master and slave as they existed in the slave states of the Union. By a vote of 120 to 11, abolitionism and the work of abolitionists were condemned in equally strong terms and two members of the Conference, who had attended and lectured at an abolition meeting in Cincinnati the preceding night, were publicly censured.[5] The Discipline, which still strongly condemned slavery, remained unchanged, although little effort was made to enforce it in this respect.

After 1830 some anti-slavery activity continued to be displayed in local churches or conferences in Kentucky, but it soon showed signs of decadence and by 1840 it had almost entirely disappeared. Occasionally special cases were brought before the local conferences for consideration, when the rules of the General Conference were necessarily taken into account. One of these cases occured in the Kentucky Conference as late as 1837, when Thomas Lasley, a prominent and influential minister, was tried by that body for having violated the rules of the church regarding slavery, as he had come into possession of a number of slaves through the will of his deceased father. The committee in charge of the case according to "former usages of the Conference in similar cases" recommended that Mr. Lasley be required to issue deeds of emancipation for the slaves in question as soon after the adjournment of the Conference as was practicable. The report of the committee was adopted by the Conference.[6]

From this date until the division of the General Conference in 1844 into the Northern and the Southern Con-

---

[4] See *supra*, pp. 20, 21, 34, 35.
[5] McTyeire: "History of Methodism," p. 602. See also Birney: "American Churches The Bulwark of American Slavery," p. 9f. Quarterly American Anti-Slavery Magazine, July, 1837, p. 378; "Report of the Second Anniversary of the Ohio Anti-Slavery Society," Pamphlet, 1837, p. 27.
[6] Redford: "Western Cavaliers," pp. 202-203.

ferences, no important action was taken on the question of slavery by the annual conferences of Kentucky. While the Kentucky delegates in the General Conference almost unanimously supported the southern churches, many of them both in the Conference and in Kentucky during the following year endeavored to re-establish harmonious relations between the contending factions.[7]   Henry Clay, although not a member of the Methodist Church, used his influence to prevent a division of the church.   His attitude, as well as that of many Methodists of Kentucky, is clearly expressed in a letter dated April 7, 1845, and addressed to a certain prominent Methodist of the South, in which he said, "I will not say that such a separation would necessarily produce a dissolution of the political Union of these states; but the example would be fraught with imminent danger and in co-operation with other causes unfortunately existing, its tendency on the stability of the Confederacy would be perilous and alarming. * * * With fervent hopes and wishes that some arrangement of the difficulty may be devised and agreed upon which shall preserve the church in union and harmony," he closed his earnest appeal.[8]

Unfortunately the efforts of Clay and others in behalf of peace were of no avail, and in 1845 the Kentucky Annual Conference by a decided majority endorsed the action of their delegates of the preceding year and definitely threw in their lot with the newly formed Methodist Episcopal Church, South.[9] There were a few instances in which individual churches continued their relations with the northern branch of the church and numerous instances in which individual members refused to affiliate with the southern branch.[10]   This was especially true of the counties along the northern border of the state.

From 1845 until the opening of the Civil War, the policy of the Kentucky Conference remained unchanged in regard to slavery, although numerous individual members of the church continued to work for constitutional emancipation.   Six members of the Emancipation Convention, which met at Frankfort, April 25, 1849, were Methodist ministers.[11]

---

[7] Niles' Weekly Register, Vol. 66, pp. 192, 208, 240, 256; Vol. 68, pp. 166, 167, 186; Vol. 69, p. 55; The Liberator, October 17, 1845.

[8] Niles' Weekly Register, Vol. 68, p. 149.

[9] Maysville Eagle, May 14, 24, 1849; Niles' Weekly Register, Vol. 68, pp. 166-167, 186.   The vote in the Kentucky Conference was 98 to 5 for separation from the Northern Church (Niles' Weekly Register, Vol. 69, p. 55).

[10] Niles' Weekly Register, Vol. 68, p. 334; The Liberator, June 27, September 12, 1845, April 17, 1846.

[11] See below, note 91, p. 130.

The same acceptance of slavery as an institution and the same reluctance to enter upon dangerous agitation are seen in the other leading churches of Kentucky. The attitude of the Baptists of Kentucky toward anti-slavery work is well stated in an editorial in the Baptist Banner in 1835. In commenting upon the action of the Northern Baptist Association which declared "the practice of holding men in slavery to be a violation of the natural rights of man and contrary to the first principles of the Gospel," the Banner objected to the statement because it "virtually declares non-fellowship for those associations and churches in which slavery is tolerated," and because "it tends to introduce among the Baptists the discussion of the most exciting and dangerous question that ever agitated the country," and lastly because it is "calculated to do the cause of emancipation itself more harm than good."[12] The Kentucky associations, since the early part of the century, had consistently refused to be drawn into the slavery controversy and used their influence to prevent the individual churches from doing so. The individual members were left free to act as their consciences dictated.[13] When the northern branches of the church found how completely their southern brethren had yielded to the powerful social pressure of their local life, they made a vigorous but vain attempt to correct the tendency. In 1844-45, the Baptists of the East and those of the upper Northwest refused to co-operate with southern churches in their insistence upon the right to send out missionaries who owned slaves. A Southern Baptist church was the immediate result.[14]

At a meeting of the Baptist clergy and laity of Kentucky at Shelbyville, in 1845, it was decided that the Kentucky Baptists should identify themselves with the southern branch of the church.[15] Little or no opposition was manifested to this action.

While the Presbyterian churches of Kentucky attracted a smaller proportion of slaves than either the Methodist or the Baptist, they were always much interested in the Negro's welfare. Their efforts in his behalf during the late twenties have been described in the preceding pages.[16] These efforts continued unabated during the remainder of the existence of

[12] The Baptist Banner, December 19, 1835.
[13] See *supra*, pp. 19ff, 37-42.
[14] Niles' Weekly Register, Vol. 66, p. 192.
[15] Maysville Eagle, June 18, 1845; Niles' Weekly Register, Vol. 68, p. 272. The proceedings, including the resolutions adopted, are given in the Frankfort Commonwealth, June 24, 1845.
[16] See *supra*, pp. 36, 37.

slavery. In 1831 the West Lexington Presbytery again reminded the churches embraced in its membership that it was the duty of masters and mistresses to have their servants taught to read the word of God. They were instructed to pay especial attention to the young slaves so that none should be permitted to grow up without being able to read and they were instructed to give a Bible to every slave as soon as he was able to read it.[17]   This is very different from the spirit manifested in the columns of the Southern Religious Telegraph, a Presbyterian paper in Richmond, Virginia, which would prohibit the instruction of slaves in reading, and prevent the circulation of the Bible among them, lest on learning to read it "they might be induced to read bad books."[18]

Sentiment in Kentucky was, however, by no means unanimous in this regard. Schools established solely for Negroes were often broken up or the promoters were intimidated, in a few instances as a result of force, into giving up the work.[19] An undated manuscript found in the Draper Manuscript collection is worthy of mention because of its frank expression in this connection of the dangers which many apprehended from the education of the slaves. "Previous to their adjournment the Grand Jury feel themselves irresistibly impelled by a sense of their duty, to present as an evil of the most serious and portentious character, the school which has recently been established in the town of Lexington for the education of the slaves. * * * The Grand Jury do not consider it either necessary or proper in this place, to detail the manifold evils which inevitably must result from enlightening the minds of those whose happiness obviously depends on their ignorance, and whose discontent, under the presence of their bonds, must keep pace with the progressive illumination of their minds.* * Solemnly impressed with these awful forebodings of future evils the Grand Jury seriously calls upon the Ministers of the law to exert their authority in suppressing the institution of which

[17] Liberator, April 30, 1831; see also Western Luminary, January 24, 1827, June 3, 1829; Rev. John Young: "The Duty of Masters," pamphlet, p. 35; Western Presbyterian Herald, January 4, 1838.

[18] The Liberator, April 30, 1831, quoted. Although there was no law in Kentucky prohibiting the teaching of slaves, the pro-slavery element always displayed considerable opposition to the practice. See John Rankin: "Letters on Slavery," p. 24; Western Citizen, October 9, 1824; J. G. Birney: "American Churches, the Bulwark of American Slavery," p. 4.

[19] Western Presbyterian Herald, September 28, 1837; Davidson: "History of the Presbyterian Church," p. 340. The acts were usually committed by "Vigilance Committees" that had been organized in various parts of the State for protection against the aggressions of the North and for putting down or preventing any slave insurrection that might result therefrom.

they complain."[20]   No other reference has been found either to the presentment of the grand jury or to any action by the government, but the complaint may have been directed against one of the schools established by the Presbyterians of Lexington, since Lexington was a Presbyterian stronghold.

Slavery came before the Synod of Kentucky in 1832 when the anti-slavery members endeavored to secure the adoption of severe rules condemning slavery. Among the proposals before the body was the following: "Resolved, That it is the view of this Synod that slavery, as it exists within our bounds, is a great moral evil, and inconsistent with the word of God, and we do, therefore, recommend to all our ministers and members who hold slaves, to endeavor to have them instructed in the knowledge of the Gospel and to promote, in every peaceable way, the interests of the Colonization Society, and to favor all proper measures for gradual voluntary emancipation." After considerable discussion, the resolution was laid on the table until the following year, when it was again brought before the Synod for consideration. By a vote of 41 to 36 the following substitute was offered and carried: "Inasmuch as in the judgment of this Synod, it is inexpedient to come to any decision on the very difficult and delicate question of slavery, as it exists within our bounds, therefore, Resolved, That the whole question is indefinitely postponed."[21]   Upon the passage of this resolution Robert J. Breckinridge, one of the most active opponents of slavery in the Synod, arose from his seat in the center of the house and taking his hat in his hands walked rapidly toward the door, saying, "God has left you, and I also will now leave you, and have no more correspondence with you."[22]

But the question of slavery was not to remain so quietly disposed of. The Synod of Kentucky, in 1833, passed a resolution, "That the Synod believe that the system of absolute and hereditary domestic slavery, as it exists among the members of our communion, repugnant to the principles of our holy religion, * * * and that the continuation of the system any longer than is necessary to prepare itself for its safe and beneficial termination is sinful." The Presbyteries and church sessions and people under their care were earnestly recommended

---

[20] Draper Collection of Kentucky Manuscripts, Vol. 7, Worsley Papers. Worsley was a newspaper owner and writer of considerable importance.

[21] Davidson: "History of the Presbyterian Church," p. 338; William L. Breckinridge signed the resolution as Moderator.

[22] Wickliffe: "Reply of Robert Wickliffe to Robert J. Breckinridge***," Pamphlet, 1841, p. 60f.

to commence immediate preparations for the termination of slavery among them, "so that this evil may cease to exist with the present generation and the future offspring of our slaves may be free."[23] Further, the Synod by a vote of 56 to 8 appointed a committee of ten to prepare a plan for the instruction and future emancipation of slaves. The committee were: Hon. John Brown, chairman; Judge Green, J. C. Young, Thomas Porter Smith, Esq., Charles N. Cunningham, Esq., J. R. Alexander, Esq., Rev. Robert Stuart, Rev. James K. Burch, Rev. Nathan H. Hall, and Rev. W. L. Breckinridge, men of strong characters and of wide influence.[24]

It is probable that this action was due in large measure to James G. Birney. Shortly before the meeting of the Synod, Birney, who was a prominent Presbyterian, sent a circular letter to the ministers and elders of the Presbyterian Church of the state, in which he bitterly attacked the institution of slavery and endeavored to point out the proper course for the church to take.[25] He also talked freely along these lines with numerous members of the Synod.[26] The action taken by the Synod compared with the ideas held by Mr. Birney at that time indicates that his influence must have been very great. The Presbyterian Church of Kentucky, although not so large in membership as either the Methodist or the Baptist, contained many of the leading men of the state. Consequently, any action by that body carried with it unusual influence.

In 1835, the committee published its proposed plan in a pamphlet of 64 pages, which had been written by J. C. Young, the president of Centre College of Danville, Kentucky, and approved by the other members of the committee. The address was an able document. It took a strong and decided stand in favor of gradual emancipation. After fearlessly pointing out the numerous evils of slavery and answering objections that were commonly raised the author recommended the following plan: "The master to retain, during a limited period, and with regard to the real welfare of the slave, that authority which he had before held, in perpetuity, and solely for his own interest. Let the full liberty of the slave be secured against all contingences, by a recorded deed of emancipation to take effect

[23] Davidson: "History of the Presbyterian Church," p. 338; Emancipator, October 26, 1837, November 4, 1834.
[24] Davidson: "History of the Presbyterian Church," p. 338; J. G. Birney: "American Churches The Bulwark of American Slavery," pp. 25-26.
[25] J. G. Birney: "Letter to the Churches, to the Ministers and Elders of the Presbyterian Church of Kentucky," September 2, 1834. Pamphlet of 24 pages.
[26] Birney: "James G. Birney and His Times," p. 146.

at a specified time. In the meanwhile, let the servant be treated with kindness—let all those things which degrade him be removed—let him enjoy means of instruction—let his moral and religious improvement be sought—let his prospects be presented before him, to stimulate him to acquire those habits of foresight, economy, industry, activity, skill and integrity, which will fit him for using well the liberty he soon is to enjoy.

"1.   We recommend that all slaves now under 20 years of age, and all those yet to be born in our possession, be emancipated as they severally reach their 25th year.

"2.   We recommend that deeds of emancipation be now drawn up, and recorded in our respective county courts, specifying the slaves whom we are about to emancipate, and the age at which each is to become free.

"3.   We recommend that our slaves be instructed in the common elementary branches of education.

"4.   We recommend that strenuous and persevering efforts be made to induce them to attend regularly upon the ordinary services of religion, both domestic and public.

"5.   We recommend that great pains be taken to teach them the Holy Scriptures; and that, to effect this, the instrumentality of Sabbath-Schools, wherever they can be enjoyed, be united with that of domestic instruction.

"These are measures which all ought to adopt; and we know of no peculiarity of circumstances in the case of any individual, which can free him from culpability if he neglects them."[27]

The report of the committee was never acted upon by the Synod of Kentucky, although it was published in the Western Luminary and various other papers in Kentucky and elsewhere. The report of the committee was far in advance of public sentiment in the slave states. The Maysville Intelligencer, a Presbyterian paper published at Maysville, Tennessee, was not permitted to publish the entire report of the committee because of a law recently passed in that state making it a penitentiary offense to receive or publish any anti-slavery paper or pamphlet in the state; and parts of this report were considered to be in this class by the state censor. In 1836, the General Assembly of the Presbyterian Church, in its annual meeting at Pittsburg, in

---

[27] "An Address to the Presbyterians of Kentucky, Proposing a Plan for the Instruction and Emancipation of their Slaves, by a Committee of the Synod of Kentucky," Pamphlet.
It is an interesting fact that the plan of gradual emancipation proposed by the gradual emancipation societies, described above, is almost identical with this plan. A comparison of the names shows that the same men were back of both movements.
Davidson: "History of the Presbyterian Church," pp. 339-340.

answer to numerous memorials on the subject of slavery, decided that slavery was a political question and that any action of the General Assembly with reference to slavery could only tend to divide the church.[28]

The position of the Presbyterian Church had come to be almost identical with that of the Baptists and the Methodist Episcopal Churches. The churches, acting partly from a fear inspired by the Garrisonian abolitionists and partly from a conviction that slavery was an established fact, were for some years to show little interest in emancipation.

The anti-abolition campaign which was so successful in preventing anti-slavery discussions and work in the state during the thirties, lost most of its force during the early forties, when free discussion was resumed and continued with few interruptions. This change in sentiment was the result partly of the renewal of the demand for the calling of a constitutional convention with which the question of gradual emancipation was associated. This subject will be discussed in Chapter IX.

The churches again took up the question of colonization and education of the slaves and used their influence to encourage voluntary emancipation. In 1845, the Synod of Kentucky adopted a resolution in favor of the education of the slaves of the state which was copied from a similar resolution adopted by the Presbytery of Georgia the preceding year.[29] In 1846, the Presbyterian Herald, the leading Presbyterian journal in the state, after approving the resolution came out in opposition to any further agitation of the question.[30]

Although the church as an organization refused to be drawn into the slavery controversy after this date, the members of this church were the leaders in the campaign in 1848 and 1849 for the constitutional abolition of slavery. In the emancipation convention held in Frankfort, April 25, 1849, thirteen of the 150 delegates were Presbyterian ministers. A writer in the Prentice Review (Louisville) in October, 1849, asserted that "the Presbyterians have taken the lead in the struggle. There is not a prominent man in the Synod of Kentucky who has not been conspicuous for his zeal and efforts in behalf of emancipation.* * * * As far as we know, there is not a single Presbyterian minister whose name is found among the advocates of slavery."[31]

---

[28] Niles' Weekly Register, Vol. 50, p. 25.
[29] The Liberator, January 17, 1845. The plan for the education of the slaves adopted by the Georgia Presbytery was printed in pamphlet form, a copy of which is in the Breckinridge papers for 1845.
[30] The Presbyterian Herald, October 22, 1846.
[31] The Prentice Review, October, 1849.

THE NON-IMPORTATION LAW OF 1833 AND THE EFFORTS TO SECURE ITS REPEAL

CHAPTER VII

Other indications of the course of public opinion with respect to slavery, in the thirties and forties, is found in the efforts in the legislature to secure the passage of laws that were intended to bring about either directly or indirectly the final abolition of slavery. These bills were of two classes—first, those intended to limit or to prohibit the importation of slaves into the state, and second, those intended to secure the abolition of slavery by means of a constitutional provision. This chapter will be concerned with the passage of the Non-Importation Law of 1833 and the efforts to secure its repeal.

The domestic slave trade does not appear to have been of much consequence in Kentucky before 1815.[1] Soon after this date, however, a considerable business seems to have grown up with the southern states where cotton planting was being developed on a very large scale. The unusual demand for slave labor caused an extensive trade to be established between the border states, where slave labor could be employed to little advantage, and the lower, or the cotton South,[2] where it was very profitable.

We have no means of determining definitely the extent to which Kentucky was engaged in this trade. As early as 1818, Estwick Evans[3] and Henry Bradshaw Fearon,[4] both of whom traveled extensively in the West, spoke of a large number of slaves that were being sent down the Mississippi River to the

---

[1] W. H. Collins: "Domestic Slave Trade," p. 40.

[2] A letter published in the Western Luminary in 1827 and copied in the Genius of Universal Emancipation, September 15, 1827, says that the border States where "tobacco or grain is the staple are now nurseries which support the cotton grounds with human flesh. In consequence of this there is nearly as great a slave trade floating annually on the Mississippi or its branches as ever was wafted across the Atlantic. The raising and transporting of slaves to perish on the cotton and sugar lands is what keeps up the value in Kentucky." J. F. Rhodes: "History of the United States," Vol. 1, p. 315. In a speech before the Colonization Society in 1829 (Report of the Executive Committee of the American Anti-Slavery Society, Pamphlet, p. 17) Henry Clay said: "It is believed that nowhere in the farming portion of the United States would slave labor be generally employed, if the proprietors were not tempted to raise slaves for the Southern markets which keeps it up in his own."

[3] Estwick Evans: "A Pedestriou's Tour," p. 216, in speaking of the extent of the traffic in slaves in the city of Natchez, says: "There is no branch of trade in this part of the country more brisk and profitable than that of buying and selling slaves. They are a subject of continual speculation and are daily brought together with other live stock from Kentucky and other places to Natchez and the New Orleans markets."

[4] Fearon: "Sketches of America," p. 268. He speaks of having seen fourteen flat boats loaded with slaves from Kentucky, where they had been collected by dealers from the border States.

southern markets. In different parts of Kentucky, dealers were located who bought up slaves in that and the adjoining states and shipped them in large gangs to the South.[5] The Hon. Robert Wickliffe, in a speech in the Kentucky Legislature, in 1840, estimated that over 60,000 slaves had been exported from Kentucky alone during the preceeding seven years.[6] This estimate is doubtless too large. The evidence, however, seems to indicate that such sales exceeded 5,000 per year. In addition to the large number of slaves annually sent out of the state, there was also a considerable importation of slaves from Virginia and Maryland as well as a large traffic in slaves within the state.

No aspect of slavery was more objectionable to the great majority of the people of Kentucky than that of buying and selling slaves for profit. There were those, however, who were willing to endure the contempt that was almost universally heaped upon the domestic slave trader in order to reap the large profits derived from the business. There were those also in every community who, though recognizing the inhumanity of the slave trade, would, when necessity demanded— and many such demands were made—buy or sell a slave or slaves as their interests might dictate.

Petitions were sent repeatedly to Congress from Kentucky and other parts of the Union asking that body, which, according to the federal constitution, had control over interstate trade, to prohibit the inhuman and odious traffic in slaves. Congress, however, adopted the theory that its authority was limited to the regulation of and not to the prohibition of interstate trade. Since slaves were regarded by the laws of the United States and of the several slave states as property, it had no power to prohibit citizens from taking them either into a state or out of it. Consequently it did not act on the subject.[7] The individual states, therefore, possessed the power of regulating all trade within their bounds. Each could also limit or even prohibit the importation of slaves, though it had no authority

---

[5] John Rankin: "Letters on Slavery," pp. 45-46. Rankin mentions a number of men who engaged in the slave trade as a regular business. (1822). See also Genius of Universal Emancipation, October, 1822, and Fearon: "Sketches of America," p. 268.

[6] Cassius M. Clay: "Review of the Late Canvass," p. 8f. Clay accepted these figures. J. C. Ballaugh: "History of Slavery in Virginia," p. 25, gives the exportation of slaves from Virginia as 6,000 annually.

[7] This position is clearly set forth by Henry Clay in a speech in the United States Senate on "Abolition Petitions," February 7, 1839, (Annals of Congress, 1839, Vol. 7, p. 354), when he said: "But I deny that the general government has any authority whatever from the Constitution to abolish what is called the slave trade, or in other words to prohibit the removal of slaves from one state to another slave state. The grant in the constitution is of a power of regulation, and not prohibition. The regulation intended was designed to facilitate and accommodate, not obstruct and incommodate the commerce to be regulated.***The moment the incontestable fact is admitted that negro slaves are property, the law of movable property irresistibly attaches itself to them and secures the right of carrying from one to another state."

over their exportation. Laws regulating and limiting the importation of slaves were passed at different times by most of the slave states. The constitution of Kentucky, adopted in 1792, instructed the legislature to prohibit the importation into the state of all slaves that had been brought into the United States from any foreign country since 1789.[8] An act designed to accomplish that end was passed in 1794[9] and amended in 1815.[10] These laws, while limiting and regulating importations from other states, embodied a long list of exceptions, which made them of little value, especially in the sections of the state where public sentiment favored a loose interpretation and a mild enforcement of them.

From the late twenties the anti-slavery workers in Kentucky directed much effort towards influencing public opinion in favor of an absolute prohibition of the importation of slaves into the state. In this they were prompted by a desire to lessen the evils of the slave system and to prevent, in so far as possible, the increase of slaves in the state, so that when a plan of gradual emancipation should be agreed upon the difficulties and the dangers of the undertaking would not be so great.

In 1827, Franklin Lodge, Number 28, of the Masonic Order, located at Danville, Kentucky, sent to each of the members of the order in the state a circular in which the commerce in slaves carried on by importations to the state from other slave-holding states was declared to be in conflict with the feelings of benevolence and philanthropy which it was the duty of every Mason to inculcate. Such business was declared to be inconsistent with the principles of Accepted Ancient York Masonry and ought, therefore, to be discontinued by every member of the fraternity. All intention of interfering with the system of slavery as it existed in the state was disavowed. The paper closed with a warning to all members of the craft against participating in any way in "that commerce which under the influence of a degrading cupidity imports from other states hundreds of slaves."[11] This circular is significant in that it shows the sentiment of the enlightened public toward the domestic slave trade.

---

[8] Littell: "Statute Laws of Kentucky," Vol. 1, p. 246.
[9] *Ibid.*
[10] "Acts of the Legislature of Kentucky, 1814-1815," pp. 435-436.
[11] This circular was issued March 3, 1827, and was published in full in the Western Luminary, October 31, 1827. It appeared also in a number of other papers in different parts of the state.

The churches of Kentucky were very pronounced in their opposition to the trade. In 1834, the Synod of Kentucky adopted a report in which they drew a thrilling picture of the cruelties and horrors of the traffic in slaves, characterizing it as a "flagrant violation of every principle of mercy, justice, and humanity."[12] Similar sentiments were expressed frequently by the other denominations.

A petition signed by a large number of citizens was presented to the legislature in 1828 requesting the passage of an efficient law to put an end to all importations of slaves except when they were brought in by immigrants removing to the state.[13] The petitioners characterized domestic slavery as a "great moral and political evil, which extends its baneful influence in a greater or less degree to the whole body of society in every county where it exists," and the large yearly importations of slaves as a "violation of an Act of the Legislature and, as we believe, of the laws of God."[14] A bill was introduced in the Senate by John Green embodying the suggestions of this petition and stating further that all slaves thenceforth brought into the state as merchandise and in violation of the act were to be given their freedom and were to be entitled to all the rights and privileges of free persons of color.[15]

In the course of his defense of the bill, Mr. Green said he believed that emancipation would take place sooner or later and that it was their duty to prepare for it. Emancipation would necessarily be gradual and would require many years from its commencement to its completion, and the fewer the slaves in the state, the more easily could it be accomplished. This consideration was said to be the most powerful argument in favor of the passage of the bill.[16] The measure was opposed particularly by Mr. McConnell on the ground that it was not only inexpedient but unconstitutional. He declared that under the section of the constitution respecting slavery, the legislature was prohibited from emancipating slaves without the consent of each individual owner. To this it was replied that emancipation or forfeiture, by way of penalty for illegal importation, was not restricted by the

---

[12] Goodell: "Slavery and Anti-Slavery," p. 152.
[13] Genius of Universal Emancipation, January 12, 1828, quoted from the Western Luminary.
[14] Genius of Universal Emancipation, January 12, 1828, quoted from the Western Luminary.
[15] Kentuckian, January 10, 1828.
[16] Spirit of Seventy-Six, January 31, 1828.

constitution.[17]   After the bill had been considered for some days, and had aroused general discussion of slavery, it came to a vote and was defeated by a very small majority.[18]   It came up again during the winter session of 1828-29, and was again defeated in the senate by a vote of 45 to 51.[19]

Within the next few years numerous articles appeared in the newspapers discussing every phase of the slavery controversy, and particularly the proposed Non-Importation Law. Three series of letters printed in 1830 deserve special mention. The first, consisting of seven letters signed "B," was written by Robert J. Breckinridge and was published in the Kentucky Reporter.[20]   The second, signed "Philo C," written by Judge John Green, for many years a member of the Kentucky legislature, appeared in the Westery Luminary.[21]   A third and much longer series, signed "C," addressed to the legislature of Kentucky was written by George Clark, a man whose talents were recognized throughout the state.[22]   These letters, advocating gradual emancipation, to be preceded by the legislative prohibition of the importation of slaves, were widely copied by papers in all sections of the state.   Mr. Breckinridge was forced to resign his seat in the legislature as a result of this expression of his anti-slavery sentiments.[23]

The Non-Importation bill was again brought before the House of Representatives in 1830.   In defending the measure Mr. Love said that the existing laws were generally evaded, that he had not known of a single conviction in his time, and that the passage of the bill would pave the way for emancipation, which he declared to be the ultimate purpose of the supporters of the bill.   He said further that if he was given an opportunity he would support either immediate or gradual emancipation.[24]   Mr. Daniels then spoke against the bill, because, he said, slaves were more humanely treated in Kentucky than in any other place in the Union.   While they remained property he was unwilling to interfere to prevent free trade in them. "If we pass this bill, what will South Carolina, North Carolina,

---

[17] Spirit of Seventy-Six, January 31, 1828; Western Luminary, January 23, 1828.
[18] Spirit of Seventy-Six, February 7, 1828.
[19] Kentuckian, December 11, 1828, December 25, 1828.
[20] These articles were called "Hints on Slavery."   The first appeared in the Kentucky Reporter, April 21, and the last June 9, 1830.
[21] Western Luminary, October 6, 1830, ff.   This series consisted of five letters.
[22] Western Luminary, September 30, 1830, ff.
[23] Kentucky Reporter, August 4, 1830.   A number of interrogatories addressed to Mr. Breckinridge were published in the Kentucky Gazette, June 4, 1830, among which was the following: "Are you the author of the numbers in the Reporter, in favor of emancipating the slaves?"   See also, "Speech of Robert J. Breckinridge delivered at Lexington, Kentucky, October 12, 1840," Pamphlet.
[24] Kentuckian, January 8, 1830.

and Georgia say? They will have the same right to prohibit the importation into their states of our hogs, our horses and our mules. This measure will open the door to that of restrictive legislation and the precedent will be a bad one."[25] Mr. Hise then took the floor in defense of the bill. He said: "There is a loud and impressive call upon every member of this body for a firm and unequivocal expression of their opinion on this subject."[26] His remarks were continued at considerable length; he enlarged particularly upon the evils of slavery and endeavored to point out the advantage of free over slave labor and to draw a striking contrast between the present condition in the free states and that in those where slavery existed. He attributed the rapid progress of the non-slaveholding states in power and in prosperity to the absence of this evil, and drew from these facts an argument against permitting as far as practicable the increase of the evil in Kentucky.[27] Mr. Elisha Smith, of Rockcastle County, spoke at length against the bill. He believed it a departure from sound policy and a violation of private rights as well as a violation of the constitution.[28] When the bill came before the House of Representatives it was defeated by a vote of 48 to 48.[29]

In Niles' Weekly Register for February 6, 1830, we find the following comment on the situation in Kentucky: "In an animated debate on a bill to prevent the importation of slaves into Kentucky, we are glad to observe much soundness of principle and freedom in expressing it. That slavery has been highly injurious to Kentucky, is undoubted; and that measures will be taken to rid the state of its slave population, so far as may be consistent with what are esteemed the rights of property, is entirely manifest to us. The first step towards that is an absolute prohibition of their importation from other states."[30]

There were two bills before the legislature of Kentucky in 1831, designed to afford some measure of relief to slaves. · One of them prohibited jailors, under pain of being removed from office and fined $50, from receiving slaves into jail, unless they were committed by due process of law. The object was to prevent slave traders from using the county jails to facilitate their operations. The second bill prohibited the importation

---

[25] *Kentuckian,* January 8, 1830.
[26] *Ibid.*
[27] *Ibid.*
[28] *Ibid.*
[29] *African Repository,* Vol. 5. p. 380.
[30] *Niles' Weekly Register,* Vol. 37, p. 399.

of slaves into the state under certain stipulated conditions.[31] The slave bill, as the Non-Importation bill was termed, passed the House of Representatives in both 1831 and 1832, but was defeated each time in the Senate by a very small majority.[32] Finally it passed both houses and was approved February 24, 1833.[33] It provided, "That each and every person or persons who shall hereafter import into this state any slave or slaves or who shall sell or buy, or contract for the sale or purchase for a longer term than one year of the services of any such slave or slaves, knowing the same to have been imported as aforesaid, he, she, or they, so offending, shall forfeit and pay $600 for each slave so imported, sold, or bought, or whose service has been so contracted for, recoverable by indictment by a grand jury on an action of debt, in the name of the Commonwealth of Kentucky, in any circuit of the county where the offender or offenders may be found."[34] These provisions were not intended to prevent immigrants to the state from bringing slaves with them for their own use, but immigrants were required to make oath within sixty days after their arrival that they had no intention of selling such slaves as they had brought with them. The law did not apply to residents of the state "deriving a title to slaves by will, descent, distribution or marriage or gift in consideration of marriage."[35]

In order to secure the efficient administration of the law, its enforcement was placed in the hands of the county attorneys, who were required to take an oath that they would faithfully prosecute all offenders against the act within their knowledge or of which they might be informed. They were further to receive twenty per cent. of all fines upon conviction. The Justices of the Peace were also given power to issue warrants

---

[31] Lexington Observer, October 21, 1831; Liberator, February 5, 1831.
In a speech in the House of Representatives in support of the slave bill, May Squire Turner spoke especially of the inadaptability of Kentucky to slave labor. He gave a great many figures to substantiate his points and made a number of comparisons between the free states and Kentucky. His speech was quoted in the Lexington Observer, October 21, 1831. Elisha Smith, of Rockcastle County, spoke in opposition to the bill. In the course of his remarks he said he believed that the bill was "unconstitutional, calculated to disturb the repose of the slave; to excite hopes that cannot be realized in some sixty or eighty years; to rivet and to draw closer the fetters that now bind him, and to lessen the price of your products and to uprip and derange the commercial intercourse of this State with her sister States." (Commentator, December 13, 1831).

[32] Western Luminary, December 28, 1831; Liberator, December 10, 1831; Shelbyville Examiner, December 29, 1832.

[33] The bill passed the House by a vote of 56 to 32 and the Senate by 23 to 12. Among those voting for the measure were Owsley, Clark, Simpson, Green, Wooley, Crittenden, Thomson, Marshall, Guthrie, Thornton, Butler and Ewing. See "Speech of Robert J. Breckinridge * * *, Lexington, October 12, 1840," pp. 16ff.

[34] Session Acts of 1835, p. 258. R. H. Collins: "History of Kentucky," Vol. 1, p. 37.

[35] Session Acts of 1835, p. 258.

for violators and the action might be begun any time within five years after the offense was committed.[36]

This law was passed to save the state from an excessive slave population and to keep open the way for emancipation at some future day. It was evident by 1840 that the first of these objects was being accomplished. The percentage of slave population had gradually increased until 1830, when it represented twenty-four per cent. of the total population. Following the passage of the Non-Importation Law of 1833 the percentage remained almost stationary and by 1840 it had decreased slightly.

The strength of the anti-slavery forces was greatly augmented in 1836 by the election of Cassius M. Clay to the legislature. Though only twenty-six years of age, he soon assumed both in the legislature and in the state as a whole that leadership of the anti-slavery workers which he held during the remainder of the slavery period. He was a nephew of Henry Clay and a son of General Green Clay of Madison County. Although a member of one of the wealthiest slave owning families in Kentucky, he acquired a very strong anti-slavery tendency during his college days at Yale College, where he heard William Lloyd Garrison and other anti-slavery workers speak. After his graduation in 1832, he returned to Kentucky and entered the legal profession, in which he soon attained prominence. In 1835, and again in 1837, he represented Madison County in the legislature.[37] The following year he moved his residence to Lexington, Fayette County, and in 1840 he was again elected to the legislature on the Whig ticket, defeating Howard Wickliffe, the son of Robert Wickliffe, the leading democratic politician and the largest slave-owner in the state.[38] His early antagonism to slavery was clearly expressed in 1840, when he declared slavery to be "an evil morally, economically, physically, intellectually, socially, religiously, politically—evil in its inception and in its duration."[39]

No sooner had the Law of 1833 been passed than the pro-slavery element launched a campaign for its repeal or modification. The leader in this movement after 1835 was Robert Wickliffe. The question of the repeal of the law came before the legislature almost annually and the bill frequently passed the

[36] Session Acts of 1835, p. 258.
[37] "Memoirs of Cassius M. Clay," Vol. 1, p. 73.
[38] *Ibid.*, p. 74.
[39] Cassius M. Clay: "Review of the Late Canvass," p. 14.

senate but was regularly defeated in the house.[40] In the elections of 1840 it was one of the leading issues before the people. In a number of places the candidates were publicly asked to state their views in regard to the measure.[41] During 1840 and 1841 a long and bitter newspaper and pamphlet controversy was waged, largely over the Non-Importation Law of 1833, in which the leading participants were Robert Wickliffe, Thomas Marshall, Robert J. Breckinridge, and Cassius M. Clay, the last three defending the law. In one of the pamphlets published in 1840, Wickliffe urged the slaveholders of the South to hold a convention for the purpose of formulating plans for the better protection of their slave interests.[42] In this he maintained that the Non-Importation Law of 1833 was part and parcel of the system of the abolitionists, which had for its main object the severance of Kentucky from the southern slave states by diminishing the number of slaves, thus increasing the proportion of non-slaveholders and free laborers, forcing the entire slave population upon the "Southern Angle," and finally terminating slavery there "by the murder of the whole white population."[43] This calamity, he believed, could be averted only by an expansion of the slave territory and by "nipping in the bud" all anti-slavery schemes.

The repeal bill came up annually[44] before the legislature, until 1849, when a bill was passed repealing the most important provisions of the Non-Importation Law of 1833.[45] This action was taken on the eve of an election of delegates to a constitutional convention, an election in which gradual emancipation was one, if not the most important issue, and was doubtless designed to counteract the growing sentiment in favor of emancipation. The Presbyterian Herald in commenting upon the vote said: "We do not know how far this action of the legislature is in accordance with the popular sentiment of the State at large. At this point we hear but one opinion

---

[40] The Maysville Eagle, December 22, 1838. In this year the bill passed the Senate by a vote of 20 to 14. See also the Philanthropist, October 28, 1840; Cassius M. Clay: "Review of the Late Canvass, 1840," Pamphlet. It was largely due to the efforts of Clay that the law was not repealed at this time.

[41] The Philanthropist, October 28, 1840.

[42] Wickliffe: "Reply to Robert J. Breckinridge * * *, 1840," Pamphlet, p. 45f.

[43] Ibid., pp. 45ff. See also Thomas Marshall: "Letters to the Editor of the Commonwealth," Pamphlet, 1840, Vol. 2, p. 22. In these letters he attempts to prove the constitutionality of the law which had been contested by Wickliffe and others. For the part taken by Robert J. Breckinridge see the Breckinridge Papers for 1840 and 1841, which contain a number of important letters on this subject.

[44] The Liberator, April 9, 1840, February 12, 1841, February 14, 1845, January 16, 1846, February 11, 1848; Niles' Weekly Register, Vol. 64, p. 4; Anti-Slavery Bugle, February 18, 1848.

[45] Niles' Weekly Register, Vol. 75, p. 113; The Liberator, March 2, 1849.

expressed, and that is that the action of the Legislature in the matter is uncalled for and unpolitic."[46]

The effort to prevent importation was one of the hopeful measures that characterized the late twenties and the early thirties, measures designed to prevent slavery from acquiring a firmer hold on the state and to facilitate, in that way, the work of gradual emancipation. The effort of pro-slavery leaders to secure the repeal of the non-importation act is to be regarded as a sign of the aggressive program to which they adhered after the threat of the Garrisonian abolitionists and it illustrates quite aptly the place which in the forties slavery had come to occupy in the political and social life of the state.

[46] The Presbyterian Herald, February 22, 1849.

GRADUAL EMANCIPATION AND RADICAL
ABOLITION
1830-1840

CHAPTER VIII

The development of sentiment in favor of gradual constitutional emancipation following the constitutional convention of 1799 has been traced in the preceding pages. It
has been seen that the question of calling a convention was
an issue in practically every legislature and that the party
favoring a convention, although it represented a minority,
was strong enough at times to control one of the houses. The
result was a constant uneasiness on the part of the slaveholders
lest slavery might be abolished if entrusted to a representative
constitutional convention.[1] Illustrative of this was a circular
addressed to the freemen of Fayette County, in 1830, by the
Hon. Robert Wickliffe, in which he bitterly opposed the calling
of such a convention. His arguments in support of this position, typical pro-slavery arguments, were based largely on his
fear of emancipation, which he considered inexpedient unless
it could be made effective in all the states of the Union. He
maintained that the attempt to emancipate the slaves of Kentucky would not succeed, but would drive the slaveholders
with their slaves to the southern states, where slavery would
continue "for centuries yet to come." He considered the
consequences of such a migration dangerous "to the wealth and
the capital of the state" and spoke especially of the inhumanity
of such a move, since the slaves would be removed "to a country
where their slavery would be more intolerable than it is at
present." He regarded the diffusion of slaves over extensive
portions of the nation as tending more to the final emancipation of the race than the gathering of them in large masses.
Furthermore, he expressed his wish that slavery should not be
perpetual, and he firmly believed that Providence would at

---

[1] There is a "Bill for the Emancipation of Slaves" in the Draper MSS. (Boone MSS.,
Original Doc., Vol. 27). On the obverse side of this Bill is a petition signed by Robert Todd,
P. Patterson, David Reid, James Crawford, Andrew McCalla, William Barber, and W. Machean,
which pronounces slavery a great political evil and moral wrong. The Legislature was asked
to pass certain laws that were designed to encourage emancipation, especially of the future
offspring of the present generation of slaves. Neither the Bill nor the petition was dated.

the proper time point out the means of effecting its extinction. He firmly believed that the calling of a convention would result in emancipation and accordingly warned the slaveholders throughout the state "of the danger to the tenure by which they hold their slaves which would result from a convention." He referred to the yearly returns of the tax commissioners and endeavored to prove that less than one voter in ten was a slaveholder.[2] "In this state of the polls," he asked, "what chance can the slaveholder have to retain his slaves, if by a new constitution he is left at the mercy of the annual legislature of the state?" The address closed with the warning "that while the constitution secures the rights of the masters to their slaves the religious societies, that abhor the principles of slavery, feel themselves restrained to be silent as to its evils; but so soon as it becomes a question to be settled in a new constitution all such feel themselves called on by the principles of their religion to act, and they will act, as their conscience dictates."[3]

Robert Wickliffe represented the radical element in the pro-slavery party, but his fears of those who favored gradual emancipation were shared by many. Millions of dollars had been invested by the citizens of the state in slave property and many of those who were interested in slavery, although they did not always regard slave labor as economical, did not wish to see the power to emancipate placed in the hands of the legislature, since the legislature might at any time pass under the control of a radical anti-slavery party that would summarily abolish the institution and without compensation. On the other hand, there were many slaveholders who actively co-operated with the anti-slavery party, because they believed that slavery was detrimental to the best interests of the state. Yet they neither desired nor anticipated radical action on the subject.

---

[2] This seems to be a fair estimate of the slaveholding population of Kentucky. Cassius M. Clay in a speech in the House of Representatives of Kentucky in 1841, said that nine-tenths of the free white population of the state were non-slaveholders or working men. "Speech of Cassius M. Clay in the House of Representatives of Kentucky in January, 1841, upon a Bill to Repeal the Non-importation Law of 1833," Pamphlet, p. 4.

[3] Kentucky Reporter, February 17, 1830. It was also published in pamphlet form and in the Western Luminary (May 26, 1830), and in other Kentucky papers. The following observation of the anti-slavery prospects in Kentucky was made by Benjamin Lundy in the Genius of Universal Emancipation, April 1, 1830, p. 3: "In addition to the evidence, so conclusive, that the good cause is there fast gaining ground, it will be recollected that the Legislature recently had under consideration a resolution to amend the Constitution of the State, when the advocates of that measure vowed that their ultimate object was the eradication of slavery from their soil. A letter from a gentleman of high standing, in Lexington, to the Hon. Charles Miner, of Pennsylvania, states that this was the principal inducement with many to support the proposition; and it will be remembered that the resolution was negatived by a majority of one vote only."

While many slaveholders advocated the calling of a constitutional convention for the purpose of providing some means for the gradual extinction of slavery in the state, a considerable number of anti-slavery workers, among them Robert J. Breckinridge, a member of the Kentucky legislature, opposed the convention bill on the ground that under the existing constitution slavery might be terminated in perfect accordance with its spirit and provisions. This point of view was advanced by Mr. Breckinridge in the fourth and fifth numbers of his "Hints on Slavery," in answer to the pamphlet by R. Wickliffe quoted above.[4] He maintained that the constitution expressly recognized two methods of emancipation: first, by consent of the owners, and second, by compensation on the part of the state. He maintained also that by a system of moderate and sustained police regulations emancipation might be ultimately accomplished without infringing the title of the owner more than had been done by multitudes of laws on other subjects.[5] He adduced the following constitutional argument concerning the post nati which he maintained was intentionally ingrafted into the constitution by the framers of that document.[6] The constitution comprehends under the single word "slaves," the total interest of the owner protected by it; and allows his total interest, whatever it may be, to be taken and paid for by the state. Now, if the possibility that a female will have children is such an interest that it vests in the master, then it is such an interest as by the force of the terms the state can pay for and control. If it is not such an interest, then there is no question that the state can control it without pay. Thus, either way, the power of the state over the post nati is complete; according to one construction with compensation, according to the other,

---

[4] Breckinridge Papers, for 1830, contain the original copy. See also Kentucky Reporter, May 12, 19, 1830. Breckinridge's "Hints on Slavery" is one of the most important anti-slavery documents in the history of Kentucky. They were copied into many of the Kentucky papers and received state-wide attention. Among other things he says: "Two out of every seven of her population are estimated to be slaves. One out of every thirteen of her white population is estimated to be a slave owner. It may be conjectured that one in every two among slaveholders are favorable to the principle of gradual abolition. Twelve out of every thirteen own no slaves, and are therefore, in every way, interested in getting rid of them. It follows, therefore, that not more than one in every twenty-six whites, upon a fair presentation of the subject, could upon any reasonable calculation, be supposed favorable to the perpetuity of negro slavery in the state." He then attempted to prove that slavery was decidedly against the true interests of the state. While he expressed confidence in colonization he maintained that the real object was to secure the freedom of the slaves. This he believed should be preceded by an absolute prohibition of all importations of slaves into the state. Furthermore, he stated that the state had a right to and should at once levy a tax on all slaves within the state, the proceeds of which were to be devoted to the removal of the freed slaves to Africa.

[5] "Hints on Slavery," Kentucky Reporter, May 12, 19, 1830. Also Breckinridge Papers (1830).

[6] See *supra*, pp. 31, 32.

without it.[7] In the summary closing his constitutional argument he said: "I cannot doubt, then, that I am authorized to give the following interpretation to the debated clause of the constitution, as embracing its plain meaning and fulfilling its intent:

"1. The General Assembly (of Kentucky) can never emancipate any slaves gradually, contingent or in any way whatever; except, first, with their owners' consent, or secondly, after having previously paid for them.

"2. * * *

"3. The General Assembly has full power, before the birth of those persons who by our Constitution and laws, are allowed to be held in slavery—so to modify existing laws, as to allow them to remain as they are born—free.

"4. It follows that the General Assembly has full power, so to modify existing laws, as to allow the condition of slavery to attach at birth to those who can be slaves, only in a qualified or limited manner; that is, to provide for the gradual prospective emancipation of the descendants of female slaves."[8]

These articles, in addition to appearing in pamphlet form, were printed in a number of the leading papers of the state. They attracted wide attention and provoked much discussion. They were written to prove that, although the legislature had no power to liberate slaves without the consent of their owners, or without first paying for them, yet it had the power to provide for emancipation of descendants of female slaves. The secondary object was to prevent the call of a convention, by showing that it was not necessary insofar as the subject of emancipation was concerned.[9]

---

[7] "Hints on Slavery," Breckinridge Papers; Kentucky Reporter, May 12, 19, 1830.

[8] *Ibid.*, May 19, 1830.
"The power to liberate persons in slavery being restricted in part, cannot be exercised in the excepted cases. The power to enforce and confirm the laws of nature, anterior to the birth of the children of slaves is not restricted, but remains complete under the general grant.* * * If it had been the intention of the Convention to put an absolute, instead of a limited restraint on the power of the Legislature to prevent forever the extinguishment of slavery, instead of guarding the interests of owners to a certain extent, a very different phraseology would naturally have suggested itself, and must have been used, 'The General Assembly shall have no power to pass laws for the extinguishment of slavery.' This was followed by a long discussion of gradual emancipation. The article ended with this significant statement: "Domestic slavery cannot exist forever; it cannot exist *long* in any condition of society or under any form of government, quiet and unbroken. It may terminate in various ways—but terminate it must." (Breckinridge Papers, Original copy.) This same idea was expressed in the "Speech of Robert J. Breckinridge * * *, October 12, 1840," Pamphlet.

[9] Robert Wickliffe, a personal and political enemy of R. J. Breckinridge, in commenting a few years later on the influence of Breckinridge: "Hints on Slavery," said: "That those articles excited in the slaves of the county and city a spirit of insubordination that filled the county of Fayette with murder, arson and rapes to such a degree that, in one year, there were about fifteen committals of slaves for capital offenses, and many executions of them, when there had not been one case of an execution of a slave for fifteen years before they commenced their operations in favor of abolition." ("Reply of Robert Wickliffe to Robert J. Breckinridge, 1841." Pamphlet, p. 20f.)

The sentiment in favor of gradual constitutional emancipation seemed to be gaining strength rapidly during the early thirties. The passage of the Non-Importation Law of 1833 is an evidence of that fact.[10] This victory only tended to encourage the anti-slavery party to greater efforts and led them to believe that the time was ripe for the submission of a plan of gradual emancipation to the people. In 1833 James G. Birney regarded Kentucky "as the best site in our whole country for taking a stand against slavery."[11] In a letter to Lewis Tappan, February third, of the same year he said: "I returned a few days since from Frankfort. I heard whilst there most of the debates on the convention bill into which the subject of slavery and emancipation always entered. I conversed on the subject with many of the members of the legislature as well as with many other intelligent gentlemen from the different parts of the state. The conclusion to which my mind has been brought is this—that emancipation in some form or another occupies the minds of the community, and that the feeling in favor of it is growing. * * * I am not without hope that the subject of emancipation will be taken up in many parts of the state by the candidates for the next General Assembly of the state. Should this be so I can entertain no doubt, that the result will be a termination of slavery in some way or another."[12]

In a speech in the legislature of Kentucky in 1835 in support of the convention bill and a gradual emancipation clause in the new constitution, J. M. Helm said in this connection: "The spirit of emancipation is abroad in the land, and you had as well try to resist electricity or control the lightnings of heaven as to attempt to check its onward march. * * * Let us now meet the question and have some constitutional assurance how long we may be expected to be permitted to hold them (slaves). * * * Let the coming generation have an opportunity of arranging their fortunes at once. * * * What disposition shall be made of our slave population is a question of grave consideration, and I will not now hazard an opinion upon the subject. But this much I will say, if that population is to be perpetually urged as an argument against altering, reforming, or abolishing our government, when experience shall point out its necessity, our country is doubly en-

---

[10] See *supra*, p. 94.
[11] Birney: "James G. Birney and His Times," p. 131.
[12] Liberator, April 4, 1835.

slaved; our slaves are slaves to us, and we are, because of them, slaves to our laws."[13]

By 1835 the sentiment in favor of emancipation had become so strong and so persistent that many slaveholders who were opposed to emancipation now supported the convention bill in order to bring about a permanent settlement of the question one way or the other. Some slaveholders, opposed to emancipation, regarded the time as opportune for testing the strength of the anti-slavery party since hundreds of moderate emancipationists had withdrawn their support either temporarily or permanently as a result of the activities of the radical abolitionists.[14] There were also other issues involved in the calling of a convention that commanded a considerable following and for a combination of reasons the legislature in 1837, by a vote of 20 to 16 in the Senate and of 57 to 42 in the House, passed the convention bill.[15]

The constitution of Kentucky provided that when a majority of all the members elected to each House of the General Assembly should concur in passing a law, "specifying the alterations intended to be made, for taking the sense of the good people of this State as to the necessity and expediency of calling a convention" elections were to be held, and if a majority of the citizens entitled to vote for representatives voted for the convention, the General Assembly was to direct that a "similar poll shall be opened and taken" at the general election the following year; and if a majority of the citizens entitled to vote for representatives again voted for the convention, the General Assembly, at its next session, was to issue a call for and order the election of delegates to a constitutional convention. But if by the vote of either year such a majority was not secured the convention was not to be called.[16] Thus the bill having passed the legislature in 1837 the first election was ordered for the fall of 1838.

It is evident, therefore, that the campaign for the gradual constitutional emancipation was only begun by the passage of the legislative act of 1837. To accomplish the desired end it would be necessary for the friends of emancipation to command a majority of the votes in the elections of 1838 and 1839,

[13] Liberator, March 7, 1835, quoted from the Lexington Intelligencer.
[14] A correspondent in the Western Presbyterian Herald, for November 30, 1837, speaks disparagingly of the tendency among the friends of emancipation to cease temporarily their efforts in its behalf as a result of the northern abolitionist propaganda. Such action, he declared, could not be justified at such a crisis by the errors of abolitionists.
[15] Western Presbyterian Herald, January 4, 1838.
[16] House Documents, 59th Congress, 2d Session, Vol. 89, p. 1288.

and also to secure the election of a majority of the delegates to the convention in 1840 to support their cause. This, under the most favorable circumstances, would be a most difficult undertaking, especially since, as we have seen, the action of the legislature in referring the question of a convention to the people was not due wholly to the efforts of the anti-slavery men.[17]

The Lexington Observer, which consistently opposed the convention bill, made the following comment on the situation in regard to slavery: "For a time we must expect this subject to control all others. The state of Kentucky is to be the theatre upon which a great battle is to be fought. It is useless to disguise the question. * * * All other imputed defects in the Constitution are mere playthings—we have not heard one pointed out which would justify this extreme resolve. It is time that the people of this state should know what their future destiny is to be. If a majority should be of the opinion that it is better to extirpate slavery, it is time it should be known. There is a restlessness in the public mind, which should be allayed, by full, free, and manly discussion. Let us discuss it in the right spirit. * * * We make war on no man for his opinion—some of the brightest ornaments of Kentucky are of the opinion that slavery is a great moral and political curse."[18]

The anti-slavery activity in Kentucky between 1830 and 1840 was viewed by the entire country with a great deal of interest. The final decision of the state upon the question of whether or not slavery should be permitted to remain touched vital interests in both the North and the South. It was frequently asked: Should Kentucky abolish slavery, would the other border states, Tennessee, Missouri, Maryland, and Virginia, follow? Should any one or all of these states voluntarily take such action, would it be possible to restore the balance of power in the national government between the North and the South as established by the Missouri Compromise in 1820, and if not would it result in the final abolition of slavery in the entire South?

An indication of the opinion of the South is given in an editorial in a North Carolina newspaper in 1837: "The legislature of Kentucky has passed a bill to take the sense of the people on

[17] Western Presbyterian Herald, for June 4, 1838, in reviewing this Act, said: "Slavery was one issue although the anti-slavery element did not control the legislature. Many desired to find out the will of the people on that and other questions."
[18] Genius of Universal Emancipation, January, 1838, quoted from the Lexington Observer. This article was also copied in the Emancipator, January 25, 1838.

the propriety of calling a Convention, the primary object of which is the abolition of slavery in that State. Such a movement, in a juncture like the present, is to be especially regretted. Its effects will not be confined to the State of Kentucky, but will have a weighty and important bearing upon the interest of all the slave States. Those in Kentucky who desire the continuation and the glory of this Union, and who participated in effecting this movement, have given by it but an ill-judged and an impolitic earnest of that desire. And the Abolitionists of the North and of that State are now doubly exulting at a prospect so favorable to the final accomplishment of their designs. Is it not time that the South were awake, and moving, by States, to the common principle, that slavery shall not be abolished?"[19] The Richmond Whig in commenting upon the coming Kentucky election said: "It assumes a consequence and importance surpassing that of any subject ever agitated in Kentucky. But the interest in the event will not be confined to the citizens of that state. * * * Every portion of the Confederacy, and the slaveholding region especially, will look with intense interest to the decision of the question."[20] The Savannah Georgian about the same time urged the South to oppose the candidacy of Henry Clay for the presidency because he came from "a state where public opinion is undergoing a change upon the subject of slavery. When it is ascertained that hemp can be grown at less expense with white than with slave labor, that state will go further against the institution than any other, on the same principle that one renegade is worse than ten Turks."[21]

The Emancipator, the official organ of the American Anti-Slavery Society, was very optimistic over the prospects of success in the Kentucky struggle.[22] It expressed the opinion that the abolition of slavery in the state, as a result of her contiguity to a number of slave states, might virtually abolish the institution in the whole South.[23] By April, 1838, it seemed to regard the struggle as won by the anti-slavery forces when it made the following comment: "In spite of all the machinations of interested politicians, Kentucky has virtually withdrawn from the

[19] Genius of Universal Emancipation, January, 1838, quoted. The name of the North Carolina paper is not given. Benjamin Lundy made the following comment on this article: "The reader will bear in mind that the doctrine which the Southern slaveholders have heretofore preached, is, non-interference with regulations of other States. But now we have a different language from them. We hope and trust, however, that the people of Kentucky will properly attend to their own concerns, whatever the besotted tyrants in the Carolinas may think or say of them."
[20] Emancipator, February 15, 1838, quoted.
[21] Emancipator, October 4, 1838, quoted from the Savannah Georgian, August 26, 1838.
[22] Emancipator, February 15, June 14, 1838.
[23] *Ibid.*, February 15, 1838.

confederacy of oppressors. The struggle may yet be severe. Slavery will die game, but it must die. Kentucky is now the battleground of abolition."[24] The expression, "Kentucky is now the battleground of abolition," was repeatedly used from this time on by the Emancipator and other anti-slavery papers, and was taken up by the pro-slavery newspapers and politicians of Kentucky and held before the public as an evidence of the undue interference of the North in the internal affairs of the state.

William Lloyd Garrison, the editor of the Liberator, expressed considerable confidence in the outcome of the election in Kentucky, although he was not so sanguine as the editor of the Emancipator.[25]

Numerous pamphlets and anti-slavery papers were sent into Kentucky by the American Anti-Slavery Society and similar societies and by various anti-slavery newspapers of the free states.[26] Efforts were made in a number of towns to exclude this material from the mails. Mr. J. J. Ficklin, the postmaster at Lexington, refused to deliver such documents to the people of that place. He informed the editor of the Emancipator that the numerous abolition pamphlets and papers sent to the citizens of that vicinity were not reaching their destination and requested that he stop sending them. He said that there were no immediate abolitionists in Kentucky and that there was no prospect of any.[27]

On the other hand, it was asserted by the Commonwealth, one of the leading Kentucky newspapers, that the Kentucky convention was making more "noise beyond the borders of the state than it was at home,*** where it was attracting no great amount of attention."[28] It reviewed at length the attempt of the northern abolitionists to make Kentucky the "battleground of abolition." The editor spoke especially of the Emancipator, a copy of which had recently come into his hands. This number he declared showed a keen observation of passing events in the state legislature. It contained a careful and accurate synopsis of the progress and the passage of the convention bill as well as a number of the speeches in the legislature. The Emancipator

[24] Emancipator, April 5, April 19, June 14, 1838.
[25] Liberator, August 31, 1838.
[26] Emancipator, February 15, 1838, June 14, 1838. In 1838 there were 1,346 abolition societies, with 112,480 members in the free states. During the year the central office in New York City issued 646,000 copies of anti-slavery publications. More than 100 abolition papers were being published in various parts of the northern states.
[27] Emancipator, April 19, 1838; Commonwealth, April 18, 1838.
[28] Commonwealth, March 28, 1838. "The abolitionists contend that it (the Convention) was forced through the legislature by the strength of abolitionism—while the Globe in large capitals heralds it as being the combined product of Federalism, United States Bankism and Abolitionism." The Commonwealth assigned the call for the convention to a number of causes, one of which was slavery.

was described as being conducted with "singular ability" and as "better calculated to work ruin to the South than all the rest of the machinery put together." The people were warned against the "designs of that growing and dangerous faction," the abolitionists of the North. Any yielding on the part of any of the slaveholding states would throw a preponderating power into the scale of the abolitionists and serve to increase their determination, already too strongly marked.[29]

The Hon. James T. Morehead, for many years an outspoken opponent of slavery in the state and an ardent advocate of colonization, in a speech in the legislature of Kentucky on the convention bill, gave the following reasons, which are typical of addresses on the subject, for opposing the calling of a convention or for the constitutional abolition of slavery: "Any man who desires to see slavery abolished—any friend of emancipation, gradual or immediate—who supposes for a moment that now is the time to carry out this favorite policy, must be blind to the prognostics that lower from every quarter of the political sky. Sir, the present is not the period to unmanacle the slave in this or any other state of the Union. Four years ago you might have had some hope. But the wild spirit of fanaticism has done much to retard the work of emancipation and to rivet the fetters of slavery in Kentucky.*** The advocates of abolition—the phrenzied fanatics of the North, neither sleep nor slumber. Their footsteps are even now to be seen wherever mischief can be perpetrated—and it may be that while the people of Kentucky are reposing in the confidence of fancied security, the tocsin of rebellion may resound through the land—the firebrand of the incendiary may wrap their dwellings in flames—their towns and cities may become heaps of ashes before their eyes and their minds drawn off from all thoughts of reforming the government to consider the means necessary for their self-preservation—the protection of their families and all that is dear to men."[30]

Even Henry Clay, who had not taken a decided stand regarding emancipation in Kentucky since 1799, wrote to his friends advising them to oppose the call for a convention and to oppose emancipation. This was a great disappointment to the

[29] Commonwealth, April 18, 1838. This paper, though pro-slavery, was by no means radical. Articles advocating gradual emancipation frequently appeared in it. In the above number, the Hon. John J. Helm, a member of the legislature, published a circular letter addressed to his constituents in vindication of his vote for the convention bill. A plan of gradual emancipation and colonization was recommended to them for their consideration. July 18, 1838, in a long article signed "C," a plan of emancipation, copied after that formerly adopted by New York, was advocated. Both Mr. Helm and correspondent "C" bitterly assailed abolitionism.

[30] Commonwealth, April 4, 1838; Maysville Eagle, April 11, 1838.

opponents of slavery and a decisive blow to the emancipation cause in the state. Because of his ardent advocacy of colonization and his repeatedly expressed belief that the institution of slavery was detrimental to the best interests of the state, it had been expected that once the question had been submitted to the people he would add his powerful influence to the cause. Clay justified his action in opposing the convention bill upon the ground of expediency. He made no attempt to defend or excuse slavery on moral or economic grounds, but his hatred and fear of abolitionists and abolitionism was intense.[31]

By the spring of 1838 the discussions of the advisability of calling a convention and of gradual constitutional emancipation were rapidly degenerating into a denunciation of abolitionism in which the friends and the foes of slavery took an equal part.[32] Scarcely an article appeared in the newspapers, scarcely a speech was delivered on either side of the question that abolition and abolitionists were not bitterly assailed. Many of the leading advocates of a convention now turned against it because in view of the interference of northern abolitionists in the affairs of the state the holding of a convention that might affect the constitutional status of slavery was thought undesirable. The northern abolitionists were ignorantly playing into the hands of the radical pro-slavery leaders and were enabling them to associate abolition, regarded by all classes as a dangerous menace to southern society, with the constitutional convention and perhaps gradual emancipation, and thus to defeat the measure. Opposition to modern abolitionism then as in later years became a popular policy regardless of the excuse for it or the issue involved.

When the question of calling a convention came before the people in the election during the fall of 1838 the supporters of the convention were defeated by a large majority.[33] Various causes contributed to this result and one of the most important was, doubtless, the suspicion and fear aroused by the growth and

---

[31] Annals of Congress, 1839, Vol. 7, p. 354. Speech on Abolition Petitions, February 7.

[32] In 1836, Robert J. Breckinridge, at that time an advocate of gradual emancipation, spoke of abolitionists as the "most despicable and odious men on the face of the earth." He said further that there were not more than ten men in the whole State holding their views. George Thompson: "Discussion of American Slavery Between George Thompson and Robert J. Breckinridge," p. 40.

In a speech before the Colonization Society of Kentucky, in 1830, Henry Clay said: "When we consider the cruelty of the origin of negro slavery, its nature, the character of the free institutions of the whites, and the irresistible progress of the public opinion, through America as well as Europe, it is impossible not to anticipate frequent insurrections among the blacks in the United States.*** By the very condition of the relation which subsists between us we are enemies of each other." (African Repository, Vol. 6, p. 11.)

[33] Henry Clay estimated this majority at four to one. Annals of Congress, 1839, Vol. 7, p. 358.

activity of the northern abolitionists. Henry Clay said, in explanation of the defeat of the convention, that the anti-slavery majority in the state had gradually increased from 1799 and was increasing "until the abolitionists commenced their operations. The effect has been to dissipate all prospects whatever, for the present, of any scheme of gradual or other emancipation. The people have been shocked and alarmed by these abolition movements. * * * The apprehension of the danger of abolition was the leading consideration amongst the people for opposing the call (of the convention). But for that, but for the agitation of the question of abolition in States whose population had no right, in the opinion of the people of Kentucky, to interfere in the matter, the vote for the convention would have been much larger, if it had not been carried."[34] Considerable evidence has been found indicating the importance of radical abolitionism in Kentucky during this period. Professor Shaler, in his "Kentucky, an American Commonwealth," sums up the matter in this fashion: "From the local histories the deliberate student will easily become convinced that if there had been no external pressure against slavery at this time (1830-1840) there would still have been a progressive elimination of the slave element from the population by emancipation on the soil, by the sale of slaves to the planters of the Southern States, and by their colonization in foreign parts."[35]

The radical abolition propaganda was also instrumental in intensifying sectional feeling which previous to 1830 had not been pronounced in Kentucky. There was a growing feeling that it was the duty of Kentucky as a slave state to support the southern states in their struggle for the maintenance of slavery, and this determination was greatly strengthened by the countenance and assistance rendered to the Underground Railroad System, by which hundreds of citizens of Kentucky were un-

---

[34] Annals of Congress, 1839, Vol. 7, p. 358. Speech on Abolition Petitions, February 7. Clay further expressed the opinion that the abolition movement had set back for half a century the prospect of any kind of emancipation in the state.
    The Liberator, for September 22, 1843, quoting from the Western Citizen, of Paris, Ky., said: "It is often cast into the teeth of abolitionists that their agitation of the slave question in the free states has prevented emancipation in Kentucky and Virginia—that those states were some ten or twelve years ago on the very eve of emancipation, but the discussion of the question by abolition fanatics at the North drove them from it." The Western Citizen, however, attributed the defeat of the emancipation to the attitude of Henry Clay, who was bidding for the Presidency.
    In a speech at Richmond, Indiana, in 1840, Henry Clay said that before abolitionists began their work the people of Kentucky were nearly, if not altogether, ready for the passage of a law for the gradual emancipation, "but the misguided, and, we believe, honest zeal of the abolitionists, had to a great extent destroyed this feeling." (The Liberator, October 21, 1842.)
    [35] Shaler: "Kentucky, Pioneer Commonwealth," p. 197.

lawfully deprived of their slaves.[36]   Thus there was developed among the slaveholders a feeling of wrong and indignation, and their determination to oppose in every way possible the efforts of the radical abolitionists in behalf of the slave was greatly strengthened.   Thousands of men who earnestly desired emancipation by some gradual constitutional measure were unwillingly driven to the support of the institution of slavery.   There was also developed a stronger and more determined opposition to all anti-slavery activities within the state, associating all such efforts with those of the northern abolitionists, whose activities had occasioned such great anxiety and economic losses within the state.

---

[36] The practice of encouraging and assisting fugitive slaves to escape to the free states or to Canada was begun in Kentucky as early as 1818 (Harris: "Negro Servitude in Illinois," p. 59; Levi Coffin: "Reminiscences," p. 107), although it was not very well established for a number of years after that date.   As early as 1827 a society composed of slaveholders was formed in Mason County for the purpose of concerting measures for the better security of their slave property.   (Maysville Eagle, July 11, 25, 1827.)   By 1835 the number of fugitive slaves that annually escaped to Ohio and Indiana had become quite large and the chance of recovering them very small.   The sentiment in the free states to the North was so strong against slavery that it was almost impossible to secure a jury that would convict a person for assisting slaves to escape and when they crossed into Kentucky their actions were so guarded that the task was equally difficult.   A striking illustration of this was the arrest, trial, and acquittal by a Kentucky jury in 1838 of the well-known Ohio abolitionist, Rev. John B. Mahan, for inciting, aiding and abetting slaves to escape, although his guilt could scarcely be questioned.   (Maysville Eagle, November 21, 1838; Western Presbyterian Herald, December 13, 1838.)   The Maysville Eagle in reviewing the trial said that: "Our fellow-citizens of Ohio will perceive from the result of this trial that there is no disposition on our part to interfere with their rights or to encroach upon the sovereignty of their state.   Have we not a right to ask, in return that they will frown down the disposition manifested, by a portion of their citizens, or to intermeddle with our rights, by inciting, aiding and abetting the escape of our slaves which we esteem property, and the possession of which is guaranteed to us by our common constitution."   (Maysville Eagle, November 21, 1838, January 26, 1839.)   The Commonwealth stated that the people of Kentucky had displayed more forebearance than might have been expected of them in the hope that "time and reflection would, of themselves, be sufficient to bring back those misguided and wicked disturbers of her repose, to a sense of justice and propriety."   This moderation, however, had led to more and greater excesses.   A solemn warning was issued against future acts of this nature which if continued might lead to a spirit of retaliation which "may, in its turn, overleap the boundaries of propriety, and go even farther for redress than they have gone to inflict injury."   (The Commonwealth, December 26, 1838.)   The Governor, in his annual message, in 1838, discussed at considerable length this particular grievance against the Northern Abolitionists and recommended an enactment to prevent the propagation of the views and arguments of the abolitionists, stating that they were professedly circulated for the conviction of the masters, but really intended to operate on the slaves.   He could see no reason why a man should be tolerated in the publication of opinions dangerous and ruinous to the security of the right to property and at the same time be restrained from a publication injurious to his character."   (Maysville Eagle, December 4, 11, 19, 1838.)   The subject was early brought before the Legislature when the numerous facts brought to light chiefly by the Mahan trial, showing the methods of assisting and the extent of the resultant losses of slaves, were fully discussed.   The outcome of the discussion was that two commissioners were appointed to proceed at once to Columbus, Ohio, where the Legislature of that State was in session to endeavor to induce that body to pass a law calculated to prevent the interference with the slave property of Kentucky by evil-disposed persons in Ohio.   (The Commonwealth, December 26, 1838.)   The commissioners were received with courtesy (The Commonwealth, February 6, 1839,) although they were not asked to speak before the Legislature as they had anticipated.   (Maysville Eagle, February 2, 1839).   The Ohio Legislature in compliance with the wishes and with the approval of the Kentucky Commissioners passed a law designed to remedy the above grievances.   (Maysville Eagle, December 4, 1839.)   Unfortunately, the matter did not end here, for neither Kentucky nor Ohio were able *to permanently break up* the work of the Under Ground Railroad System; in fact the number of slaves who annually escaped increased alarmingly.

THE FAILURE OF EMANCIPATION IN THE CONSTITUTIONAL CONVENTION OF 1849.

CHAPTER IX

The failure to secure the calling of a constitutional convention in 1838 did not end anti-slavery efforts in Kentucky. The pro-slavery feeling could not be kept at the heat of 1837-1838 in view of the relatively slight direct interest of most Kentucky people in slavery, a fact which left the way open for the anti-slavery element to resume their activities. This was recognized by the anti-slavery leaders, who early took advantage of it. By 1840 the cry of radical abolition, which during the thirties had counteracted anti-slavery sentiment, had lost most of its force so that many openly advocated emancipation.[1]

Cassius M. Clay in 1840, in discussing the slavery issue in the state and the nation, said, "There are two classes of fanatics in these states; one the anti-slavery fanatics, the 'abolitionists,' the other the slave fanatics, the 'disunionists.' In one class are those reckless spirits who, to free the slave, would violate the national constitution and plunge the country into civil war. The other class are those enemies of human liberty and the progressive civilization who would destroy the same ever-glorious palladium of freedom and equal rights among men, to perpetuate slavery. They are both the outlaws of nations and the enemies of mankind. The North has her 'abolitionists,' her Garrisons, her Tappans. The South has her 'disunionists', her McDuffies and her Wickliffes. From such malign influences may Heaven in its mercy preserve my native land."[2] A comparatively small number of either of these classes lived in Kentucky.

Cassius M. Clay was one of the most enthusiastic, outspoken and determined anti-slavery sympathizers in the state during the forties. During the early part of his political career, he held himself decidedly on the defensive against both the abolitionists and the slaveholders. Against the abolitionists he appealed to the legal rights of the slaveholder, and on the ethical side of the

---

[1] As in the preceding period numerous plans of gradual emancipation were proposed and their merits discussed. Most of these proposals were conservative and they were made in many instances, by slaveholders. Of especial interest was a pamphlet published at Paris, Kentucky, in 1837, "Remarks on Slavery and the Slave Trade by a Slaveholder," addressed to the Hon. Henry Clay.
[2] Cassius M. Clay: "Review of the Late Canvass," p. 7.

question he demanded freedom of conscience. Against the slave-holders he invoked the limits set to slavery by the constitution, the law and the public will, because of his belief that from every point of view slavery exerted a malign influence upon the development of the state.[3]

A thoroughly honorable and deeply moral nature, such as that of Cassius M. Clay, could not long remain in an ambiguous position. He was never a clear thinker. His impelling force was, and remained, feeling, which reacted to every stimulus too vigorously not to involve him in frequent and glaring inconsistencies in thought and action.

After his extended speaking trip through the northern and eastern states in 1843, in which slavery was his chief subject of discussion, he returned to his native state a much more pronounced opponent of slavery. He now formally submitted to the whole "People of Kentucky" his confession of faith in an address, the substance of which was, "I proudly aver myself the eternal enemy of slavery," and "Kentucky must be free."[4] He would no longer be content with attacking slavery at one point or another, but, in so far as concerned his own state, he would open fire along the whole line, and would end the struggle only with the destruction of slavery. His assertion that Kentucky had not the same interest as the plantation states in the maintenance of slavery and that the ninety per cent. or more of her people who were not slaveholders had the highest interest in the abolition of slavery was too positive and too clear not to cause anxiety to slaveholders. His position was forcefully stated, in 1843, in a speech before a mass meeting at White Sulphur Springs, in Scott County, for the purpose of advocating the annexation of Texas in which he maintained that the most important object of those who desired the annexation of Texas was to extend the slave territory of the United States. Such action, he believed, would seriously threaten the Union, in which Kentucky was more vitally interested than any other state. All her "interests, temporal and eternal, demand of her speedily to extinguish slavery within her borders, and to unite her destiny with the northern states: who relying upon God, Liberty and Equality, will be able to stand against the world in arms."[5] And in

---

[3] "The writings of Cassius Marcellus Clay," edited by Horace Greeley, pp. 87, 88. As late as 1843 he says: "They (the abolitionists) are few indeed, and deserve, as they receive, the execration of good men in both the North and the South."

[4] *Ibid.*, p. 174f. Soon after his return to Kentucky Clay freed his own slaves, giving them employment on his estate at the prevailing wages.

[5] Cassius M. Clay, "Speech on the Annexation of Texas," 1843, Pamphlet, p. 17f.

case of dissolution of the Union he expressed his intention of casting in his lot with the North. After expressing his belief in compensated emancipation he said: "I thus far pledge myself that whenever Kentucky will join me in freeing ourselves from this curse which weighs us down even unto death, the slaves I own, she shall dispose of as to her seems best. I shall ask nothing in return but the enhanced value of my land which must ensure gradually from the day that we become indeed a free and independent state. I will go still further—give me free labor and I will not only give up my slaves, but I will agree to be taxed to buy the remainder from those who are unwilling or unable consistently with a regard to pecuniary interests to present them to the state—and then I shall deem myself and my posterity richer in dollars and cents than we were before."[6] He further asserted that emancipation in the English West Indies had proved that the great majority of the freed men could be employed economically in the same offices at small wages as they were then holding, with more ease and safety than under the existing conditions.[7]

Of the two leading political parties in the state in 1840, the Democrats and the Whigs, the latter had by far the largest number of members who favored emancipation. Cassius M. Clay and Henry Clay were both Whigs. The former in 1840 and 1841 represented in the legislature Bourbon County, one of the largest slaveholding counties in the state.[8] While the slavery issue did not figure in all the political contests in the state during the forties it was not unusual for the candidates for Congress and the state legislature voluntarily or by request to state their positions on the question of emancipation. A typical instance of this is found in Fayette County in 1845, when 120 citizens belonging about equally to both the Whig and the Democratic parties signed a communication which they presented to the candidates for the state and the national offices, asking them "to let their fellow citizens know their present views, and what will be their future course, if elected, upon the following important questions as follows:

"1. Are you or not, in favor of the abolition of slavery in Kentucky, and if you are, please give a synopsis of your course and plan and when it is your wish to see it effected?

---

[6] Cassius M. Clay, "Speech on the Annexation of Texas," Pamphlet, p. 20ff.

[7] *Ibid.*, p. 18.

[8] In 1843 the Whig candidate for Congress from the Louisville district, Mr. Thomasson, an ardent and active anti-slavery worker, was elected.

The Louisville Public Advertiser (Dem.), Sept. 29, 1843, in commenting upon the election, characterized Thomasson as "about as thorough an abolitionist in theory as can be found outside the Liberator Office or the World's Convention."

"2. Are you or not, in favor of emancipation in Kentucky, either gradual or immediate; if you are, we should be pleased to hear your views on the subject in full, and how you desire to see them consummated.

"3. If slavery is to cease in Kentucky either by abolition or present or gradual emancipation, we respectfully ask you to let us hear what you are in favor of doing with the slaves after they are freed and are they to remain amongst us here or be removed.

"4. Are you or not, in favor of the change of the constitution of Kentucky, and if you are, what changes do you desire?

"5. Are you or not, in favor of the entire repeal of the negro law, usually called the 'Negro Law of 1832-3' now on our statute books?"[9]   Robert Wickliffe, the candidate for the legislature from Fayette County, refused to answer the inquiry or to take the pledge required to oppose the repeal of the Law of 1832-3 and as a result was defeated. In a circular addressed to the "Freemen of Fayette County," he stated that the abolitionists had "ruled and governed" the county from 1840 to 1845 and "put up or put down whom they pleased."[10]   "When this has been your subserviency to the mandates of these clubites," he continued, "are you astonished that the abolitionists have located in your city, and in other cities and towns in the county?"[11]

Early in 1845 Cassius M. Clay, in co-operation with some other Kentuckians, made proposals to publish a paper, "The True American," devoted to free discussion of gradual emancipation in Kentucky. In this statement, which attracted nation-wide attention, he attempted to show that slavery was morally wrong and opposed to the economic interest of Kentucky.[12]   He advised the organization of the anti-slavery forces in all the counties of the state and the nomination of candidates pledged to support a call for a convention. These candidates were to "run again and again till victory shall perch on the standard of the free."[13]   As early as February 18, in a letter to Gerrit Smith

[9] The Liberator, August 15, 1845. Quoted from the Lexington Inquirer.
[10] R. Wickliffe: "A Circular Addressed to the Freemen of the County of Fayette, Kentucky," Pamphlet (1845), pp. 6-7.
[11] Ibid., p. 18.
[12] The Liberator, Feb. 21, 1845. He said further: "Kentuckians will be richer in dollars and cents by emancipation, and slaveholders will be wealthier by the change. I assert from my own knowledge, that lands of the same quality in the free, are from one hundred to one hundred and fifty per cent. higher in value than in the slave states—in some cases six hundred per cent. higher. Lands six miles from Cincinnati, in Ohio, I am credibly informed, are worth sixty dollars per acre, whilst in Kentucky, at the same distance from that city, and of the same quality are worth only ten dollars per acre. Now the slaveholders of the state with rare exceptions are the land owners of the state; they, therefore, absolutely increase their fortunes by liberating their slaves, even without compensation."
[13] The Liberator, Feb. 21, 1845.

he said that he had already received 240 subscribers in his home county and was expecting five or six thousand from the North.[14] During May, W. C. Bell secured in New England subscribers for the paper, among whom Daniel Webster was one of the first.[15] After reading the prospectus, William Lloyd Garrison predicted that Clay would not long be permitted to continue the publication.[16]

The first number of The True American, which was published weekly, appeared in Lexington, June 3, 1845. The declared purpose was to accomplish, by discreet argument and by legal means, the gradual abolition of slavery in Kentucky. The first leading article was devoted to a denunciation of those who demanded the suppression of the paper in the interest of suppressing discussions of slavery.[17] At the outset, The True American had about 300 subscribers within the state and about 1,700 in other states and a few weeks more sufficed to dispel any doubt that it would shortly exert influence and power. At the end of the first two months of its existence, the subscription list had increased to 700 in Kentucky and to 2,700 in other states. Not only did the number of its subscribers grow with rapidity, alarming to its enemies, but its influence became very apparent upon the Kentucky press.[18] The Greenfield Gazette (Mass.) said that the paper was destined to exert a powerful influence "particularly in the slave states, in bringing about the downfall of the accursed institution of slavery in this country.***This paper, if continued, and we hope that it will be, will effect in one year more than can be accomplished by a hundred Garrisons and his coadjutors in the space of ten."[19] The True American made a strong appeal to the non-slaveholders of the state and won considerable favor with them.

Plans for holding a great emancipation convention on the 4th of July, 1846, met with the approval of many of the prominent citizens of the state, many of whom were slaveholders.[20] The pro-slavery leaders became very much alarmed and determined to take steps at once to stop the movement before it was too

14 The Liberator, April 4, 1845.
15 Ibid., May 2, 1845.
16 Ibid., Feb. 28, 1845.
17 "Appeal of Cassius M. Clay to Kentucky and the World," Pamphlet, p. 14f. Clay was especially bitter in the denunciation of some of his enemies, particularly Robert Wickliffe, and he declared his willingness to meet them with the bowie-knife or the pistol. Garrison, in The Liberator, June 20, 1845, while approving the general spirit of the paper said that these denunciations were "in bad taste, as well as in the wrong spirit, and may lead to bloody results."
18 Ibid. The anti-slavery leaders at Louisville took the initiatory steps for the establishment of a similar paper there.
19 The Liberator, August 1, 1845.
20 "Appeal of Cassius M. Clay to Kentucky***," p. 5.

late. On the 14th of August, 1845, "a number of respectable citizens" of Lexington resolved to "request" Clay to cease the publication of his paper, because it endangered the peace of the Commonwealth and the safety of their families. A committee upon which two of Clay's most bitter enemies had been placed was appointed to acquaint him with this resolution. They called at his home and explained that they did not approach him in the form of a threat, but exhorted him to consider well that his own safety depended upon his answer.[21] Clay was ill at the time and unable to leave his house, but he made a vigorous reply: "Traitors to the laws and constitution cannot be deemed respectable by any but assassins, pirates, and highway robbers.*** I treat them with the burning contempt of a brave heart and a loyal citizen. I deny their power and defy their action."[22] Following this communication, he made a number of appeals to the people by means of the publication of hand bills and pamphlets, which were widely distributed. In these he attempted to prove that he was not as black as he had been pictured; that all his actions had been strictly legal; and, furthermore, that he desired to bring about the abolition of slavery only in a constitutional way. He repudiated a number of articles that had appeared in his paper during his illness, of which he knew nothing before their publication, and he promised that in the future the paper would be managed with more moderation and discretion and that the discussions in its columns would be within narrower limits. A few days later he appeared unexpectedly before a large mass meeting of his enemies and in a passionate speech attempted to justify his conduct as editor of the paper. These appeals had no effect upon Clay's enemies, who had already assembled a determined mob from the surrounding country to make sure the accomplishment of their plan. A committee of sixty men, among them James B. Clay, a son of Henry Clay, demanded the keys of the printing office from the Mayor of the city, to whom they had been delivered in accordance with a judicial order. After admonishing the committee that they were about to commit an unlawful act, the Mayor surrendered the keys. The committee proceeded at once to the office of The True American which had been fortified by Clay with two four pound brass cannon and other arms and was defended by six men employed for that purpose. Clay decided at the last moment not to offer any resist-

[21] "The writings of Cassius M. Clay," Vol. 1, p. 290. See also "Appeal of Cassius M. Clay to Kentucky***," p. 5.

[22] "The writings of Cassius M. Clay," Vol. 1, p. 110. "Appeal of Cassius M. Clay to Kentucky***," p. 11f.

ance, and the committee in a very orderly way packed up the press and the types and sent them to Cincinnati in care of a reliable firm. All the private papers found in the office were carefully bound and mailed to Clay at his residence.[23] Clay at once filed suit against the leaders and three years later received a judgment against James B. Clay and T. H. Waters for $2,500. This sum was secured by subscription on the part of the Committee of Sixty in Fayette and the adjoining counties.[24] The action of the "Lexington mob" did not put an end to The True American, for Clay remained in Lexington and The True American continued to be written and dated there, but was thenceforth printed in Cincinnati. A few weeks after the removal of his press to Cincinnati, Clay published in pamphlet form an "Appeal to Kentucky and the World" in which he attempted to explain and justify his part in connection with The True American.[25]

Mass meetings were held in various parts of the state, endorsing the actions of the "Lexington mob."[26] Many of the leading newspapers justified the act, but a number were noncommittal and some actually condemned it as an infringement of the freedom of speech and the press. The papers discussed at length the advisability of passing a law providing for strict censorship of the press with a view to excluding all anti-slavery literature from the state. A bill to that effect was introduced during January, 1846, and passed the Senate, but was defeated in the House, largely by the members from the non-slave holding counties.[27]

During the controversy just related the Mexican War broke out and, although Clay had bitterly condemned the annexation of Texas, he enlisted in the army and at the head of a company of Kentucky troops marched to the front. He gave the following justification of this action: "In the slave states the political forces were quite different from those of the Free states. In the former the great mass of the voters could not read; and they were led by political speakers on the stump, when the orators of both parties made their appeals. It was, therefore, to the suc-

---

[23] "Appeal of Cassius M. Clay to Kentucky * * *," p. 11f. E. S. Kinkead, "Story of Kentucky," p. 154. See also, The Liberator, Aug. 29, Sept. 12, Oct. 31, 1845; The Anti-Slavery Bugle, Aug. 29, Sept. 5, Oct. 31, 1845; and Niles' Register, Vol. 68, p. 408, Vol. 69, pp. 13-15.
[24] "Writings of Cassius M. Clay," Vol. 1, p. 108. See also Liberator, Oct. 17, 1845; July 14, 1848.
[25] "Appeal of Cassius M. Clay to Kentucky * * *," Sept. 25, 1845. Appeared in The True American, Sept. 5, 1845.
[26] A meeting was called at Washington, Mason County, by a notice signed by 456 citizens. The meeting, one of the largest ever held in the county, adopted strong resolutions approving the actions of the "Lexington mob." Maysville Eagle, Oct. 5, 1845.
[27] The Liberator, March 20, 1846, quoted from The True American.

cessful progress of my cause that I should add to the liberty of the press the liberty of public discussion.***Kentuckians being exceptionally, from their early history, fond of military glory, I hoped by the Mexican War, to strengthen myself so that I could take the stump, when I would be an overmatch for all my foes; when, if deemed necessary, The True American could be located at some point secure against mobs, and act as an ally of public discussion.   The result proved that I was right."[28]

Clay left his friend, John C. Vaughan, a South Carolinian by birth, in charge of the paper during his absence, with his brother Brutus J. Clay as his financial manager.   The subscription list fell off considerably after the opening of the War and in view of the uncertainty of Clay's return it was thought best after several months to give up the publication of the paper.[29]   Thereupon Vaughan took the materials and list of subscribers and located in Louisville, where associated with F. Crosley, a Kentuckian, he started the publication of an anti-slavery paper on the order of The True American, The Examiner,[30] which first appeared June 19, 1847.[31]

In the first number the objects were given in the following words: "The necessity of such a paper as The Examiner seems clear enough to our friends, Because:

"First, of the extent of the anti-slavery sentiment in Kentucky. There never was a period when our people did not feel it.   At the formation of our constitution the convention came within a few votes of inserting in it a gradual emancipation clause, and in 1832 public opinion was almost ripe for such a step.   The feeling is not apparently as strong now.   It is still, however, in its outspoken form an energetic element and if all causes of interest were removed we believe it would be overwhelming in its action.   Shall this sentiment have no organ?***The object of The Examiner will be to represent the anti-slavery sentiment in Kentucky, and as far as it can, to extend it—to inquire into and to discuss all reform measures and to advocate, to the best of its ability every claim of humanity.***If a single person labors by

---

[28] Henry Clay and the majority of the Whigs of Kentucky opposed the annexation of Texas.   In 1847 Henry Clay, as presiding officer of a great mass meeting at Lexington, spoke for two hours and a half against President Polk's action in sending General Taylor into the disputed territory, thus precipitating hostilities.   Resolutions were adopted opposing the annexation of any territory which might be secured as a result of the war. (Anti-Slavery Bugle, November 26; December 16, 1847.)   The Cleveland Herald, in commenting upon Clay's speech said that the speech "would do more good than 10,000 abolition lectures to help forward the glorious era of emancipation." (Anti-Slavery Bugle, December 10, 1847.)
[29] "Writing of Cassius M. Clay," Vol. 1, p. 175.
[30] "Writings of Cassius M. Clay," Vol. 1, p. 109f.
[31] The Examiner, June 19, 1847.   A file of this paper is in the Library of the University of Chicago.   See also The Examiner, Sept. 11, 1847.   John Heywood and Noble Butler were later added to the staff.

himself, the power which consists in union is wanting. A drop of rain will produce no moisture òn the dry clod; but when it is united with other drops, the copious shower revives the dying plant and gladdens the whole face of nature. If thus we are united, we shall make Kentucky the home of the free, as well as as of the brave, and awaken in our sister states of the South the spirit which will not tire until crowned with the glory of universal emancipation."[32] A few weeks later the editor asserted that The Examiner was "strictly an anti-slavery paper, and the organ and exponent of the emancipation movement in Kentucky."[33]

In the first number was begun a long series of articles signed "A Carolinian" and entitled an "Inquiry into the causes which have retarded the accumulation of wealth and increase of population in the southern states."[34] A little later was printed the speech of David Rice before the Constitutional Convention of Kentucky in 1792 in support of a proposed amendment providing for gradual emancipation.[35] A number of other articles appeared from time to time, mostly of an economic character, running through several issues of the paper.[36] The most important of these was a serial in twenty-five parts on "Thoughts of Emancipation."[37] Many of these articles were copied into other Kentucky papers and found in that way more extensive circulation.

A comparatively small amount of opposition on the part of the Kentucky press was manifested to the publication of The Examiner. The Louisville Journal, a Democratic paper, said of it: "We take pleasure in saying from our personal knowledge of the editors of The Examiner, we are confident they will discuss it (slavery) with ability, and in a spirit of calmness and moderation offering no occasion for offense to any portion of the community."[38] The other Louisville papers maintained the same attitude with the single exception of the Baptist Banner and Pioneer, which stated that "The Examiner is, we take

---

[31] The Examiner, June 19, 1847. Clay, in a letter to the Examiner dated Dec. 18, 1847, said, "The Examiner has succeeded The True American. My detention in a Mexican prison delayed my return longer than was anticipated; the editor of The Examiner has forestalled my wishes, and is now fulfilling all my obligations to my subscribers by substituting his paper for mine. Those who have seen both papers will not regret the change. I ask for him the continuance of that generous support in that cause which was in me shown dear to so many noble Americans."

[32] The Examiner, Sept. 11, 1847. See also March 4, 1848.

[33] The Examiner, June 19, 1847, July 3, 1847.

[34] Ibid., Aug. 28, Sept. 4, 14, 1847.

[35] Ibid., September 2, 1847. Number 3 of "Elements of Progress" appeared September 2; Number 1 of "Effects of Slavery on Industry" appeared February 6, 1848.

[36] "Thoughts on Emancipation," September, 1847, to June 10, 1848. They were signed "A," the real author being Jas. M. Pendleton, of Bowling Green.

[37] The Louisville Journal, June 22, 1847.

it, 'The True American' revived," and "they will mistake the spirit of our citizens, if they encourage an avowed notorious abolitionist of a neighboring city, to come here or to remain in Cincinnati (Mr. Vaughan was at that time a resident of that place), where he now resides, and throw firebrands into the community."[39] The confidence of the Louisville press was justified. The Examiner was at all times conducted in a spirit of fairness and retained in consequence the respect and the friendship of the majority of the papers of the state. At the end of the first year of the existence of the paper, the opposition, which in some sections had been pronounced at first, had practically subsided.[40] The Journal and the Courier of Louisville, and the Shelbyville News spoke in the highest terms of The Examiner and frequently copied articles from it. The Journal declared that it was the best paper of its class in the Union and said that the editors were "gentlemen of the most decided ability, and some of the ablest men in the state are contributors to its columns."[41]

All this agitation could not go on without producing some effect politically. In fact, the anti-slavery workers, undiscouraged by the defeat of the convention in 1838, had persistently labored to have the question of a convention again submitted to the people. Inasmuch as the constitution of 1799 had many defects which needed remedying, and since the anti-slavery forces did not seem to be strong enough to make a convention dangerous, the pro-slavery men joined with anti-slavery men in demanding that the question of a convention be submitted to a vote. During the early part of January, 1846, a bill to this effect passed the House of Representatives, but was rejected in the Senate.[42] In the following year, it passed both Houses and the first vote was set for August, 1847. In the interval between the issuance of the call and the first vote on the convention, the anti-slavery element was very active in some sections of the state, especially in and around Louisville, which, due largely to the industrial character of the city, had become the stronghold of anti-slavery in the state. In other sections the slavery question seemed to be of minor consideration. In the August election, the people supported the call for a convention by a majority of about 30,000 votes.[43] The Examiner, in re-

---

[39] The Baptist Banner and Pioneer, June 23, 1847.
[40] The Examiner, June 17, 1848. October 28, it was stated that "The day has gone by when a frown, a threat or a curse was sufficient to paralyze the human tongue."
[41] The Louisville Journal, October 21, 1848.
[42] The Commonwealth, Jan. 20, 1846; The Presbyterian Herald, Jan. 15, 1846. The vote in the House was 56 to 40 and in the Senate, 18 to 20.
[43] Niles' Register, Vol. 72, p. 400; The Examiner, August 4, September 4, October 9, 1847.

viewing the results of the election, said: "We do not say that all who voted for the convention are in favor of emancipation; but this we do say, that the great majority are."[44] The Louisville Courier also maintained that the anti-slavery men had forced the call for a convention.[45] The mountainous counties in the eastern part of the state, where but few slaves were held, and the counties along the Ohio River gave the largest majorities for the bill.[46]

In the second election held a year later, the people again sanctioned the calling of a constitutional convention by about the same majority.[47] It then became the duty of the legislature, which did not meet until January, 1849, to arrange for the election of delegates and the time and the place for the meeting of the convention.

The year 1848 was marked by a revival of interest in emancipation and this interest increased with the approach of the time for the election of delegates. Discussions of emancipation in the newspapers and on the stump became much more general. For the first time in the history of the state, the question of local option as a means of abolishing slavery was now seriously advocated. A large number of similar proposals appeared in The Examiner, which, as was to be expected, entertained a kindly feeling toward the idea. By this plan two-thirds of the vote in any county might abolish slavery in that county.[48] The Examiner maintained that if such a plan should be adopted in all the slave states it would be only a question of a few years until eastern Kentucky, eastern Tennessee and western Virginia, western North Carolina and western South Carolina would abolish slavery, as well as a number of the river counties of Kentucky. Louisville, it was believed, would not delay such action a single year.[49] The Examiner spoke encouragingly of the growing emancipation sentiment in the state.[50]

---

[44] The Examiner, August 4, 1847.
[45] The Louisville Courier, August 6, 1847.
[46] The Examiner, October 9, 1847.
[47] Niles' Register, Vol. 74, p. 277. The Louisville Courier, February 21, 1849, in commenting on the recent election said, "We should like to know what particular object those gentlemen, who are fighting so much against emancipation think the people of Kentucky had in voting in favor of a convention. What great evil did the people feel pressing upon them to require the immense vote of 101,828 in favor of remodeling the constitution? The magistracy has never been felt as an oppression, the mode of appointing sheriffs is not very disastrous to the people, nor have the clerkships ever been felt as a serious oppression. What great predominant idea was upon the public mind, if it was not the principle of emancipation? Scarcely a solitary friend of perpetual slavery can be found among the 101,828 votes in favor of a convention.* * * All attempts to hinder discussion, to choke off free inquiry, or to paralyze public sentiment will recoil on the heads of those who make the attempt. The people of Kentucky know their rights and will maintain them."
[48] The Examiner, January 8; March 25; June 10, 1848.
[49] The Examiner, March 25, 1848.
[50] The Examiner, April 8, 1848.

In February of 1848, emancipation meetings composed of many of the leading men of both political parties were held in Louisville and committees were appointed for the purpose of forming plans for the coming elections. A general address was issued to the people of Kentucky advocating the adoption of some plan of gradual emancipation.[51] As the question of emancipation attracted more and more attention throughout the state, numerous plans were proposed, most of which called for some slow conservative plan of gradual emancipation.[52] During the summer of 1848 Ex-Governor Letcher, of Kentucky, in a speech at Indianapolis, Indiana, in discussing the question of emancipation in his own state declared that only the radical element of the extreme South desired the extension of slavery and that he believed that the people of Kentucky, in the coming constitutional convention, would provide some plan for the gradual emancipation of slaves.[53] A number of the leading newspapers of the state came out for emancipation about this time. The Lexington Atlas prided itself on being the only Whig newspaper in the state which had taken a decided stand against emancipation.[54] While the Louisville Courier was an enthusiastic supporter of emancipation, the Louisville Journal took little part in the campaign, believing that there was little chance for the success of emancipation at that time.[55] This was also the position of the Lexington Observer and other newspapers in the state.

The editor of The Examiner said that the subject of emancipation was becoming more and more the engrossing topic throughout the state. Even in neighborhoods in which the discussion of the subject had been unusual, men now expressed their opinions freely. It was the duty of the friends of emancipation to promote these discussions, but a warning was issued to be "extremely careful to keep aloof from angry and embittered controversy, which always confirms the prejudices of the opponent. Be gentle, discreet, and yet firm. Do not hazard any wild propositions. Keep attention fixed on those evils which result from slavery and are sufficiently manifest in every section of the state. Let slavery in the abstract, as it is called, alone, and talk of

[51] The Examiner, March 3, 17, 1848. William L. Breckinridge was one of the most active of the Louisville anti-slavery members.
[52] One plan called for the freeing of all males born after 1850, at the age of 25, and of all females at the age of 21. (Anti-Slavery Bugle, September 15, 1848.) See also, The Examiner, October 28, 1848. A series of 12 articles addressed to the "Mechanics Workingmen of Kentucky," was running at this time.
[53] Indianapolis Journal, October 9, 1848.
[54] The Examiner, January 27, 1849.
[55] The Louisville Journal, January 23, 1849.

slavery as it exists around us."[56]   During the latter part of 1848, a number of the most prominent men in the state issued[57] a long "Address to the People of Kentucky," advocating the adoption of a plan of emancipation similar to the plan by which Pennsylvania, New York, and New Jersey had abolished slavery.   They expressed the hope that this plan might be accompanied by a system of African colonization that would remove the blacks from Kentucky as fast as they were freed.[58]   The Western Kentuckian, in commenting upon the address, said: "We again invoke the attention of our readers to this document.   Its authors are men of talents and character whose interests are all bound up in the fortunes of the state.   What they would propose for her amelioration, therefore, may well be supposed worthy of the notice, if not of the approbation, of her citizens."[59]

The pro-slavery leaders were equally active during this time. To counteract the influence of The Examiner and other newspapers supporting emancipation they decided to establish in Louisville a newspaper, The Chronicle, for the express purpose of opposing any form of emancipation whatever.[60]   While as a rule they upheld free discussion,[61] there were occasional threats of violence and a few cases in which an attempt was made to suppress discussion of the subject in the press and on the platform.[62] Cassius M. Clay and other anti-slavery leaders made it their special business to uphold the freedom of the press and not to be intimidated, because they realized that if they were not permitted to speak freely according to their constitutional rights, their whole scheme of emancipation would certainly fail.   Clay made it a policy to speak publicly in every town where violence had occurred.   When John G. Fee was prevented by violence from preaching near Crab Orchard, Lincoln County, because he opposed slavery, Clay at once arranged to speak in the same place on slavery and had posters widely circulated.   Armed and surrounded by armed followers he delivered the address without any disturbance.[63]   In another instance, in the same county, the pro-slavery element met at Stanford, the county seat, and

[56] The Examiner, November 25, 1848.

[57] The address was signed by Chancellor S. S. Nicholas, Pat. Maxcy, D. L. Beatty, Reuben Dawson, William P. Boone, T. S. Bell, W. W. Worsley, William Richardson, W. E. Glover, Bland Ballard, and James Speed.

[58] The Examiner, December 30, 1848.   The address covered six columns of the paper.

[59] The Examiner, February 3, 1849.   Quoted.

[60] Georgetown Herald, December 30, 1848.

[61] During the late fall of 1848, Geo. W. Johnson addressed a long letter to the citizens of Scott County opposing constitutional abolition.   He was one of the leading lawyers of the state.   His main objection to emancipation was the problem of the free Negro.   The Examiner, October 28, 1848.   Anti-Slavery Bugle, November 10, 1848.

[62] The Louisville Courier, August 14, 1848; Niles' Register, Vol. 75, p. 125; Wegham: "Anti-Slavery Cause in America," pp. 47-51.

[63] "Writings of Cassius M. Clay," Vol. 1, pp. 75-78.

adopted resolutions threatening with death anyone who might discuss slavery. This was done with reference to Clay, rather than to Fee. Clay at once made an appointment to speak in the court house at Stanford. Knowing that he would speak or die, a committee of the best citizens of Stanford was sent thirty miles to Clay's residence to persuade him to cancel the appointment. After patiently listening to their appeal, he said, "Gentlemen, say to your friends that I appreciate their kindness in sending you to advise with me; but, God willing, I shall speak in Stanford on the day named." On the day named surrounded by several friends, with a pistol on the desk in front of him, he delivered a long address without a single interruption before one of the largest crowds ever assembled in the county.[64] The result of this policy was a more free discussion of slavery than ever before. Many of the leading pro-slavery men and pro-slavery papers now desired to have the question thoroughly threshed out and permanently settled.

With the desire to secure a full expression of opinion on the subject of slavery, a bill was introduced in the legislature requiring the election officials to submit to each voter at the next regular election in the state the question: "Are you in favor of the indefinite continuance of slavery, or of a system of gradual emancipation with a constitutional provision for the ultimate removal of the African race." Both The Examiner and the Louisville Courier strongly advocated a direct vote on the question of emancipation. The Courier said: "We dare the enemies of emancipation to put this question to the people of Kentucky so that they may vote on that question alone."[64a] The bill failed of passage and the House of Representatives by a unanimous vote proceeded to adopt the following expression of opinion: "Resolved that we, the representatives of the people of Kentucky, are opposed to abolition or emancipation of slavery in any form or shape whatever, except as now provided for by the constitution and laws of the state."[65] The legislature then ordered the election of delegates to the constitutional convention. The elections were to be held in August and the convention was to assemble the first Monday in October, 1849.[66]

No sooner had the date of the election been set than both pro-slavery and anti-slavery men began to hold meetings, draw

[64] "Writings of Cassius M. Clay," Vol. 1, p. 177f.
[64a] The Louisville Courier, February 5, 1849; The Examiner, February 10, 23, 1849.
[65] Journal of the House, February 3, 1849. Louisville Journal, January 20, 1849; Niles' Register, Vol. 75, p. 108. The Whigs had a decided majority in both houses of the legislature.
[66] Niles' Register, Vol. 75, p. 256.

up resolutions and nominate candidates.   As early as February, a call, signed by 270 citizens of Mason County, was issued for a pro-slavery convention to "oppose meddling with the slavery question."[67]   A similar meeting was held in Woodford county about the same time.[68]   The emancipationists were equally active.   Early in February, 523 citizens of Mason county signed a call for an emancipation convention to be held at Maysville on February the 12th.   The meeting was unusually well attended and among those present were many of the oldest and most prominent men in the county.   Resolutions were adopted expressive of the opinion "that a gradual and prospective system of emancipation accompanied by colonization should be adopted by our state," and that the meeting regarded such a "project as practical, politic and humane and earnestly desire to see it accomplished."   The members pledged themselves not to support any man for the convention who would not pledge himself to the principle set forth in the resolution adopted in the meeting.[69]   Of even more importance was an emancipation meeting held at Louisville, February 1.   After approving emancipation through a change in the constitution a committee was appointed to draft resolutions expressive of the sense of the meeting which should be considered at a second meeting to be held at Louisville, February 12, and which upon approval should be issued as a public address to the people of Kentucky.[70]   At the meeting on the 12th a series of five resolutions endorsing emancipation as reported by the committee was adopted and a long address was issued to the friends of emancipation throughout the state urging them to send delegates to a state convention to be held at Frankfort, April 25, for the purpose of uniting on some plan of emancipation and perfecting a state organization to secure the election of delegates favoring emancipation to the constitutional convention.[71]   Anti-slavery workers were warned against making radical utterances.[72]   William L. Breckinridge in an able address urged the centering of all attention upon emancipation and emancipation

---

[67] Anti-Slavery Bugle, February 16, 1849.
[68] The Examiner, February 17, 1849; Niles' Register, Vol. 75, p. 256.
[69] The Presbyterian Herald, March 1, 1849; The Examiner, February 24, 1849.   Among the signers of the resolution were Henry Waller, Gen. Richard Collins, F. T. Hord, Hon. John Chambers, Edward L. Bullock, Adam Beatty, E. C. Phister, Granville Young, John C. McClung.
[70] The Louisville Journal, February 2, 1849.   W. W. Worsley presided over the meeting. The committee was composed of James Speed, Bland Ballard, Robert Dawson, Thomas H. Shreve, W. E. Glover, and William L. Breckinridge.
[71] The Examiner, February 17, 1849; The Presbyterian Herald, February 15, 1849, in speaking of this meeting said: "The greatest harmony prevailed and it is but seldom that the proceedings of a meeting as large and as enthusiastic is conducted with so much decorum." See also Niles' Register, Vol. 75, p. 256.   Both the address and the resolutions are quoted in The Presbyterian Herald for March 1, 1849.
[72] The Presbyterian Herald, March 1, 1849.

was to be accompanied always by some plan of colonization.[73] He asserted that the main reasons for the defeat of emancipation in the constitutional convention of 1799 were the radical utterances and the radical plans of many of the emancipationists.[74]

The emancipation cause received a powerful impetus about this time as a result of a letter written by Henry Clay from New Orleans, February 17, to Richard Pindell, of Kentucky, in which he recommended that measures be taken for the extermination of slavery by the adoption of some plan for gradual emancipation in the coming constitutional convention. The letter was written for publication and was an answer to a request from Pindell and certain of his friends for an expression of opinion on emancipation.

After stating his belief in emancipation, Clay said that three principles should regulate the establishment of a system of gradual emancipation: First, that it should be slow in its operation, cautious and gradual so as to occasion no convulsion or rash or sudden disturbance in the existing habits of society; second, that, as an indispensable condition, the emancipated slaves should be removed from the state to some colony; and third, that the expenses of their transportation to this colony, including an outfit for six months after their arrival, should be defrayed by a fund to be secured from the labor of each freed slave. He believed that any change in the condition of society should be marked with extreme care and circumspection. Consequently, any plan for emancipation that he might favor would necessarily be conservative. He believed that all slaves born after a certain period should be free at a specified age, and that all born before should remain slaves for life. That period, he believed, should be 1855 or even 1860. All slaves born after the date decided upon should be free at the age of twenty-five, but should be liable to be hired out, under the authority of the state, for a term not exceeding three years in order to raise a sum sufficient to pay the expense of their transportation and an outfit for six months following their arrival at the colony. The offspring of this class were to be free at birth, but were to be apprenticed out until they were twenty-one years of age, when they were liable to be hired out for three years to secure money to meet the expenses of their transportation. He regarded the colonization of the freed men as indispensable to any scheme of emancipation.

---

[73] Breckinridge Papers, W. L. Breckinridge to R. J. Breckinridge, February 12, 1849.
[74] *Ibid.*

"The color, passions and prejudices," he said, would forever prevent the two races from living together in a state of cordial union. Social, moral and political degradation would be the inevitable lot of the colored race." Clay could see no reason why the freed slaves could not be successfully transported to some colony without any great economic loss to the state. In fact, he maintained that the enhanced value of their lands and the benefits derived from free labor would more than compensate the state for any losses which might be incurred. In speaking of the political effects of emancipation in Kentucky he said: "It may be urged that we ought not, by the gradual abolition of slavery, to separate ourselves from the other slave states, but to continue to share with them in all their future fortunes.***The government of each slave state is bound, by the highest and most solemn obligations, to dispose of the question of slavery, so as best to promote the peace, happiness and prosperity of the people of the state. Kentucky being essentially a farming state, slave labor is less profitable than in other states. If in most of the other slave states they find that labor more profitable, in the culture of the staples of cotton and sugar, they may perceive a reason in that feeling for continuing slavery, which it cannot be expected should control the judgment of Kentucky, as to what may be fitting and proper for her interest." In conclusion he said "Kentucky enjoys high respect and honorable consideration throughout the Union and throughout the civilized world; but, in my humble opinion, no title which she has to the esteem and admiration of mankind, no deeds of her former glory, would equal, in greatness and grandeur, that of being the pioneer state in removing from her soil every trace of human slavery, and in establishing the descendants of Africa within her jurisdiction in the native land of their forefathers."[75]

The southern papers were particularly bitter in their denunciation. The Richmond Inquirer (Virginia) said: "Henry Clay's true character now stands revealed. The man is an abolitionist. He takes his position with Giddings and Hale. Those are the sentiments long ago expressed by all the organs of abolition. That is the spirit which breathes in all their writings and speakings. And the letter has been received with rapturous applause by all the abolitionist newspapers and by all the abolitionist people in the United States."[76] The Augusta Banner,

[75] The Examiner, March 10, 1849; Cincinnati Chronicle, March 6, 1849.
[76] The Liberator, May 4, 1849. Quoted.

even more antagonistic, said, "Of course, then his doctrines, if carried out, would lead to the abolition of slavery in every state in which it now exists. We differ in opinion from Mr. Clay. Slavery is a blessing rather than an evil.***The doctrine is generally entertained at the South as well as at the North, that any state has the right to abolish slavery. We do not concur in this opinion, however popular or general it may be   We think that even Mr. Clay's great influence will fail to make Kentucky adopt his plan, however plausibly cautious it may be.***If Kentucky should take measures to place herself in a position hostile to the institutions of the other Southern States, it will devolve upon them to devise the most proper means for self-protection."[77]   The New Orleans Crescent said: "That slavery will be abolished in Kentucky by the coming convention there is now no doubt. All the leading men in the state are in favor of it; it is for the obvious interests of the state to substitute free for slave labor; the scheme may be carried out without much if any loss, and with a show of liberality which will gain the praise of magnanimity from the unthinking. If Kentucky will abolish slavery she should take all the responsibilities for the act—if she will join the Northern allies let her do so at her own risk—if she be anxious no longer to make common cause with the south, she has a right to go over, but there is no reason why the other Southern States should build a bridge to facilitate her passage."[78]

In the North the Modern Abolitionists, of whom William Lloyd Garrison was the chief representative, also condemned Clay's program as only a half-way measure, but its moderation secured the approval of many anti-slavery workers.

In Kentucky Clay's letter secured by no means uniform approval. In the county of Trimble, a people's meeting adopted a series of resolutions offered by John Robert, a Whig, requesting Henry Clay to resign his seat in the United States Senate in consequence of the sentiments expressed in his letter to Richard Pindell on the subject of slavery.[79] Nor was Clay unprepared for this condemnation. In a letter to his son James, March 3, 1849, he said, "As you were absent I sent to Richard Pindell a letter on the Emancipation Question. As I regret to hear that it was not popular, I suppose that my letter will bring on me

[77] The Liberator, July 27, 1849. Quoted.
[78] The Examiner, April 7, 1849. Quoted.
[79] Niles' Weekly Register, Vol. 75, pp. 185, 384.

some odium. I nevertheless wish it published. I owe that to the cause, and to myself, and to posterity."[80]

The Pindell letter was reprinted in all sections of the country by newspapers of every class, and the editors generally, whether they approved it or not, agreed in considering it a document of great importance, destined to wield a vast influence. In Kentucky, as in the country as a whole, Clay's influence was very great, and consequently his support of emancipation at least greatly encouraged and emboldened the anti-slavery workers and helped to ensure a free discussion of the subject.[81]

In the slavery controversy in Kentucky, two main issues appear—the interest of Kentucky, as Clay and others represented it, as being hostile to slavery, on the one hand; and on the other, the reluctance to desert the South, a feeling based partly on political sympathy and partly, perhaps, on a fear of economic retaliation. This conflict appears in the campaign elections preparatory to the constitutional convention.

It has been shown that the state convention was proposed for the purpose of furthering emancipation and that it was to meet at Frankfort on the 25th of April. In March a mass meeting of emancipationists was held in Danville, and delegates were elected to this convention. The meeting was a large and enthusiastic one with at least 500 men, one-half of whom were slaveholders, present.[82] A similar meeting was held at Frankfort in the same month, when 50 delegates were elected to the convention.[83] A meeting of citizens of Lexington and Fayette county "opposed to the perpetuation of slavery," was held in April.[84] The object of the meeting was explained by Henry Clay in a long address. On motion of Robert J. Breckinridge, it was resolved that slavery was contrary to the rights of mankind, opposed to the fundamental principles of free government, inconsistent with a state of sound morality, hostile to the pros-

---

[80] Clay's Private Correspondence, p. 585.

[81] About this time the Presbyterian Herald, as well as other papers, came out in support of emancipation. On March 1 it said: "We are equally well convinced that slavery is an incubus upon the prosperity of the state in all its interests. Its climate, its soil, its geographical position surrounded as it is by a cordon of free states, which are outstripping it in population, wealth and enterprise, all proclaim that it must eventually become a free state." (The Presbyterian Herald, March 1, 1849.) William L. Breckinridge, who was associated with this paper, and who was a large slaveowner himself, wrote many articles advocating emancipation, which appeared in a number of papers throughout the state. In these he proposed the absolute prohibition of the importation of slaves, the freeing of all slaves born after a fixed date upon their reaching the age of twenty-five and lastly the holding of all slaves upon receiving their freedom under the control of the state and the hiring them out until enough money was secured to pay for their transportation to Africa. (The Examiner, March 3; April 7, 16, 1849. See also The Paris Citizen, February 28, 1849.)

[82] The Presbyterian Herald, March 15, 1849; The Examiner, March 31, 1849.

[83] The Examiner, March 31, 1849. Dr. W. A. McDowell acted as presiding officer of the meeting.

[84] The Lexington Atlas, April 17, 1849. Edward Oldham acted as president of the meeting and W. A. Dudley as secretary.

perity of the Commonwealth and that in the forthcoming constitutional convention steps should be taken to ameliorate the condition of slaves, "in such way as shall be found practicable in itself, just as regards the masters of slaves, and beneficial to the slaves themselves."[85]   Thirty men were named as delegates to the Frankfort Convention.[86]   Similar conventions were held in many of the counties of the state and delegates were elected.[87]   Candidates were also nominated or endorsed for the election of delegates to the constitutional convention in October.

The Frankfort convention assembled at the appointed time with more than one hundred and fifty delegates from 24 different counties present.[88]   Among the delegates were Henry Clay, from Bourbon County; Robert J. Breckinridge, from Fayette county; J. G. Fee, from Lewis County; Cassius M. Clay, from Madison county; and Senator J. R. Underwood, from Spencer county.[89]   Both political parties and all classes of the population were represented.   A majority of the delegates were slaveholders, who owned in all about 3,000 slaves.[90] The Frankfort Commonwealth, an opponent of emancipation, said of the convention: "It is perhaps the first general convention of the citizens of Kentucky favorable to the organization of an emancipation party, ever held in the state, and a regard for truth compels us to say that we have never seen, on any occasion, here or elsewhere, a more intelligent and respectable body of men."[91]   Twenty-one, or nearly one-seventh of the total membership of the convention, were ministers.[92]

The convention was called to order by J. R. Thornton, of Bourbon county, after which Henry Clay was elected Presi-

---

[85] The Lexington Atlas, April 17, 1849.   See also The Examiner April 14, 1849; The Presbyterian Herald, April 19, 1849.

[86] The Lexington Atlas, April 17, 1849.   The delegates were Edward Oldham, Samuel Shy, M. C. Johnson, Robert J. Breckinridge, H. P. Lewis, A. Vanmeter, C. H. Barkley, John A. Hull, John Hurd, E. C. Dudley, George R. Trotter, William Rhodes, James Turner, W. Pullen, John W. Clark, Carter R. Harrison, O. D. Winn, George W. Sutton, O. D. McCullough, John T. Bruce, J. J. Hunter, William K. Wallace, Richard Pindell, James Ashton, George P. Jouett, Matthew T. Scott, T. Dolan, B. Keer.

[87] The Examiner, April 7, 1849, stated that the following counties had elected delegates to the Frankfort Convertion: Boone, Bourbon, Boyle, Barren, Fayette, Jefferson, Lincoln, Logan, Lewis, Mecklenburg, Muhlenberg, Madison, Mason, McCracken, Mercer, Nelson, Oldham, Scott, Shelby, Warren, and Woodford.   For details of the various meetings, see The Examiner, April 7, 14, 18, 21, 28, 1849.

[88] The Examiner, April 28; May 5, 1849.   The latest number gives the number of representatives from the different counties as follows: Barren, 1; Bath, 1; Boone, 6; Bourbon, 14; Boyle, 8; Fayette, 19; Franklin, 19; Garrard, 2; Henry, 5; Jefferson, 6; Kenton, 1; Lewis, 2; Lincoln, 1; Louisville, 22; Madison, 3; Mercer, 6; Nelson, 5; Nicholas, 3; Oldham, 3; Owen, 1; Pulaski, 2; Scott, 5, Shelby, 17; Spencer, 4; Warren, 1.

[89] The Examiner, April 25; May 5, 1849.   T. F. Marshall, Adam Beatty, S. S. Nicholas, W. L. Breckinridge and J. A. McClung were in attendance.

[90] The Presbyterian Herald, May 5, 1849.

[91] Ibid.   Quoted.   Thirteen of the ministers were Presbyterians, six Methodists, one Baptist, one Unitarian, and one Campbellite.

[92] Ibid.   There was also considerable talk of holding a meeting of the ministers of the state who favored emancipation.   See Breckinridge Papers for 1849.

dent, and Henry Wingate, of Franklin, was made vice-president.[93] Although harmony and enthusiasm prevailed in the convention, the members could not agree upon a plan of emancipation. Opinions ranged all the way from immediate compensated emancipation without colonization to the mere colonization of those voluntarily emancipated; but the majority of the members desired some plan of gradual emancipation to be followed by colonization.[94] While the convention adopted no scheme of emanciaption, it made the following declaration by a vote that lacked but one of being unanimous: "Believing that involuntary, hereditary slavery as it exists by law in this state is injurious to the prosperity of the Commonwealth, inconsistent with the fundamental principles of free government, contrary to the natural rights of mankind, and adverse to a pure state of morals; we are of the opinion that it ought not to be increased, and that it ought not to be perpetuated in the Commonwealth." Accordingly, it was resolved to work for the election of delegates to the constitutional convention who would be in favor of the absolute prohibition of further importation of slaves into Kentucky, and who would favor a constitution which would give the people unlimited authority to adopt a system of gradual emancipation.[95]

After the convention had adjourned, the emancipationists began at once to canvass the state for the election of delegates favorable to emancipation. A central executive committee, appointed by the Frankfort convention, had general control of the state campaign, with Louisville as its headquarters.[96]

Local emancipation conventions were held in many counties in the state. Most of these adopted the "Frankfort Platform," and in some cases nominated candidates for the constitutional convention.[97] There were differences of opinion in the various parts of the state as to just what program the emancipationists intended to adopt. In some cases the emancipationists did not go beyond the demand for the insertion of the law of 1833 into the constitution.[98] Many desired a constitutional

[93] The Presbyterian Herald, May 3, 1849. See also Niles' Register, Vol. 75, p. 301.
[94] Many wanted the laws of 1833 incorporated into the constitution. See Breckinridge Papers for 1849; W. O. Smith to Robert J. Breckinridge, April 29, 1849, and Garret Davis to Robert J. Breckinridge, April 27, 1849.
[95] Anti-Slavery Bugle, May 11, 1849; Niles' Weekly Register, Vol. 75, p. 301.
[96] The Examiner, May 5, 1849, May 12, 19, 26; June 2, 9, 16, 23, 1849. The following were members of the committee: Wm. Richardson, W. W. Worsley, W. E. Glover, David Beatty, Bland Ballard, Thomas McGrain, Reuben Dawson, Patrick Dawson, W. P. Boone, James Speed. In addition to the counties mentioned previously as having held emancipation conventions were Wayne, Clarke, Crittenden, Caldwell, Ohio and Trimble.
[97] Breckinridge Papers, James Matthews to Robert J. Breckinridge, May 30, 1849; Ibid., Frank Ballanger to Robert J. Breckinridge, May 7, 1849.
[98] Ibid., Letter from Citizens of Taylorsville to Robert J. Breckinridge, June 8, 1849.

provision for gradual emancipation, while others wished only to give the legislature power to provide for emancipation any time that it saw fit to do so.[99]　This lack of unity lost the emancipationists hundreds of votes and may have been a determining factor in the election.[100]

The pro-slavery party generally adopted the policy of nominating as delegates to the convention "their ablest, wisest, and most virtuous citizens."[101]　This, it was hoped, would lessen the strength of the emancipationists, as it most assuredly did. Most of the pro-slavery candidates took a mild, conciliatory attitude toward slavery.[102]　In a number of counties where the emancipationists were strong, the pro-slavery Whigs and the pro-slavery Democrats united on one candidate.[103]　With untiring persistence they approached all classes and appealed to all motives that promised aid.[104]　Especially earnest were their appeals to the prejudices and apprehensions of the non-slaveholding whites who were made to believe that "to emancipate the black man was to enslave the white man."　The arguments which they used most successfully were: (1) that the emancipationists had offered no practical method for emancipating the slaves or of colonizing them once they had been freed and (2) that emancipation by Kentucky and an alliance with the North, which would necessarily follow, would result in the dissolution of the Union.

Both United States senators from Kentucky, Henry Clay and J. R. Underwood, as well as Robert J. Breckinridge, Cassius M. Clay, T. F. Marshall, T. J. Boyle and others, stumped the state for emancipation.　There was a great demand for speeches by Robert J. Breckinridge, a man of high standing and of great ability as a speaker, whose numerous writings on the subject of slavery had attracted wide attention.[105]　During the month of June, 1849, he published a "Platform of Emancipation," of which hundreds of copies were distributed throughout the state.[106]　In part it was as follows: "The people of Kentucky

---

[99] Breckinridge Papers, Geo. Blakey to Robert J. Breckinridge, July 10, 1849. The Examiner, July 21, 1849.

[100] The American Citizen, April 7, 1849.

[101] The Louisville Journal, January 23, 1849.

[102] Breckinridge Papers, W. O. Smith to Robert J. Breckinridge, April 7, 1849; The American Citizen, April 27, 1849.

[103] Breckinridge Papers, Citizens of Taylorsville to Robert J. Breckinridge, June 8, 1849. The Examiner, March 31, 1849.

[104] The Examiner, August 4, 11, 1848; July 7, 14; August 18, 1849.

[105] Breckinridge Papers, Letters to Robert J. Breckinridge from George Blakey, July 10; A. F. Scott, July 23; R. C. Grundy, May 19; William Garnett, May 22; A. M. Brown, May 21; Six Citizens of Clark county, May 28; James Matthews, May 30; W. O. Mills, May 30; E. Stevenson, May 31; William Hewett, May 8; B. Mills, May 11.

[106] Lexington Observer and Reporter, June 30, July 4, 1849.　The original manuscript is in the Breckinridge Papers.

ought by means of that convention: 1. Absolutely to prohibit the importation of any more slaves into the state: And through it retain in their own hands the complete power, now held by the call of that convention, to enforce and perfect, in or under the new constitution, a system of emancipation, And still further, this power of emancipation, thus retained, should be so guarded in the constitution itself that it will be exercised, (a) only prospectively, (b) only gradually, (c) only in connection with the removal from the state of the emancipated slaves, and finally this power of emancipation, and all exercise of it, should be, not of ordinary legislation, but of the community itself, by an expression of its sovereign will: (1) Either by means of a provision in the constitution allowing specific amendments, if such a clause should be inserted according to the original plan of the Convention party; (2) or, under the Constitution, by means of an express provision in it, allowing the sense of the people to be taken on the question, if the new constitution should be procured without what is called the open clause."[108]   Breckinridge regarded this plan as a reasonable concession to the pro-slavery party, especially since the slaveholders of the state were outnumbered nearly ten to one and were divided among themselves, the most prominent leaders of the emancipation movement being slaveholders.[109]

There was also a great demand for speeches from Cassius M. Clay. He made a special effort to reach the non-slaveholders. In his address before the (Frankfort) convention he said: "For myself I am in favor of agitating this question.* * *We must convince the people—the real people—of its importance, before it can be done. How can we get at the non-slaveholders but by agitation? The newspapers, as a general thing, do not reach the non-slaveholders. We must seek them out at the cross roads and places of public resort in their neighborhoods. The newspapers are already open. But we want something more than the press. We want men on the stump. We want to get at the ear of the people."[111] Clay had great personal magnetism, which drew many people to him, but he also had a stinging tongue which made many enemies for himself and for his cause.[112]

---

[108] Breckinridge Papers for 1849.
[109] "Writings of Cassius M. Clay," pp. 183, 186, 175ff.   Spencer County Journal, April 16, 1849.   The Examiner, June 9, 1849.
[111] "Writings of Cassius M. Clay," pp. 183, 186, 175ff.
[112] *Ibid.*, pp. 186, 211.   The Examiner, June 23, 1849.
    Upon one occasion while he was speaking before a large audience, one of his enemies took offense at some of his remarks and called Clay a liar, whereupon a fight ensued in the assembly room, in which Turner, his opponent, was killed and Clay was seriously injured. Turner was clearly the aggressor and consequently Clay was never even indicted for the offense.

The campaign, as a whole, although bitter, was comparatively free from acts of violence. In many instances the opposing candidates engaged in public debate, often on the "Frankfort Platform." In these debates the pro-slavery leaders were usually the aggressors, although the emancipationists made it a policy never to refuse a challenge to meet publicly an opponent in debate.[113] In speaking of the sections of the state where the emancipationists were strong The Examiner said: "In those counties in which the proportion of slaves is largest—for instance, in Jefferson, Fayette and Bourbon—notwithstanding the supposed large pecuniary interests of the people in slaves, the hostility to slavery is most efficient."[114] This was one of the peculiarities of the anti-slavery movement in Kentucky, not only at this time but during the entire history of the state.

The hopes of the emancipationists were far from being realized in the election of delegates to the constitutional convention. In the twenty-nine counties where emancipationists had made nominations, they were unable to elect a single candidate, although they polled about 10,000 votes.[115] In commenting upon this vote, The Examiner said that according to this proportion the emancipationists could poll in the one hundred counties of the state about 30,000 votes. It expressed the belief also that "thousands of the friends of emancipation in Kentucky were deterred from voting by various reasons,"[116] but no specific instances of intimidation or violence were given.

Several influences contributed to reduce the number of emancipation votes. Many opponents of slavery thought that no feasible plan of emancipation and colonization had been proposed or that the time for emancipation was not ripe. Others believed that in the bitter sectional struggle between the slave and the free states it was the duty of Kentucky to stand by the South. Furthermore, the majority of the non-slaveholders in the state had not been reached by the emancipation appeals and contrary to their own interests adhered to the conservative party. On account of the strong emancipation feeling, the pro-slavery leaders adopted a conciliatory attitude and nominated candidates who were known to be men broad in their opinions and highly esteemed in their communities. This fact in part accounted for the lack of emancipation candidates in nearly

[113] Breckinridge Papers, Presbyterian Herald, May 28, 1849.
[114] The Examiner, June 16, 1849; Anti-Slavery Bugle, July 28, 1849.
[115] The Examiner, September 8, 15, 1849; The Presbyterian Herald, September 20, 1849.
[116] The Examiner, September 15, 1849.

three-fourths of the counties. Both the Whig and the Democratic parties were so opposed to emancipation that, in those counties where the emancipationists were strongest, they laid aside their political differences and united on a single candidate to the constitutional convention. Still another reason for the small number of emancipation votes was the fact that the emancipation candidates represented only one issue while their opponents stood for several of the issues involved in the coming convention, thus appealing to a wide constituency.

Notwithstanding the failure to elect emancipationists as delegates, there is abundant evidence of interest on the part of the members of the convention in slavery and emancipation. In the reports of the convention nearly one-fourth of the space is devoted to the debates on slavery, far more than was alloted to any other subject. If we may judge from the reports of the press and the frequent complaints of the members on the floor, the discussions of slavery had become a burden to the convention. The Frankfort correspondent of the Louisville Journal said: "The slavery question in the constitutional Convention has been discussed to death. The mind of the delegates is made up and cannot be changed, and when a delegate gets the floor and proceeds to make a speech upon it, as he cannot be stopped, all that the others can do is to kill the time as well as they can until he sits down."[117]

Although much time was given to the discussion of slavery it was evident that the convention was in the hands of proslavery men and that the institution was not in danger. A delegate from Fleming county said: "What is the history of this convention since it assembled here? We are asked for the incorporation of the law of 1833 into the constitution. We are told that it conflicts with the interests of the slaveholder—that it is the first step toward emancipation; that, therefore, it must be sacrificed. The ballot system of voting is called for. Again we are told that it will prove injurious to the slave interests. The specific mode of amending the constitution, which the spirit of the nineteenth century evidently calls for, is suggested. Still the cry is that slave property is endangered by it. Driven in at all points, we ask that representation shall be equal and uniform throughout the Commonwealth. Even at this point they meet us and say that we must yield. They tell us that the dearest

---

[117] "Debates in the Kentucky Convention, 1849," p. 485. See also the Presbyterian Herald, November 1, 1849.

right of Kentucky freemen must yield to the slave, that the time has arrived when one section of the state must be deprived of representation, must be disfranchised, to protect the interest of another. Where is this matter to stop? How far shall the ideal interests of one section of the state control the absolute rights of another? Are 110,000 non-slaveholder voters to be disfranchised for fear they will emancipate the slaves? I stand here the warm advocate of the rights of the people.*** The people of northern Kentucky are as conservative upon the question of slavery as any other section of the state. Look at the Northern Counties and Cities and tell me what indications of radicalism the late election has shown.***I came not from the region of the shuttle and spindle on the one hand, nor do I represent the Bluegrass on the other, but I came as the representative of the free constituency of Fleming and I feel called upon by that constituency to maintain the rights of the people at large."[118] This was further emphasized by a Mr. Dixon, of Henderson County, in one of the discussions when he said: "Beware, how you trample on the rights of the non-slaveholding community. I have the utmost confidence in that community, and I take leave to say, were it not for their forbearance, their high sense of justice, and their noble and elevated attachment to principle, the institution would have been very greatly endangered. They know that you are entitled to the property that you have inherited and purchased, and they fully recognize the great principle in our constitution, that no man's property shall be taken without a full and fair compensation.***I believe that there is not a single emancipationist returned here to proclaim the wishes of that portion of our people who believe in the propriety of emancipating the negroes with compensation."[119] The contention of Dixon is well supported by contemporary evidence as well as by the constitution itself.

M. P. Marshall, of Fleming County, a man of wide influence and a large slaveholder, said in the convention: "There are not a dozen balanced minds in this house that believe slavery to be a blessing. With few exceptions, you believe it to be a social and political evil. Few of you, indeed, under the broad light which experience has thrown on the subject, were the question

---

[118] "Debates in the Kentucky Convention, 1849," p. 485. Speech of Mr. Garfield, of Fleming County. He was a New Englander by birth and education.
[119] "Debates in the Kentucky Convention, 1849," p. 564.

of the introduction of slavery now open, few of you indeed, I am persuaded, would impose it upon Kentucky."[120]

Page after page attests that these sentiments were quite generally shared by the delegates. A few, indeed, argued for the institution as right and just, but the majority saw in it much to condemn, although they were not yet ready for emancipation.

The work of the convention was finished in December, 1849, and in May of the following year the new constitution was ratified by a popular majority of 51,351, in a total vote of 91,955. June 3 the convention again assembled and adopted several amendments. The third constitution of Kentucky was then proclaimed and the convention permanently adjourned.[121]

The new constitution in addition to retaining most of the provisions in the slave clause of the old constitution provided that "no slave shall be emancipated but upon condition that such emancipated slave be sent out of the state."[122] Another clause forbade free Negroes to emigrate to the state and another inserted in the bill of rights gave further emphasis to the argument which had proved so powerful in the convention campaign, namely, that "the right of property is before and higher than any constitutional sanction; and the right of the owner of a slave, and its increase, is the same and is as inviolable as the right of the owner to any property whatever."[123] Thus the convention itself not only failed to adopt any plan of gradual emancipation, but, on the contrary, the new constitution asserted, in the strongest terms, the right of property in slaves and their increase.

The Examiner in reviewing the campaign and the work of the convention said: "Of the ultimate success of the cause of emancipation in Kentucky, we have never for a moment, doubted. The friends of the cause, during the past few months, have had much occasion for anxiety, but none for despondency, and though at present success has been denied, the certainty of final success was never clearer than now. The star of hope shines in the heaven with undimmed lustre. The subject has been freely discussed, and many of the best minds and purest hearts of the state have committed themselves gladly, unreservedly, and forever to the cause of freedom. We doubt not that when the subject shall come up again for action, to be decided upon its own merits, and without reference to political considerations a

[120] "Debates in the Kentucky Convention, 1849," p. 840.
[121] Collins: "History of Kentucky," Vol. 1, p. 332.
[122] "Journal of the Convention, Debates," etc., pp. 1087-1089. See also pp. 867-874.
[123] *Ibid.* See Constitution of Kentucky, 1850, Article 10, Sections 1, 2, 3.

result will crown the efforts of the friends of freedom which will cause their hearts to thrill with joy."[124]

The fact that in Kentucky, where four years previously Cassius M. Clay had been prevented, by pro-slavery men, from publishing an emancipation newspaper, a movement such as this could be set on foot and the whole question of slavery so unreservedly discussed, was assuredly great progress. The freedom of discussion thus secured was never lost.[125]   From this date until the abolition of slavery in Kentucky by the thirteenth amendment to the Constitution of the United States in 1865, the free discussion of slavery both in the press and in public discussions prevailed to a greater extent than in any other slave state; and this, one of the most important of the accomplishments of the anti-slavery workers of Kentucky, was in some measure responsible for the loyalty of the state to the Union and the North during the Civil War.   It must be said, however, that the anti-slavery agitation in spite of the most eminent support completely failed to gain its chief end.   On the contrary the constitution of 1849 made emancipation more difficult than before and more firmly established and safeguarded the institution of slavery in the state.

---

[124] The Examiner, December 8, 1849.   This paper was discontinued after the publication of this number, due largely to the lack of support.

[125] Cassius M. Clay was a candidate for Governor on an emancipation ticket in 1851. He canvassed the entire state and encountered but little opposition.

CONCLUSIONS

CHAPTER X

While slavery was introduced into Kentucky with the first settlers, the slaves constituted a comparatively small and unimportant element of the population before 1792. The early settlers, although coming largely from the slave state of Virginia, were men of moderate means and were consequently small or non-slaveholders. Furthermore, the prevalent pioneer conditions were not conducive to the development of so aristocratic an institution as slavery. Since the country was ill adapted to the plantation system, domestic slavery generally prevailed. And since the cultivation of tobacco, which alone of the chief agricultural products was suited to the extensive application of slave labor, was ruinous to the soil, considerable opposition was early manifested to its wide production in the state.

In Kentucky, as in other sections of the country before 1792, people generally were hostile to slavery and anxiously looked forward to its final abolition. It was condemned not only by Washington, Adams, Jefferson, Madison, Marshall, Jay, and other prominent men but by the leading religious denominations of the country, many of which took vigorous action toward its ultimate elimination. As long as Kentucky remained an integral part of Virginia, there was little opportunity for anti-slavery effort. No sooner, however, had the question of the admission of Kentucky into the Union as an independent state been settled and the election of delegates ordered in 1792 to the convention to frame Kentucky's first constitution than the opponents of slavery launched a movement for constitutional emancipation. In many of the convention elections, the slavery issue received considerable attention and several candidates favorable to emancipation were elected. Under the leadership of the Rev. David Rice, they made a vigorous fight in the convention against the recognition of slavery in the new constitution, but were defeated by a vote of 26 to 16. The pro-slavery element was ably led by Col. George Nicholas and was supported by a majority of the political leaders of the state.

After the adoption of the constitution, anti-slavery effort continued unabated, especially in the churches. The Baptist

Associations while condemning slavery regarded the question of emancipation as political and as such attempted to prevent its discussion in the local churches and associations. In this, however, they were not wholly successful, for widespread dissensions arose and in a few instances caused the formation of independent emancipation churches. While the Presbyterian church was more pronounced in its opposition to slavery than the Baptist Associations, it suffered less from dissensions and secessions. Less strongly anti-slavery sentiment found expression in the Methodist Episcopal and other religious denominations of the state.

In 1797 the first emancipation societies west of the Alleghany Mountains were organized in Kentucky. They were small in numbers, limited in influence, and conservative in policy, advocating gradual emancipation. After an existence of two or possibly three years they were dissolved.

In the controversy over the calling of a constitutional convention in 1797 and 1798 and in the convention elections of the following year, the question of constitutional emancipation was one of the leading issues before the people. In most of the convention elections the candidates either voluntarily or by request expressed their views in regard to slavery, and in a few instances the campaign appeared to have been waged on this issue alone. Among those who favored emancipation at this time and labored to secure its adoption was Henry Clay, who was just beginning his long and eventful political career. While the anti-slavery forces displayed great activity and strength, they were unable to secure control of the convention and to prevent the new constitution's reaffirming with a few minor changes the slave provisions of the constitution of 1792.

During the three following decades, anti-slavery sentiment continued to find expression in a number of ways. In the legislature repeated attempts were made to secure the passage of laws designed to encourage voluntary emancipation, to safeguard the rights and interests of free Negroes, to prevent the importation of slaves into the state, and to secure the calling of a constitutional convention for the purpose of adopting some plan of emancipation. While the religious denominations were still hostile to slavery, there was a pronounced tendency to regard the question as outside the jurisdiction of the church. Nevertheless, during the first quarter of the nineteenth century, Baptist dissensions were numerous and a number of seceding emancipation churches were organized into an association. The general at-

titude of the churches was a contributing cause of the formation
in 1808 of gradual emancipation societies, which furnished an
outlet for the expression of anti-slavery feeling. These societies
had an active existence of about twenty years. During this
time they embraced more or less of the colonization idea and
finally they were either dissolved or merged into colonization
societies.

One of the great difficulties in connection with emancipation was the problem of the freed slave. Should he be colonized?
Or should he be permitted to live a free man in the former slave
states? This latter solution, the southern people generally viewed
with the greatest apprehension and alarm. Believing, as they
did, in the decided inferiority of the Negro as compared with the
white man, they could see only chaos, anarchy, and bloodshed
following emancipation without colonization. This belief was
based largely upon their observation of the free Negroes who
were criminal, immoral, and depraved and were undesirable members of the population in the North as well as in the South. Hence
to the people in the slave states, where the Negroes constituted
a large percentage of the population, colonization was an exceedingly important consideration. With a desire to solve this problem, the American Colonization Society was founded in 1816.
Its principles, approved by Congress, many state legislatures,
religious denominations, and other organizations, spread rapidly.
In Kentucky and the other border states, where the anti-slavery
workers were conservative gradual emancipationists, it became
from the beginning very closely associated with the emancipation movement, although all emancipationists did not necessarily
favor colonization, neither did all colonizationists support
emancipation. In Kentucky the colonization movement was
very popular. It received the repeated approval of the legislature and the active support of the religious denominations as
well as that of the political leaders of the state, chief among whom
was Henry Clay. During the forties, from funds raised within
the state, a large tract of land known as "Kentucky in Liberia"
was purchased in Liberia for the purpose of colonizing the free
Negroes of the state as well as those Negroes who might be freed
for the purpose of colonization. Although receiving the general approval of people in the state, the movement was very dis-
appointing in its results. Because of the lack of funds and the
indisposition of the free Negroes to present themselves to the
society for transportation, not a great deal was accomplished in

the way of ridding the state of the free Negro population or in preparing the state for emancipation. It served, however, as a means for the expression of anti-slavery sentiment through which the evils of slavery and the question of emancipation were kept constantly before the people.

As a result of the general philanthropic and reform movement which swept over the country about 1830, in Kentucky there was an increased interest in the slave and the free Negro and a pronounced renewal of anti-slavery agitation. Emancipation became a popular topic of discussion and the Kentucky newspapers gave the subject more attention than at any time in the history of the state. A sentiment, supported largely by slaveholders, favoring emancipation was rapidly developing, which found expression in part in the formation of gradual emancipation societies composed of slaveholders, who pledged themselves voluntarily to emancipate their slaves and to work for the adoption of constitutional emancipation in the state. While the number of these societies was small, as a result of the prominence of many of the members they exerted an influence far out of proportion to their numbers. The dissolution of these organizations after an existence of less than five years was due in no small degree to the rise of the modern Garrisonian abolition movement and the formation in 1835 of a society in Kentucky auxiliary to the American Anti-Slavery Society. This branch, although under the able leadership of James G. Birney, continued only a few months. Both the society and The Philanthropist, an abolition newspaper published by Birney, called forth from all classes of the population, even the gradual emancipationists, such violent opposition that he was forced to discontinue his publication in Kentucky. With the discontinuance of this paper, the modern abolition movement in the state, which had become a great drawback to the real anti-slavery work and in many instances caused its cessation altogether, collapsed.

The increased anti-slavery activity during the early thirties brought the question of emancipation constantly before the religious denominations of the state. Although they regarded slavery more and more as a political question with which they should not interfere, a strong attempt was made in the Presbyterian church to force a decided stand in favor of emancipation. While the attempt failed, the controversy attracted wide attention, since in this church were many of the leading political leaders and large slave owners of the state. In all the religious denominations, interest was being diverted from the original issue to the question of the general well-being of the slave population. Particularly the Methodist Episcopal, the Presbyterian, and the Baptist churches made special efforts to educate and Christianize the slaves. When the divisions occurred in the Methodist and the Baptist churches during the forties, the Kentucky churches almost unanimously supported the southern wing of the church.

From the very beginning, opposition to the importation of slaves from other states and from foreign countries was pronounced in Kentucky, which upon receiving statehood enacted a number of laws designed to regulate and, to a limited extent, to restrict the importation of slaves. But since inadequate provisions were made for their enforcement, they accomplished little. Anti-slavery workers, in their endeavors to make slavery as humane as possible while it lasted, not only opposed the ordinary traffic in slaves but diligently sought to secure the enforcement of the existing importation laws and, further, to restrict importations of slaves from other states. This, it was maintained, would check the increase of the slave population and consequently lessen the difficulties of emancipation. About 1830, wider interest was manifested in favor of the adoption of a new stringent importation law. After a thorough discussion of the subject for three years in the legislature and throughout the state, the law was passed in 1833. Unfortunately, the controversy did not end here. The supporters of slavery at once launched a campaign to secure the repeal of this law. The question came before the legislature annually until 1849, when the most important features of the law of 1833 were repealed. This controversy was especially important in connection with the anti-slavery movement in Kentucky because in these annual debates on the subject almost every phase of slavery and emancipation was most thoroughly discussed.

While anti-slavery workers labored in every way possible to counteract the many evil effects of slavery, the ultimate object of their efforts was constitutional emancipation. For more than three decades after the ratification of the constitution of 1799, the question of calling a constitutional convention came before the legislature nearly every year, almost unanimously supported by the anti-slavery workers, although many other advocates of the convention were opposed to emancipation. During the early thirties, the convention bill became one of the leading issues before the legislature. Believing that the time was ripe for emancipation, the opponents of slavery pushed the bill with all their energy and were largely instrumental in causing the legislature, in accordance with a constitutional provision, to submit the question to the people in 1837. The anti-slavery workers throughout the country were very optimistic concerning the result and pro-slavery leaders in Kentucky and the South were much alarmed. While the anti-slavery workers of the North pronounced Kentucky "the battleground of freedom" and concentrated their efforts there, openly predicting that the abolition of slavery in Kentucky would be followed in the near future by similar action in Missouri, Arkansas, Tennessee, Virginia, Maryland, North Carolina, and then the states of the lower South, the pro-slavery leaders of Kentucky and the South appealed to Kentucky to remain loyal to her sister slave states, from which came threats of commercial retaliation and even secession in case she deserted them and allied herself with the North. Sectional feeling, which was probably stronger than at any previous period in the history of the state, played an important part in the convention elections. Henry Clay, the most influential man in the state, was joined by many other prominent men in opposing the convention and emancipation largely on the ground that due to the antagonism aroused by the radical abolition movement it was not expedient to abolish slavery at that time. Many of the conservative emancipationists, also, took this attitude with the result that the convention bill and consequently constitutional emancipation were defeated by a large majority. Henry Clay and other Kentuckians of that period expressed the belief that had it not been for the interference of radical abolitionists and northern support of the Underground Railroad System, by which hundreds of Kentuckians were deprived of their property in slaves, Kentucky probably would have adopted some plan of gradual emancipation. This assumption seems to be borne out by the historical evidence.

For a few years following the defeat of the convention bill, anti-slavery activity was not conspicuous. But during the early forties, the bold, fearless, and energetic Cassius M. Clay, nephew of Henry Clay, and a member of one of the wealthiest and most prominent slave-owning families in the state, assumed the leadership of the anti-slavery forces and gave new life to the movement.

Believing that the anti-slavery sympathizers of Kentucky should have some medium for the expression of their views, since the columns of many of the newspapers were closed to anti-slavery discussions, he established at Lexington, in 1845, an anti-slavery newspaper, The True American. The circulation of the paper increased rapidly; but after the appearance of a few numbers the pro-slavery element, fearing its influence, particularly upon the non-slaveholders, to whom it made an especial appeal, by force compelled Clay to discontinue its publication in Kentucky. The press was moved to Cincinnati, where the paper was printed for a few months. Soon after Clay's enlistment in the army at the opening of the Mexican War, some of the men associated with him in the publication purchased the press and moved to Louisville, where they began in 1847 the publication of The Examiner, a weekly anti-slavery paper modeled after The True American. This, although a pronounced anti-slavery paper, encountered but little opposition during the two years of its existence.

When the legislature, due to the demand for constitutional reform, in 1846 submitted the question of calling a constitutional convention, the people in the elections of 1848 and 1849 returned large majorities in favor of it. It is impossible to say just what part anti-slavery workers had in this result. It is certain, however, that emancipation was the leading issue in some counties and one of the important issues in many others. Since emancipation had been one of the troublesome questions in the state for more than half a century, there was a general desire on the part of both pro- and anti-slavery men to force a definite and final settlement. This fact was of importance in the elections.

Immediately after the election of delegates had been ordered for the convention, the anti-slavery men began to organize and held emancipation meetings throughout the state. In April, 1849, there was a great state convention, presided over by Henry Clay, who had come out openly in favor of gradual emancipation in the new constitution, which adopted a series of resolutions condemning slavery and advocating gradual emancipation and colonization. After this meeting, emancipation candidates were nominated in many counties and the candidates in many of the remaining counties were forced to state their positions in regard to emancipation. United States Senators Henry Clay and J. R. Underwood, together with many other prominent Kentuckians, canvassed the state in the interest of emancipation. The question was freely discussed both on the platform and in the press.

One of the weaknesses of the anti-slavery cause was the lack of agreement upon any specific plan of emancipation and colonization out of the hundreds of plans proposed and discussed. There was much talk of the submission of the question of emancipation to the people for a referendum vote; and local option as applied to slavery found many supporters. But the plan that attracted the most attention provided that all slaves in 1849 should remain slaves for life but that all children of slaves born after a fixed date, as 1855, should be free, males at the age of twenty-five and females at the age of twenty, and upon acquiring freedom should be colonized in Africa at the expense of the state.

The pro-slavery leaders were equally active and far better organized. They nominated for convention delegates their best men,—men who were recognized as conservative and safe and who held the confidence of the people.

The result of the campaign was the election of pro-slavery candidates in every county in the state. The convention which assembled a few months later, instead of providing some plan of gradual emancipation, added a number of provisions to the slave clause of the old constitution making voluntary emancipation more difficult and safeguarding the rights of slaveholders to their property in slaves.

With the defeat of the emancipation party in the convention election of 1849 and the ratification of the new constitution, the possibility of the abolition of slavery in Kentucky for many years vanished. While the anti-slavery leaders did not lose confidence in the ultimate success of their efforts, they realized both that a long and systematic campaign was necessary to convince the people that slavery should be abolished because it was not only morally wrong but economically harmful to their interests, and that some definite, practical plan of emancipation and colonization must be brought forward to command the support of all the elements in the anti-slavery ranks.

During the fifties, the anti-slavery party gradually increased in strength and influence through the addition to their numbers of many prominent men. As in the preceding decade, emancipation was in many counties an important issue. And in one instance Cassius M. Clay canvassed the state as an emancipation candidate for governor.

As the hostility between the North and the South increased after 1850, the sectional lines in Kentucky became more closely fixed and the national questions such as the extension of slavery into the territories of the United States and the right of secession attracted more and more attention. Because of the loyalty of the great majority of Kentuckians to the Union, slavery in Kentucky became so closely associated with these national questions that were rapidly dividing the Union into two hostile camps that it is exceedingly difficult, if not impossible, to treat them separately. For this reason it has been thought advisable to consider the period after 1850 in a second volume.

BIBLIOGRAPHY.

ACTS OF THE GENERAL ASSEMBLY OF KENTUCKY. Published by the authority of the Government. 1809-1850.

ADAMS, ALICE DANA: The Neglected Period of Anti-Slavery in America. 1808-1831. Radcliffe College Monographs, No. 14. Boston, 1908.

ALDER, GEORGE HENRY: New Governments West of the Alleghanies before 1780. Wisconsin Historical Bulletin, No. 2.

ALLEN, JAMES LANE: The Blue Grass Region of Kentucky. New York, 1892.

ALLEN, WILLIAM B.: A History of Kentucky, embracing gleanings, statistical and biographical sketches. Nashville, 1878.

AMBLER, CHARLES H.: Sectionalism in Virginia. Chicago, 1910.

AMES, H. V.: Slavery and the Constitution, 1789-1845. New York, 1906.

ANDREWS, ISRAEL WARD: Kentucky, Tennessee and Ohio, Their Admission into the Union. Pamphlet. New York, 1887.

ARMSTRONG AND COMPANY: The Biographical Encyclopaedia of Kentucky. Cincinnati, 1878.

ASBURY, FRANCIS: An Extract from the Journal of Francis Asbury, Bishop of the Methodist Episcopal Church in America. Philadelphia, 1792.

BACON, LEONARD WOOLSEY: Anti-Slavery before Garrison. An address before the Connecticut Society of the Founders and Patriots of America, New Haven, September 19, 1902. Pamphlet. New Haven, 1903.

BAIRD, SAMUEL G.: A Collection of the Acts, Deliverances and Testimonies of the Supreme Judicatory of the Presbyterian Church. Philadelphia, 1856.

BALLAGH, JAMES CURTIS: The History of Slavery in Virginia. Baltimore, 1902.

BANGS, NATHAN: A History of the Methodist Episcopal Church. 2 Vols. 3rd. Edition. New York, 1839.

BARNES, ALBERT: The Church and Slavery. Philadelphia, 1857.

BARROW, REV. DAVID: Involuntary, Absolute, Hereditary Slavery Examined on the Principals of Nature, Reason, Justice, Policy and Scripture. Pamphlet. Lexington, Ky., 1808.

BARTON, W. E.: Life in the Hills of Kentucky. Oberlin, 1890.

BENEDICT, REV. DAVID: A General History of the Baptist Denomination. 2 Vols. Boston, 1813.

BIOGRAPHICAL SKETCHES OF THE HON. LAZARUS W. POWELL of Henderson, Kentucky, and of the HON. JOHN L. HELM, both Governors of the State of Kentucky. Frankfort, Kentucky, 1868.

BIRNEY, JAMES G.: American Churches, the Bulwark of American Slavery. Pamphlet. London, Eng., 1840.

BIRNEY, JAMES G.: Correspondence between the HON. F. H. ELMORE, one of the Southern Delegates in Congress, and JAMES G. BIRNEY, one of the Secretaries of the American Anti-Slavery Society. Pamphlet. New York, 1838.

BIRNEY, JAMES G.: Letter on Colonization Addressed to the Rev. Thornton J. Mills, Corresponding Secretary of the Kentucky Colonization Society, July 15, 1834. New York, 1838.

BIRNEY, JAMES G.: Letter to the Churches, to the Ministers and Elders of the Presbyterian Church of Kentucky, September, 1834. Pamphlet.

BIRNEY, WILLIAM: James G. Birney and his Times. The Genesis of the Republican Party with some Accounts of the Abolition Movement in the South before 1828. New York, 1890.

BISHOP, ROBERT H.: Outline of the History of the Church in the State of Kentucky during a period of forty years, containing the Memiors of Rev. David Rice and Sketches of the Original and Particular Churches and of the Lives of the Men who were Eminent and Useful in their Day. Lexington, Ky., 1824.

BLAKE, W. O.: The History of Slavery and the Slave Trade, * * * and the Political History of Slavery. Columbus, 1858.

BRECKINRIDGE, ROBERT J.: Discussion on American Slavery between George Thompson, Esq., Agent of the British and Foreign Society for the Abolition of Slavery throughout the World, and Rev. Robert J. Breckinridge, Delegate from the General Assembly of the Presbyterian Church in the United States to the Congressional Union of England and Wales, held at Glasgow, Scotland, June, 1836. Boston, 1836.

BRECKINRIDGE, ROBERT J., Speech of, Delivered in the Court House Yard at Lexington, Ky., October 12, 1840, in reply to the speech of Robert Wickliffe in defense of his personal character, his political principles and his religious connections. More particularly in regard to the questions of the power of the legislature on the subject of slavery; of the importation of slaves; of abolition, etc. Pamphlet. Baltimore 1841. Lexington, Ky., 1840.

BRECKINRIDGE, ROBERT J., Speech of, Delivered in the Court House at Lexington, Ky., November 9, 1840, in answer to notorious charges brought against him by Robert Wickliffe. MSS. Copy in Breckinridge Papers.

BRECKINRIDGE, Robert J.: Hints on Slavery. Series of 7 articles published in the Kentucky Reporter, 1830. MSS. Copy in Breckinrigde Papers.

BRECKINRIDGE, Robert J.: The question of Negro Slavery and the new Constitution of Kentucky. Princeton Review, 1849, pp. 582-608.

BROUSSEAU, KATE: L'Education des Nigres aux Etats Unis, Paris, 1904.

BROWN, JOHN MASON: The Political Beginnings of Kentucky. A Narrative of Public Events Bearing on the History of that State up to the time of its Admission into the American Union. Filson Club Publication, No. 6, Louisville.

BUCKINGHAM, J. S.: The Slave States of America. 2 Vols. London, Eng., 1842.

BUTLER, MANN: A History of the Commonwealth of Kentucky from its Exploration and Settlement by the Whites to the Close of the Northwestern Campaign in 1813. 2nd Edition. Louisville, 1836.

CAIRNES, J. E.: The Slave Power; Its Character, Career and Probable Designs: being an attempt to explain the real issues involved in the American contest. New York, 1862.

CARPENTER, W. H.: The History of Kentucky from its Earliest Settlement to the Present Time. Philadelphia, 1858.

CARTWRIGHT, PETER: Fifty years as a Presiding Elder, edited by W. S. Hooper. Cincinnati, 1871.

CARTWRIGHT, PETER: Autobiography of Peter Cartwright, the Backwoods Preacher, edited by W. P. Strickland. New York, 1857.

CASSEDAY, BEN: The History of Louisville from its Earliest Settlement till the year 1852. Louisville, 1852.

CHANNING, WILLIAM E.: Letter from William E. Channing to James G. Birney, Nov. 1, 1836. Pamphlet. Boston, Mass., 1836.

CLARK, WALTER: The Colony of Transylvania, Containing also the Journal of Col. Richard Henderson, Relating to the Transylvania Colony. In The North Carolina Booklet, January, 1904, Vol. 3, No. 9.

CLARKE, JAMES FREEMAN: Anti-Slavery Days. A sketch of the struggle which ended in the abolition of Slavery in the United States. New York, 1884.

CLARKE, LEWIS: Narrative of the Sufferings of Lewis Clarke during Captivity of more than twenty-five years among the Algerines of Kentucky. Boston, 1845.

CLAY, CASSIUS M.: A Letter of Cassius M. Clay, of Lexington, Kentucky, to the Mayor of Dayton, Ohio, with a Review of it by Gerrit Smith, of Petersboro, New York. Pamphlet. New York, 1844.

CLAY, CASSIUS M.: Appeal of Cassius M. Clay to Kentucky and the World. Lexington, Kentucky, September 25, 1845. Boston, Mass., 1845. Pamphlet.

CLAY, CASSIUS M.: History and Record of the Proceedings of the People of Lexington, and its vicinity, in the suppression of The True American, from the commencement of the movement of the 14th of August, 1845, to its final termination on Monday, the 18th, of the same month. Lexington, Ky., 1845. Pamphlet.

CLAY, CASSIUS M.: Speech of Cassius M. Clay at Lexington, Kentucky, delivered August 1, 1851. Lexington, Ky., 1851. Pamphlet.

CLAY, CASSIUS M., The Writings of; including Speeches and Addresses. Edited by Horace Greeley. New York, 1848.

CLAY, CASSIUS M.: Facts for the People. Lexington, Ky., Pamphlet undated.

CLAY, CASSIUS M.: A Review of the Late Canvass and R. Wickliffe's Speech on the Negro Law, September, 1840. Pamphlet. Lexington, Ky., 1840.

CLAY, CASSIUS M.: Memoirs, Writings and Speeches, Showing his Conduct in the Overthrow of American Slavery. 2 Vols. Cincinnati, 1886.

CLAY, CASSIUS M.: Speech of Cassius M. Clay against the Annexation of Texas to the United States of America in reply to Col. R. M. Johnson and others in a Mass Meeting of Citizens of the Eighth Congressional District at the White Sulphur Springs, Scott County, Kentucky, December 30, 1843. Pamphlet. Lexington, Ky., 1844.

CLAY, CASSIUS M.: Speech of Cassius M. Clay, of Fayette, in the House of Representatives of Kentucky, January, 1841, upon a Bill to Repeal the Law of 1833, to Prohibit the Importation of Slaves into the State. Pamphlet. Lexington, Ky., 1841.

CLAY, HENRY: Letters of Henry Clay written (in 1833) thirty years before the War giving his views on slavery. Ky. Hist. Rec. May, 1906.

CLEVELAND, CATHERINE C.: The Great Revival in the West, 1797-1805. University of Chicago Press. Chicago. 1916.

COFFIN, LEVI: Reminiscences of Levi Coffin, the Reputed President of the Underground Railroad. Cincinnati, 1880.

COLEMAN, ANNA MARY: The Life of John J. Crittenden, with selections from his correspondence and speeches. 2 Vol. Philadelphia, Pa., 1873.

COLLINS, LEWIS: Historical Sketches of Kentucky Embracing its History, Antiquities, and Natural Curiosities, Geographical, Statistical and Geological. Maysville, Ky., 1847.

COLLINS, RICHARD H.: History of Kentucky. 2 Vols. Covington, Ky., 1894.

COLLINS, WINFIELD H.: The Domestic Slave Trade of the Southern States. New York, 1905.

COLTON, REV. CALVIN: Abolition, a Sedition. Philadelphia, 1839.

COLTON, CALVIN: The Life and Times of Henry Clay. 2 Vols. New York, 1846.

COLTON, CALVIN: The Works of Henry Clay. 6 Vols. New York, 1857.

CONNELLY, EMMA M.: The Story of Kentucky. Boston, 1890.

COOK, REV. J. F.: Old Kentucky. New York, 1908.

COTTERILL, R. S.: Pioneer History of Kentucky. Cincinnati, 1917.

CRAIK, JAMES: Sketches of Christ Church, Louisville, Diocese of Kentucky. Louisville, 1862.

CRUM, FRED STEPHEN: The Life of Edward Coles with Special Reference to his Influence against Slavery in the Northwest. Manuscript. Ph. D. Thesis in Cornell University, 1893.

DANBRIDGE, DANSKE: George Michael Bedinger: A Kentucky Pioneer. Charlottesville, Va., 1909.

DAVIDSON, REV. ROBERT: The History of the Presbyterian Church in Kentucky. New York, 1857.

DAVIESS COUNTY, KENTUCKY, The History of. By the Interstate Publishing Company. Chicago, 1893.

DEBOW, J. D. B.: The Industrial Resources, etc., of the Southern and Western States. 3 Vols. New Orleans, 1853.

DRAKE, DANIEL: Pioneer Life in Kentucky. A Series of Reminiscential Letters. Cincinnati, 1870.

DRESSER, AMOS: The Narrative of Amos Dresser with Stone's Letter from Natchez, Relating to the Treatment of Slaves. Pamphlet. Publ. 1836.

DUNCAN, JAMES: A Treatise on Slavery in which is Shown Forth the Evil of Slaveholding both from the Light of Nature and Divine Revelation. Vevay, Ind., 1824.

DUNLEVY, A. H.: History of the Miami Baptist Association from its Organization in 1797 to a Division in the Body on Missions in the Year 1836. Cincinnati, 1869.

DUNN, J. P.: Indiana Redemption from Slavery. New York, 1905.

DURRETT, R. T.: The Centenary of Kentucky. Filson Club Publications. Louisville, 1872.

EARLE, THOMAS: The Life, Travels and Opinions of Benjamin Lundy, Including his Journey to Texas and Mexico, with a Sketch of Contemporary Events and a Notice of the Revolution in Hayti. Philadelphia, 1847.

EMORY, JOHN: History of the Discipline of the Methodist Episcopal Church. New York, 1840.

EVANS, ESTWICK: A Pedestrious Tour of 4000 miles through the Western States and Territories during the Winter and Spring of 1818. Concord, N. H., 1819. Also in Thwaites: Early Western Travels. Vol. 8.

FEARON, HENRY BRADSHAW: Sketches of America. Narrative of a Journey of 5000 miles through the Eastern and Western States of America. London, Eng., 3rd edition, 1819.

FEE, JOHN G: Colonization. The Present Scheme of Colonization Wrong, Delusive, and Retards Emancipation. Cincinnati, 1853.

FEE, JOHN G.: Non-Fellowship with Slaveholders the Duty of Christians. New York, 1851.

FEE, JOHN G.: Sinfulness of Slaveholding shown by Appeals to Reason and Scripture. Pamphlet. New York, 1851.

FINLEY, REV. JAMES B.: Sketches of Western Methodism. Biographical, Historical and Miscellaneous. Cincinnati, 1854.

FLINT, JAMES: Letters from America. London, Eng., 1822.

FLINT, TIMOTHY: The History and Geography of the Mississippi Valley to which is Appended a Condensed Physical Geography of the Atlantic States and the Whole American Continent. 2nd edition. 2 Vols. Cincinnati, 1832.

FREE PEOPLE OF COLOR AND DECENDENTS OF THE AFRICAN RACE: An address to the, in the United States, by the American Convention for Promoting the Abolition of Slavery and Improving the Condition of the African Race. Pamphlet. Philadelphia, 1819.

GANO, JOHN: Biographical Memoirs of the late Rev. John Gano, of Frankfort, Kentucky. New York, 1806.

GARRISON, FRANCIS J. AND WENDELL P.: Life of William Lloyd Garrison, 1805-1879. The Story of his Life told by his Children. 4 Vols. Boston, 1894.

GEORGE, J. Z.: Political History of Slavery in the United States. Washington, 1915.

GREELEY, HORACE: The Life of Cassius M. Clay. Memoirs, Writings and Speeches. Cincinnati, 1886.

GREEN, BERIAH: Sketch of the Life of James G. Birney. Utica, 1844.

GRIGSBY, HUGH B.: Virginia Convention of 1829-1830. Richmond, 1854.

GOODWIN, M. S.: Special Report of the United States Commissioner of Education. 1871.

HART, ALBERT BUSHNELL: Slavery and Abolition, 1831-1841. In the American Nation Series. New York, 1906.

HARVY, WILLIAM H.: The Mountain People of Kentucky. An account of the present conditions with the attitude of the people toward improvements. Cincinnati, 1906.

HOWE, D. H.: Political History of Secession to the Beginning of the American Civil War. New York, 1914.

HUME, JOHN F.: The Abolitionists. 1830-1864. New York, 1905.

HURD, JOHN C.: The Law of Freedom and Bondage. 2 Vols. New York 1858.

IMLAY, GILBERT: A Topographical Description of the Western Territory. London, Eng., 1797.

JEFFERSON, THOMAS: Notes on Virginia. Philadelphia, 1825. Original edition was published 1782.

JEWELL, HENRY: Life and Writings of Rev. Enoch M. Pingree who died in Louisville, Ky., January 6, 1849. Cincinnati, 1850.

JOHNSON, E. POLK: A History of Kentucky and Kentuckians; the leaders and representative men in commerce, industry and modern activities. New York, 1912.

JOHNSON, LEWIS FRANKLIN: A History of Franklin County, Ky. Frankfort, Ky., 1912.

JOHNSON, OLIVER: William Lloyd Garrison and his Times, or Sketches of the Anti-Slavery Movement in America. Boston, 1881.

JOHNSON, COLONEL RICHARD M., OF KENTUCKY: Authentic Biography of. New York, 1823.

KING, RUFUS: Ohio; First Fruits of the Ordinance of 1787. Cambridge, Mass., 1888.

KINKEAD, ELIZABETH SHELBY: A Story of Kentucky. New York, 1896.

LEBANON, JOSIAH MORROW: Tours into Kentucky and the Northwest Territory. Three Journals by the Rev. James Smith of Powhatan County, Virginia, 1783, 1790, 1797. Publ. in Ohio Archaeological and Historical Quarterly, July, 1907, Vol. 16, No. 3.

LEGGETT, J. C.: Address delivered by J. C. Leggett at Ripley, Ohio, May 5, 1892, on the Occasion of the Dedication of a Bronze Bust and Granite Monument to the Memory of John Rankin. Pamphlet.

LITTELL, WILLIAM: The Statute Laws of Kentucky, with notes and observations on the public acts, comprehending also the laws of Virginia, and acts of Parliament in force in this Commonwealth. Frankfort, Ky., 1790-1812.

LITTELL, WILLIAM, AND JACOB SWIGERT: Digest of the Statute Laws of Kentucky being a collection of all the Acts of the General Assembly of a public and permanent nature from 1792-1812. Frankfort, Ky., 1822.

LOCKE, MARY STOUGHTON: Anti-Slavery in America from the Introduction of African Slaves to the Prohibition of the Slave Trade. (1619-1808.) Boston, 1901. Radcliffe College Monographs, No. 11.

MACCABE, JULIAN P. BOLIVAR: The Directory of the City of Lexington and the County of Fayette for 1838, 1839. Lexington, Ky., 1838.

MAHAN, JOHN B.: The Trial of John B. Mahan for Felony in the Mason Circuit Court of Kentucky, 1838. Pamphlet. Cincinnati, 1838.

MARSHALL, HUMPHREY: The History of Kentucky to 1811, Exhibiting an Account of the Modern Discovery; Settlement; Progressive Improvement; Civil and Military Transactions, and the Present State of the Country. 2 Vols. Frankfort, Ky., 1824.

MARSHALL, THOMAS F.: Letters to the Editors of the Commonwealth, Containing the Argument in Favor of the Constitutionality of the Law of 1833, "Prohibiting the Importation of Slaves into the Commonwealth," and also Defending the Propriety of the Law and Policy of that Law, in reply to a Pamphlet of Robert Wickliffe, Sr., and to the Views Taken by Other Enemies of the Law. Pamphlet. Frankfort, 1840.

MATLACK, L. C.: The Anti-Slavery Struggle and Triumph in the Methodist Episcopal Church. New York, 1881.

MATLACK, L. C.: The History of American Slavery and Methodism. 1708-1849.

MAYES, HON. DANIEL: The Proceedings of the Colonization Society of Kentucky with address of the Hon. Daniel Mayes at the Annual Meeting at Frankfort, December 1, 1831. Pamphlet. Frankfort, Ky., 1831.

McDOUGALL, MARION GLEASON: Fugitive Slaves, 1619-1865. Fay House Monographs. Boston, 1891.

McELROY, ROBERT McNUTT: Kentucky in the Nation's History. New York, 1909.

McFerran, John B.: History of Methodism in Tennessee. Nashville 1869. 3 Vols.

M'Clung, John A.: Sketches of Western Adventure Containing an Account of the most Interesting Incidents Connected with the Settlement of the West, 1755-1794. Cincinnati, 1839.

McMaster, John Bach: A History of the People of the United States from the Revolution to the Civil War. 8 Vols. New York, 1896.

McTyeire, Holland N.: A History of Methodism. Nashville, 1904.

McTyeire, Holland N.: Duties of Christian Masters. Nashville, 1859.

Methodist Episcopal Church: Journals of the General Conferences of the, 1796-1844. Vols. I and II. New York.

Minutes and Proceedings of the American Convention for Promoting the Abolition of Slavery and Improving the Condition of the African Race. A practically complete file for 1794-1830 is in the Cong. Libr.

M'Nemar, Richard: The Kentucky Revival, or a Short History of the Late Extraordinary Outpouring of the Spirit of God in the Western States of America. Cincinnati, 1808.

Moorehead, C. S., and Mason Brown: A Digest of the Statute Laws of Kentucky of a Public and Permanent Nature. 1792-1834. 2 Vols. Frankfort, Ky.

Morehead, James T.: An Address in the Commemoration of the First Settlement of Kentucky, Delivered at Jonesboro, the 25th of May, 1840. Frankfort, Ky., 1840.

Narrative of the Late Riotous Proceedings against the Liberty of the Press in Cincinnati, with Remarks and Historical Notices Relating to Emancipation Addressed to the People of Ohio by the Executive Committee of the Ohio Anti-Slavery Society. Pamphlet. Cincinnati, 1836.

Needles, Edward. An Historical Memoir of the Pennsylvania Society for Promoting the Abolition of Slavery; the Relief of the Free Negro Unlawfully held in bondage and for Improving the Condition of the African Race. Philadelphia, 1848.

Nelson, David: Lectures on Slavery delivered in February, 1839, at Northampton, Mass. Pamphlet. Cincinnati, 1840.

Newman, A. H.: A History of the Baptist Church in the United States. New York, 1894.

Northcott, H. C.: Biography of Benjamin Northcott, a Pioneer Local Preacher for more than sixty-three years in the Methodist Episcopal Church in Kentucky. (1770-1854.) Cincinnati, Ohio, 1875.

Ogden, George W.: Letters from the West Comprising a Tour through the Western Country and a Residence of Two Summers in the States of Ohio and Kentucky. In Thwaites Early Western Travels, Vol. I.

Paxton, John D.: Letters on Slavery Addressed to the Cumberland Congregation, Virginia. 16 Letters. Lexington, Ky., 1833.

Peters, Dr. Robert: History of Bourbon, Scott, Harrison and Nicholas Counties. Edited by W. H. Perrin. Chicago, 1882.

Poole, William Frederick: Anti-Slavery Opinion before 1800. Cincinnati, 1873.

Presbyterians of Kentucky: An address to the, Proposing a plan for the Instruction and Emancipation of their Slaves. By a Committee of the Synod of Kentucky, 1836. Pamphlet. Newburyport, 1836. Also Louisville, 1844.

Putnam, Mary B.: The Baptists and Slavery, 1840-1845. Ann Arbor, 1913.

Quillin, Frank D.: The Color Line in Ohio. University of Michigan History Studies. Ann Arbor, 1913.

Rafinesque, C. S.: Ancient History or Annals of Kentucky with a Survey of the Ancient Movements of North America. Pamphlet. Frankfort, Ky., 1824.

Ranck, George W.: The History of Lexington, Kentucky. Cincinnati, 1872.

Rankin, John: Letters on Slavery Addressed to Thomas Rankin. 13 Letters. Boston, 1833.

REDFORD, REV. A. H.: The History of Methodism in Kentucky. 3 Vols. Nashville, 1868.

REDFORD, A. H.: Western Cavaliers, Embracing the History of the Methodist Episcopal Church in Kentucky from 1832-1844. Nashville, 1876.

RICE, REV. DAVID: Slavery Inconsistent with Justice and Good Policy. A Speech delivered in the Constitutional Convention at Danville, Kentucky, in 1792. Pamphlet. Philadelphia, 1792.

ROBERTSON, GEORGE: Scrap Book on Law and Politics, Men and Times. Lexington, 1855.

ROBINSON, REV. JOHN: The Testimony and Practice of the Presbyterian Church in Reference to Slavery. Cincinnati, 1852.

ROOSEVELT, THEODORE: The Winning of the West. 4 Vols. New York, 1889-1896.

ROTHERT, OTTO A.: A History of Muhlenberg County, Kentucky. Louisville, 1913.

RUSSELL, JOHN R.: The Free Negro in Virginia, 1619-1865. J. H. U. S. Series 31, No. 3.

SCHURZ, CARL: Life of Henry Clay. 2 Vols. In the American Statesman Series. Boston, 1899.

SEMPLE, ROBERT B.: History of the Rise and Progress of the Baptists of Virginia. Richmond, Va., 1810.

SEVERN, EARL G: Letters on the Condition of Kentucky in 1825. New York, 1917.

SHALER, N. S.: Kentucky, an American Commonwealth. Boston, 1900.

SIEBERT, WILBUR H.: The Underground Railroad from Slavery to Freedom. New York, 1898.

SILL, W.: The Underground Railroad. Philadelphia, 1872.

SMITH, WILLIAM H.: A Political History of Slavery: being an account of the slavery controversy from the earliest agitations in the 18th century to the close of the Reconstruction Period. New York, 1903.

SMITH, HON. Z. F.: The History of Kentucky. Louisville, 1886.

SPAULDING, M. J.: Sketches of the early Catholic Missions of Kentucky from their commencement in 1787 to the Jubilee of 1826-1827. Louisville, 1844.

SPEED, THOMAS: The Political Club, Danville, Kentucky, 1786-1790. Being an account of an early Kentucky Society from the original papers recently found. Filson Club Publications, No. 9. Louisville, 1894.

SPENCER, J. H.: A History of the Kentucky Baptists from 1769-1886. 2 Vols. 1886.

TAYLOR, REV. JOHN: The History of the Ten Baptist Churches of which the author has been alternately a member, in which will be seen something of a Journal of the Author's Life for more than Fifty years. Frankfort, Ky., 1823.

TOWNSEND, JOHN WILSON: Kentuckians in History and Literature. New York, 1907.

TREXLER, HARRISON ANTHONY: Slavery in Missouri, 1804-1865. J. H. U. S. Series 32, No. 2. Baltimore, 1914.

TUCKER, ST. GEORGE: A Dissertation on Slavery with a proposal for the Gradual Abolition of it in the State of Virginia. Philadelphia, 1796.

TURNER, FREDERICK JACKSON: The Rise of the New West. The American Nation Series. New York, 1906.

UNDERWOOD, HON. JOSEPH R.: An Address delivered to the Colonization Society of Kentucky at Frankfort, January 15, 1835. Pamphlet. Frankfort, Ky., 1835.

UNION COUNTY, KENTUCKY: The History of. By the Courier Company. Evansville, Ind., 1886.

VAN METER, B. F.: Dead Issues and Live Ones. Lexington, Ky., 1914.

VON HOLST, DR. HERMAN: The Constitutional and Political History of the United States. 1750-1861. 8 Vols. Chicago, 1876-1892.

WASHBURN, E. B.: Sketches of Edward Coles, Second Governor of Illinois, and the Slavery Struggle of 1823-1824. Chicago, 1882.

WATTS, WILLIAM COURTNEY: Chronicles of a Kentucky Settlement. New York, 1897.

WEBB, HON. BEN. J.: The Centenary of Catholicity in Kentucky with Details of Catholic Emigration to the State from 1785-1814, with Life Sketches of the more Prominent among the Colonists. Louisville, 1884.

WEBSTER, DELIA A.: A History of the Trial of Miss Delia Webster at Lexington, Kentucky, December 17-18, 1844, before the Hon. Richard Buckner, on a charge of aiding Slaves to escape from the Commonwealth. Pamphlet. Vergennes, 1845.

WEEKS, STEPHEN B.: Anti-Slavery Opinion in the South; Unpublished Letters from John Stuart Mills and Mrs. Stowe. In the Publications of the Southern History Association. Vol. 2, 1898.

WEEKS, STEPHEN B.: Southern Quakers and Slavery. In the Johns Hopkins University Studies. Vol. 15. Baltimore, 1896.

WICKLIFFE, ROBERT: Speech of Robert Wickliffe in reply to the Rev. R. J. Breckinridge delivered in the Court House, in Lexington, on Monday, the 9th of November, 1840. Pamphlet. Lexington, 1840.

WICKLIFFE, ROBERT: Reply of Robert Wickliffe to Robert J. Breckinridge, addressed to the freemen of Fayette County. Lexington, Ky., 1841. Pamphlet.

WICKLIFFE, ROBERT: A circular addressed to the Freemen of Fayette County, Ky., Lexington, Ky., 1845. Pamphlet. Cong. Libr.

WILLIAMS, GEORGE W.: The History of the Negro Race in America from 1619 to 1880. 2 Vols. New York, 1883.

WILSON, HENRY: The Rise and Fall of the Slave Power. 3 Vols. Boston, 1873.

WOODSON, C. G.: The Education of the Negro prior to 1861: A History of the Education of the Colored People of the United States, from the Beginning of Slavery to the Civil War. New York, 1915.

YOUNG, REV. JACOB: Autobiography of a Pioneer, or the Nativity, Experience, Travels and Ministerial Labors. Cincinnati, 1857.

YOUNG, REV. JOHN C.: Scriptural Duties of Masters. A Sermon Preached in Danville, Kentucky, in 1846. Pamphlet. Boston, 1846.

MANUSCRIPTS.

The Lyman C. Draper Collection of Manuscripts, in the Wisconsin State Historical Society Library, contains much valuable material on Kentucky history. Of special use in the preparation of this volume were the Daniel Boone Manuscripts, Vols. 3-11, and the Kentucky Manuscripts, Worsley Papers, Vols. 5-8, of this collection.

A recent contribution to the library of the University of Chicago is the collection of the R. T. Durrett Manuscripts, the papers of a number of prominent Kentuckians. It is one of the largest, as well as one of the most valuable manuscript collections on Kentucky history in existence.

The Breckinridge Papers, donated to the Library of Congress by Miss Sophonisba Preston Breckinridge and Mr. Desha Breckinridge, in 1905, subject to certain conditions which have prevented their being thrown open to the general public, contain the papers of John Breckinridge, 1760-1806, John Breckinridge, his son, 1797-1841, Robert Jefferson Breckinridge, another son, 1800-1871, and William Campbell Preston Breckinridge, son of Robert, 1837-1905. In addition there are papers of many other members of the family. In the collection there are between 25,000 and 30,000 papers which are arranged chronologically. Much valuable material for this study was obtained from this collection.

The papers of J. J. Crittenden, about 2,500 in number, marking his long and distinguished career as a public servant, are in the Library of Congress. The papers covering the period from 1840 to 1850 were useful in connection with this work.

Valuable for the early period of Kentucky history were the Harry Innis Papers, in the Library of Congress, containing about 3,000 pieces.

ANTI-SLAVERY NEWSPAPERS.

The Anti-Slavery Bugle,
  Salem, Ohio, 1845-1850.
The Abolition Intelligencer and Missionary Magazine,
  Shelbyville, Ky., 1822-1823.
The African Observer,
  Philadelphia, Pa., 1827-1828.
The African Repository,
  Washington, D. C., 1826-1850. A Colonization Paper.
The Anti-Slavery Almanac,
  Boston, Mass., 1836-1844.
The Anti-Slavery Examiner,
  New York, N. Y., 1836-1839.
The Emancipator,
  New York, N. Y., 1834-1850.
Freedom's Journal,
  New York, N. Y., 1827-1828.
The Genius of Universal Emancipation,
  Mount Pleasant, Ohio, 1821.
  Greeneville, Tenn., 1822-1824.
  Baltimore, Md., 1824-1830.
  Washington, D. C., 1830-1836.
  Philadelphia, Pa., 1836-1839.
The Herald of Freedom,
  Concord, N. H., 1836.
The Liberator,
  Boston, Mass., 1831-1850.

THE PHILANTHROPIST,
  Cincinnati, Ohio, 1837-1838.
THE QUARTERLY ANTI-SLAVERY MAGAZINE,
  New York, N. Y., 1836-1837.

NEWSPAPERS.

THE AMERICAN REPUBLIC,
  Frankfort, Ky., 1810-1812.
THE ARGUS OF WESTERN AMERICA,
  Frankfort, Ky., 1816-1830.
THE COMMENTATOR,
  Frankfort, Ky., 1823-1832.
THE COMMONWEALTH,
  Frankfort, Ky., 1834-1850.
THE CROSS (Baptist),
  Frankfort, Ky., 1834 * * *
THE GUARDIAN OF FREEDOM,
  Frankfort, Ky., 1799-1805.
THE KENTUCKIAN,
  Frankfort, Ky., 1828-1831.
THE SPIRIT OF SEVENTY-SIX,
  Frankfort, Ky., 1826-1828.
THE KENTUCKY GAZETTE,
  Lexington, Ky., 1794-1836.
THE KENTUCKY REPORTER,
  Lexington, Ky., 1812-1832.
THE LEXINGTON OBSERVER,
  Lexington, Ky., 1831-1832.
STEWART'S KENTUCKY HERALD,
  Lexington, Ky., 1795-1802.
THE WESTERN LUMINARY,
  Lexington, Ky., 1824-1835.
THE WESTERN MONITOR,
  Lexington, Ky., 1814-1825.
THE LOUISVILLE CORRESPONDENT,
  Louisville, Ky., 1814-1815.
THE LOUISVILLE HERALD AND COMMERCIAL GAZETTE,
  Louisville, Ky., 1832-1834.
THE FARMER'S LIBRARY,
  Louisville, Ky., 1802-1807.
LOUISVILLE LITERARY NEWS LETTER,
  Louisville, Ky., 1838-1840.
THE LOUISVILLE PUBLIC ADVERTISER,
  Louisville, Ky., 1818-1850.
THE LOUISVILLE JOURNAL,
  Louisville, Ky., 1840-1850.
THE PRENTICE REVIEW,
  Louisville, Ky.
THE WESTERN PRESBYTERIAN HERALD,
  Louisville, Ky., 1836-1838.
THE PRESBYTERIAN HERALD,
  Louisville, Ky., 1846-1850.

THE MAYSVILLE EAGLE,
   Maysville, Ky., 1823-1850.
THE RIGHTS OF MAN, OR THE KENTUCKY MERCURY,
   Paris, Ky., 1797.
THE WESTERN CITIZEN,
   Paris, Ky., 1824-1831.
THE ADVOCATE OF POPULAR RIGHTS,
   Shelbyville, Ky., 1833-1834.
THE BAPTIST BANNER,
   Shelbyville, Ky., 1835-1836.
THE POLITICAL EXAMINER AND GENERAL RECORDER,
   Shelbyville, Ky., 1832-1833.
THE MIRROR,
   Washington, Ky., 1797-1798.
THE KENTUCKY ADVERTISER,
   Winchester, Ky., 1816-1818.
NILES' WEEKLY REGISTER,
   Washington, D. C., 1812-1849.
THE CINCINNATI CHRONICLE,
   Cincinnati, Ohio, 1830-1850.

INDEX